POEMS OF THOMAS HARDY

A New Selection

ALSO PUBLISHED BY MACMILLAN

The Collected Poems of Thomas Hardy
  Fourth edition 1930; latest reprint 1972
  (This edition is the first to contain all
  of Hardy's poems.)

Selected Poems of Thomas Hardy, edited with
  an Introduction by G. M. Young.
  First edition 1940; first printed in
  The Golden Treasury series 1950; latest reprint 1971

Selected Poems of Thomas Hardy, edited with an
  Introduction and Notes by P. N. Furbank, in
  Macmillan's English Classics – New Series.
  Second edition 1967; latest reprint 1971

Selected Shorter Poems of Thomas Hardy, chosen
  and introduced by John Wain.
  First edition 1966; second edition, revised,
  in the New Wessex series 1974

POEMS OF
THOMAS HARDY

A New Selection

Selected, with an Introduction and Notes, by
T. R. M. CREIGHTON

'So various in their pith and plan'

Macmillan

First published 1974 by
THE MACMILLAN PRESS LTD
London and Basingstoke
Associated companies in New York Dublin
Melbourne Johannesburg and Madras

SBN 333 11839 1 (hard cover)
333 13682 9 (paper cover)

Printed in Great Britain by
THE ANCHOR PRESS LTD
Tiptree, Essex

CONTENTS

Let me enjoy the earth no less
Because the all-enacting Might
That fashioned forth its loveliness
Had other aims than my delight.

Collected Poems, p. 222

INTRODUCTION

HARDY appears as his own best interpreter in Appendixes I and II of this volume. To make room for these in a book whose length is inevitably governed by economic considerations, I have dispensed with a full critical introduction. I offer some commentary in the Introductory Notes on pages 332-7, 338-9, and 342-4, and in the notes themselves, though, to make a clean page, there are no references. I have space below only for explanation of the principles of selection and arrangement, and some primitive guidelines into the poetry. I thank Basil Creighton, Dr Mara Kalnins and Richard Taylor for invaluable advice and my wife for unfailing encouragement.

By nature and choice Hardy was a poet. He read, studied and wrote poetry intensively before he 'dreamt of novels', beginning in his early twenties in the 1860s and stopping only at his death at 88 in 1928. Prose fiction was a profession, a 'temporary' but economically 'compulsory' interruption of his poetic career (L 299).* Though he devoted a quarter of a century to it and wrote some of the best novels ever written, he never had a very high opinion of the novel as an art form, considering that 'in verse was contained the essence of all imaginative and emotional literature' (L 48). When, after *Jude*, he abandoned prose for ever, he had published only three or four poems ephemerally but had perhaps 200 unpublished in his desk. His first volume, *Wessex Poems* (1898), produced when he was 58, was a selection from the hoarded work of over thirty years. With characteristic briskness, vitality and versatility (his second wife, in a letter, wrote of him sitting late in life in his study writing a most dismal poem with great spirit), he spent the next thirty writing one of the longest poems in any language, *The Dynasts* (finished 1908) – there are no extracts in this volume; it must be taken whole or not at all – and 700 or 800 more lyrics and a number of dramatic monologues and narratives. Seven more volumes came out at irregular intervals between 1902 and 1928, and all were printed in series in the *CP* (1930),† which contains 920 poems composed over more than sixty years. Each was arranged without consistent regard to chronology of composition or homogeneity of subject, kind, tone or length of individual poems, but as a painter might hang a representative exhibition selected from a

---

* *L* = F. E. Hardy, *The Life of Thomas Hardy* (London, Macmillan, 1930 and 1962).
† *The Collected Poems of Thomas Hardy*, 4th edn (London, Macmillan, 1930).
For other abbreviations and references, see note, p. 331.

lifetime's labour to give a total impression of his art up to that moment. Each contains poems from the 1860s interspersed with many more from all periods up to its preparation. About one in ten bears a date, either of composition (at the end) or of the event, experience or impression it arose from (at the beginning); but these are never arranged in consistent order of either kind or date. The undated 90 per cent occur apparently haphazardly among them. In four volumes Hardy introduced tentative classifications – 'War Poems', 'Poems Of Pilgrimage' or 'More Love Lyrics', for instance – but none is fully classified. Each contains dozens of disconnected, heterogeneous pieces; and poems intimately related by subject, period or both come in different volumes hundreds of pages apart in the *CP*. Though Hardy chose out each volume with care as an exhibition, the system behind their sequence is hard to discern. The *CP* makes an impression of enormous, uncharted bulk arranged arbitrarily or at random. The difficulty simply of using it and finding one's way about has done much to deter readers, to confuse the critical reputation of his art and to obscure its greatness.

I. PRINCIPLES OF SELECTION

The object of this selection is to allow Hardy's art to reveal itself by reducing its bulk and defining its main kinds and preoccupations, irrespective of his volume divisions: not to present 'the best of Hardy' but a cross-section of all he wrote in reduced compass and systematic arrangement. It is not a substitute for the *CP*, and if it leads readers on to an easy familiarity with all his work it will have fulfilled its intention. It is still a popular fallacy – for which F. R. Leavis (*New Bearings*, 1932) bears a grievous responsibility – that Hardy is that inconceivable chimera, a poet who by luck or chance wrote twelve (unspecified) masterpieces and hundreds of very undistinguished verses. In fact, the slightest or oddest poem he wrote has the power over language, intensity of apprehension, acuteness of observation and distinction of imagination of the greatest, and could only have been written by a great and true poet. Hardy may have published more than has been good for his standing with critics who have not understood the nature and unity of his art, but there are no 'failures' in the poems any more than in the novels, though many shots at things previously unattempted. Gosse's remark that 'the worst chapter in *Ethelberta* is recognisable in a moment as written by the author of the best chapter in *The Return*' (*The Speaker*, 13 September 1890) is exactly applicable. My reason for exclusions – and of course I shall have omitted some of everyone's favourites – was to achieve a length manageable by the new reader and economically feasible for the publisher. The ideal would be the whole *CP* arranged as I shall now describe.

1. *Arrangement.* In a passage in the 'Apology' to *Late Lyrics* (311)

Hardy mentions the misunderstandings that may arise 'from miscellanies ... of various character like the present and its predecessors. ... I must admit that I did not foresee such contingencies as I ought to have done.... I must trust for right note-catching to those finely-touched spirits ... whose intuitiveness is proof against all the accidents of inconsequence.' Confronting the series of eight such miscellanies, the most finely-touched reader must read, re-read, mentally cross-refer and meditate on the whole work for years to see its themes 'in graduated kinship'. To rearrange is only to make this easier and does not, I think, do violence to the poetry. I have been guided by Hardy's tentative classifications or by the manifest nature of his work. The mysterious relation between nature and man, the numinous but indifferent, the lovely, inscrutable, untrustworthy, evolutionarily ruthless but in some contradictory sense almost mystically significant, face of nature, have a place on nearly every page he wrote. Love is predominant in all his work (see 332–7). Memory, nostalgia, the presentness of the past to those who live awarely in the present, the pastness of the past, the tragedy of its pastness, its irreplaceableness and sanctity, are among his leading themes (see 338–9). Religion, its necessity and impossibility, the indispensableness but incredibility of the old beliefs, have never been explored more fully or less dogmatically – and in this, as in much else, Hardy's is an essentially 'modern' sensibility using traditional forms (see 342–4). In two of his prefaces Hardy wrote that his poems were 'dramatic and personative' and, though this is partly his innate reticence defending itself against his equally strong impulse to self-revelation, he often resolves their opposition by attributing to imagined characters what was or might have been in his own life. The intrinsically dramatic character of all his poetry needs no emphasising. In the ballads and narratives Hardy is not just telling stories but recording impressions of the nature of things, of love, infatuation, violence, deceit, selflessness or devotion, probing reality and reaching as ever tentative conclusions. My broad classifications – Nature, Love, Memory and Reflection, Dramatic and Personative, and Narrative – can claim almost canonical authority. I have allowed the poems to arrange themselves and have remained as passive under their guidance as I could. They seemed to require to begin with the universal themes of nature and love rather than in biographical order with childhood.

2. *Order.* This has been the hardest problem because Hardy was careless of it. To arrange the contents of each section in chronological order of composition was impossible because the majority of the poems cannot be dated, often within thirty or forty years. Chronology is anyhow less relevant to Hardy, who can write two very similar poems about an experience of 1870 in 1890 and 1926 respectively, than to most poets. Nevertheless there is a perceptible development. In each successive volume one finds, among much that might have been written at any time,

some poems which, it strikes one, could not have occurred in previous volumes, and enough of them can be dated to substantiate this hunch. Hardy went on assimilating new techniques and devices, new subjects for and attitudes to poetry to the end of his life, proceeding as a tree grows, not as a river runs. His experiments move increasingly towards 'mean' and familiar subjects, a 'low', colloquial diction, angular, 'unpoetic' forms, and emphasis on stress scansion rather than on metrical regularity – as in 'Throwing A Tree' (20), which is known to be late, or 'No Buyers' (246) or 'An East-End Curate' (247), which resembles it – and towards a kind of deliberate doggerel which produces some witty poems – e.g. 'A Watering-Place Lady' (249) or 'A Philosophical Fantasy' (172) – which it is not irreverent to call reminiscent of MacGonagall because Hardy knows exactly what purpose he is using it for.

Order of appearance, then, has some connection with order of composition if only because a poem cannot have been written after it appeared, and does to a limited extent illustrate a development in Hardy which many critics have denied him. I have been driven to adopt two different systems of order in different areas of this selection as the least tiresome, confusing and inconsistent solution of an intractable problem. Up to the end of Part III, Section 2, 'Travel' (107), subjects have been allowed to dictate the order of poems, with no other consideration except that poems Hardy arranged as a set (e.g. 'Poems Of Pilgrimage' or *Poems of 1912–13*, whether given *in toto* or in selection) retain his order. From the beginning of Part III, Section 3, 'Memory and Reflection' (107), the poems in each *section* are in order of composition when this can be established, and of appearance when it cannot. (See note, 340, and notes on order of each section up to Part III, Section 2.) Space does not allow citing authority for dates of composition when these differ from date of appearance. Purdy and Bailey (to whom my debt is gratefully acknowledged) would be the chief. I hope this order will show Hardy's two facets: his timeless possession of his gift and experience, and his continual capacity for experiment; and that Part IV in particular will re-create the adventure of working through the *CP* – the uncertainty whether the next poem will be a lament or a burlesque, an irony or a celebration – as earlier Parts show its fundamental coherence.

All dates, place-names and notes in the text of the poems are Hardy's.

II. HARDY'S VERSIFICATION

Hardy possesses the prime requisites of a great poet: an unfailing control over the resources of language in verse, and a wide range of profound response to life. He adapts the traditional disciplines of versification to his new and independent purpose as Yeats did (though their sources, methods and purposes are enormously different) rather than evolving new modes of expression from them, as Pound and Eliot did. The following qualities especially may be indicated to the new reader, not as unique to Hardy but as acquiring a unique voice in his poetry.

1. *Rhythms* of inexhaustible variety and tunefulness form delicate patterns in themselves. Hardy's understanding of the relation of speech rhythm and underlying metre extends from the classic regularity of 'The Darkling Thrush' (14) to the stress-scansion of 'Afterwards' (18). Rhythms are always organically part of the meaning. The metrical calm of 'The Darkling Thrush' matches its mood; the dactylic movement of 'The Voice' (57) is in ironic contrast – a favourite device: cf. 'Wessex Heights' (119) or 'In Tenebris II' and 'III' (117 f.) – like Bach's use of dance rhythms for some of the most intense arias in the *Passions*, and emphasises its own collapse in the last stanza.

2. The *sounds* of words expound Hardy's subjects, whether ono-matopoeically ('Wind oozing thin through the thorn from norward') or by their own music ('when frost was spectre-gray'; 'the wind his death lament'). Try repeating these lines aloud and hear the vowel-sounds at work producing effects more subtle than consonantal alliteration and dissonance.

3. *Stanza forms* endlessly varied and inventive are always part of the meaning they convey, not superimposed on it, and declare why they are so and not otherwise. The number of lines in a stanza modifies its expressiveness. Relations between lines of similar or different lengths always say something. The sharp contrasts in 'A Wasted Illness' (112) create tension; the metrical distinction between lines of nearly similar lengths produces the elegiac feeling of 'Afterwards'. The final words of lines form patterns, not only of masculine and feminine endings, but of their own syllabic length. In 'The Year's Awakening' (2) five masculine polysyllabic endings interrupt the monosyllabic ones and the mainly monosyllabic texture of the poem dramatically. In 'Afterwards' two polysyllabic endings place a nimbus round 'mysteries' and 'outrollings'. Every aspect of *rhyme* is used suggestively. The simple rhyme of 'The Darkling Thrush' reinforces the effect of its regular metre. The complex rhymes of 'Proud Songsters' (4) mirror the mobility of the birds and their repetition over two stanzas the confused unity of nature in which they live. The triple rhymes of 'The Voice' ('call to me, all to me', etc.), in contrast to the heavy single rhymes ('were', 'fair', etc.), continue the opposition between subject and rhythm. Internal rhymes, unrhymed lines and changes of stanza within a poem always say something.

4. *Imagery* in Hardy is sparing and restrained,* eschewing extended simile, metaphor or symbolism. Overt imagery is simple, illustrative but

---

* 'He seems often bent on showing how much poetry can do without and yet be poetry', writes MacDowall (205): an interesting anticipation of a remark of Eliot's in quite a different context, that some great poets show us 'what poetry can do without – how *bare* it can be' (Henrietta Hertz Lecture, 1947).

often daring: 'like the wind on the stair' in 'I Sometimes Think' (85) or 'like the lid of a pot that will not close tight' in 'Suspense' (257). But imagery is inherent in Hardy's language as it is in most poets'. In 'The Darkling Thrush' not only the 'strings of broken lyres' (epitomising the nineteenth century) is imagery but also 'spectre-gray', 'winter's dregs', 'eye of day' and the funereal complex around the landscape and the century in the second stanza. Similarly, 'the primrose pants' in 'A Backward Spring' (3), 'the wind is blurting' in 'An Unkindly May' (4), 'much tune have I set free' in 'Haunting Fingers' (234), and the rain 'bent the spring of the spirit' in 'She Charged Me' (221). A technical term, 'beheaped', affords a marvellous image at the end of 'Places' (63). Imagery is embedded in Hardy's words and the way he uses them, not as a decoration but a function of language. Sometimes the objects in a poem form a field of imagery. In 'The Place On The Map' (27) the (undrinkable) sea, the drought, the woman's unweeping eyes combine to portray a dry situation. The solid natural creatures – leaves, moth, hedgehog, stars – in 'Afterwards' function as images of the speaker's sensibility in connection with the verbal imagery, 'postern' and 'quittance', and are all extinguished by the bell signifying his end.

5. *Syntax*. Hardy's verse sentences vary flexibly between brief simplicity and complex length, moving closely with the verse or opposing it in free enjambment over lines and stanzas as the poem requires, but never restricted by it. The easy prose syntax of 'The Darkling Thrush', or the strict formal structure of 'Afterwards' (every stanza but the last, where the order is inverted, beginning with a subordinate clause leading to a delayed verb), serve artistic purposes; as do the baffling sixth stanza of 'A Sign-Seeker' (142) or lines 2–4 of 'The Voice' ('Saying that now you are not as you were / When you were changed from the one who was all to me, / But as at first, when our day was fair.'). Syntactical complexities generally reflect confusion or distress, a kind of grammar of grief; see also 'After A Journey' (60), stanza 2. Hardy does not shun poetic inversions and other traditional usages – his practice in this respect is 'mixed', like his vocabulary – neither does he depend on them. No poet can better employ straightforward modern English in verse when he wants to.

6. *Vocabulary*. (See also note, 317.) Although it is closely related to questions of grammar and syntax, I have isolated this aspect of Hardy's diction because it has often been criticised as uncouth and affected. There is little in the poems to support the view that his diction in either sense is cumbersome or out of control, or that he was unaware of its effect. He uses a 'mixed' vocabulary in two ways. First, in a number of poems – though by no means all – he mixes 'poetic', archaic, obscure or dialect words, a good many compounds ('spectre-gray', 'blast-beruffled') and a few coinages ('outleant', 'wistlessness') of his own invention, into simple modern English. The test of this vocabulary must be whether it works to

produce the result – often of surprise, evocation or allusion – it seeks to achieve, to create the unique texture of his verse, not whether it is conventional or has precedents. Second, he mixes poems that have an unusually pure, consistent and restrained diction and vocabulary among others that have features just the reverse. 'Lying Awake' (17) and 'Four In The Morning' (5) are examples. When he is odd, it is to achieve compression or precision, or to say, as he often does, things other poets have not wanted to say. 'Cerule' is an odd word but when you have read 'Earth is a cerule mystery . . . At four o'clock', no other seems possible. (Try substituting 'azure'.) If you want to say in verse 'I wanted to be out at 4 a.m. but didn't like getting up so early', could it be better done than: 'Though pleasure spurred, I rose with irk'? It is inconceivable that the poet capable of controlling the first poem is unaware of the strangeness of the second or out of control of either. The argument may be extended to larger structures – 'The Souls Of The Slain' (180), 'In Front Of The Landscape' (120), 'To Shakespeare' (232) ['some townsman (met maybe / And thereon queried by some squire's good dame / Driving in shopward'), and the strange amalgam of cliché and fantasy in the last stanza] – to the comedy of 'Genoa' (101), where a carefully inflated and absurd diction clashes with the 'chrome kerchiefs, scarlet hose, darned underfrocks'. If what such poems say could not have been said, these effects and contrasts not produced, by other means, then Hardy's diction and vocabulary justify themselves and we may be sure he knew what he was doing. The same is true of his frequent use of clichés. His mother's death was 'a deft achievement' in 'After The Last Breath' (90); in 'The Voice' she 'was all to me' and 'our day was fair'. It is not that, at a loss for a striking phrase, he reached unconsciously for a cliché but that in the context of the poem he gives the cliché, because we are so familiar with it, a light of feeling that no more studied expression could have enjoyed.

III. HARDY'S MIND AND FEELING

The *CP* present the composite picture of a poet's mind: a mind concerned not to explain but to declare itself, able to sustain logical discrepancies within an intuitive framework. It is not an intellectually conceived picture, though Hardy possessed a powerfully incisive intellect, and can reconcile such rationally incompatible statements as that life is an unmitigated evil and is greatly to be enjoyed, within the context of feeling. 'The mission of poetry', Hardy wrote (*L* 377), 'is to record impressions, not convictions'; and, as he repeatedly says in the *Life*, he had no convictions in the normal sense. He reasons from deep emotional predispositions: an intense love and reverence for life in all its forms, a profound tenderness for all living things, a hatred of violence

cf. Larkin.

and cruelty, and an innate need for a religious explanation of the universe. These predispositions, though reduced by his experience of reality to a sense of tragedy, colour all his work. What give unity to the inconsistent, conflicting and often mutually contradictory impressions he records in his poems are the sensibility, the cast of mind, which received them and the art which sets them down. To see the poems as a whole is quite a different experience from admiring some of the best-known anthology pieces and being surprised at the slightness, oddness or apparent triviality of some of their neighbours. All the poems illuminate each other, casting reciprocal light backwards and forwards, so that quite small pieces attain a glow which might otherwise be imperceptible – e.g. 'Sacred To The Memory' (97), with its wonderfully resonant central line 'In bare conventionality', refracts rays from all the poems of family piety, of belief and unbelief, of memory and reflection, and of human life and values – and the whole work achieves a greatness beyond the sum of its parts, great as some of them are. I hope this volume, though a selection, re-creates this picture of a mind.

We cannot avoid forming a personal relation with its owner, just as in fact we cannot in the novels. Readers and critics who share T. S. Eliot's austere views about the impersonality of poetry and the creative process are unlikely to get further with Hardy than he did. (See 'Tradition and the Individual Talent' and 'Thomas Hardy' in Eliot's *Selected Prose*.) I suppose Hardy's sadness, his dark cast of mind, will strike new readers most. Eliot, discussing Hardy as a personality, not specifically as a poet, finds him neither 'wholesome' nor 'edifying' but self-absorbed, and says that he is 'interested not at all in men's minds but only in their emotions'. It is truer to say that Hardy, though always interested in mind in himself and his fictive characters, sees emotion – or some even deeper, more mysterious force of being, the awareness of which he shares with D. H. Lawrence – as what ultimately controls men's lives; and that his sadness is both wholesome and edifying, neither negative not enervating, because it is a product of the positive predispositions mentioned above. Hardy's enormous strength, which Eliot denies him, is to enunciate his sense of the value of life, his concern for the happiness of all living things in a universe which he sees as destructive of the first and indifferent to the second. Even when he ostensibly deplores the fact of consciousness, as in 'Before Life And After' (156), it is sorrow at the suffering and transience of things, not at their existence, that emanates from the poem. He cannot explain why the universe is as it is; and in not attempting to do so he may show as much strength as others who have explained. He mourns, though he never fears, death and the passage of time because they consume the vitality and possibilities of the present which he loves. He leaves us, as Day Lewis writes ('Birthday Poem', *Collected Poems*), 'warmer-hearted and brisker-eyed'. He enhances life and dwells 'in tenebris' because it seems marred by a 'thwarted purposing', 'an unfulfilled intention'. It may be a metaphysically naïve attitude but Hardy is not the only poet to have made poetry out of mutability. It is hard to see why his 'pessimism', which is in other cases called a tragic sense of life, has attracted opprobrium. Perhaps it is because he faces and discharges the task of making poetry out of what Hynes (40) calls 'experience which has no invested meaning' without investing it with a private mythological or religious significance. I do not think it true, as Hynes goes on to say, that Hardy tries 'to make poetry of monistic materialism' or of scientific humanism or of determinism. His belief in these was provisional, based on emotion and often qualified: see note, 342–4. (No one really 'convinced' about them could have chosen the words on p. 327 as the last he wished to hear in life.) His poetry is sometimes conformable to his ideas, sometimes not; and paradoxically he invests experience with a wide range of meaning by recording, as he said, 'impressions, not convictions'.

It is customary to praise the 'fidelity to life' with which Hardy does this. Certainly his delicate, acute and accurate observation of nature, of people, of emotional and psychological situations is conveyed with minute precision and extraordinary boldness – e.g. 'A Countenance' (114), written astonishingly in 1884 – and his humour, whether darkly ironic or straightforwardly comic, plays a larger part in the deeply serious body of his work than in much poetry. But his penetration of all he touches seems to me to transcend these qualities. In exploring the waste and the fertile spaces of human experience he enlarges our knowledge and understanding of them, whether we agree with his outlook or not. He is, to use his own description of a poet who puzzled him, 'a great seer and feeler' (321) and, as fully as any poet has ever been, a man speaking to men. Occasionally his sorrow at a creation of such blighted promise leads him to expressions of gloom that seem perverse and gratuitous, that make one smile in a way not intended; sometimes his relish for life takes him to the scandalous or sensational; and momentarily he loses touch with reality. But this occurs (only in a minority of poems, not, as Blackmur suggests, as a dominant characteristic) because he did not choose to censor his impressions or falsify his consciousness for public view. (He wrote his poems 'because he liked doing them, without any ulterior thought; because he wanted to say the things they contained and would contain': see L 302.) In the context of our personal relation it is seen as a complementary aspect, a kind of necessary by-product of a creative sensibility whose prevailing qualities are profundity and sensitiveness, generosity and majesty of imagination – 'his hawk's vision, his way of looking at life from a very great height', as Auden puts it.

Most academic critics from Leavis to the present express doubts about the 'greatness' of Hardy's poetry. (Hynes, the most searching, compromises by calling it 'a high poetic achievement'.) One can see why. Hardy conforms to no academically recognisable type. His art, though rooted in tradition, defies analysis in terms of historical influence. His independence of contemporary trends and fashions fits into none of the pigeon-holes reserved for his age. His own casual and unselfconscious attitude to his verse, reflected in the quotation just above, shocks expositors of other twentieth-century poets. His poetic imagination does not seek to transmute reality but to present it as he saw it and to penetrate deeply into his experience of it. His meanings offer no ambiguities for ingenious explication. But 'greatness' is a quality much easier to withhold than to define. It is hard to see how poetry which communicates intense and varied emotion with supreme articulacy can be anything but very great. The most illuminating critics of the poetry are MacDowall (chapters XI to XIV), Auden, Brown, Hillis Miller (in a book which places poems and novels in a single perspective) and, in his song-cycle *Winter Words*, Benjamin Britten.

PUBLISHER'S NOTE

The texts used are the standard ones of *CP* and *L*; a few misprints in *CP* have been corrected. Single quotation-marks have been used in accordance with current practice. Asterisk, dagger, etc., indicate editorial footnotes; Hardy's (and *CP* editor's) footnotes are printed with arabic figures.

T. R. M. C.

PART I

NATURE AND MAN

THE YEAR'S AWAKENING

How do you know that the pilgrim track
Along the belting zodiac
Swept by the sun in his seeming rounds
Is traced by now to the Fishes' bounds
And into the Ram, when weeks of cloud
Have wrapt the sky in a clammy shroud,
And never as yet a tinct of spring
Has shown in the Earth's apparelling;
    O vespering bird, how do you know,
      How do you know?

How do you know, deep underground,
Hid in your bed from sight and sound,
Without a turn in temperature,
With weather life can scarce endure,
That light has won a fraction's strength,
And day put on some moments' length,
Whereof in merest rote will come,
Weeks hence, mild airs that do not numb;
    O crocus root, how do you know,
      How do you know?

February 1910

AT MIDDLE-FIELD GATE IN FEBRUARY

THE bars are thick with drops that show
    As they gather themselves from the fog
Like silver buttons ranged in a row,
And as evenly spaced as if measured, although
    They fall at the feeblest jog.

They load the leafless hedge hard by,
    And the blades of last year's grass,
While the fallow ploughland turned up nigh
In raw rolls, clammy and clogging lie –
    Too clogging for feet to pass.

How dry it was on a far-back day
    When straws hung the hedge and around.
When amid the sheaves in amorous play
In curtained bonnets and light array
    Bloomed a bevy now underground!

Bockhampton Lane

A BACKWARD SPRING

THE trees are afraid to put forth buds,
And there is timidity in the grass;
The plots lie gray where gouged by spuds,
    And whether next week will pass
Free of sly sour winds is the fret of each bush
    Of barberry waiting to bloom.

Yet the snowdrop's face betrays no gloom,
And the primrose pants in its heedless push,
Though the myrtle asks if it's worth the fight
    This year with frost and rime
    To venture one more time
On delicate leaves and buttons of white
From the selfsame bough as at last year's prime,
And never to ruminate on or remember
What happened to it in mid-December.

April 1917

'I WATCHED A BLACKBIRD'

I WATCHED a blackbird on a budding sycamore
One Easter Day, when sap was stirring twigs to the core;
  I saw his tongue, and crocus-coloured bill
  Parting and closing as he turned his trill;
  Then he flew down, seized on a stem of hay,
And upped to where his building scheme was under way,
As if so sure a nest were never shaped on spray.

PROUD SONGSTERS

THE thrushes sing as the sun is going,
    And the finches whistle in ones and pairs,
  And as it gets dark loud nightingales
        In bushes
  Pipe, as they can when April wears,
        As if all Time were theirs.

These are brand-new birds of twelve-months' growing,
  Which a year ago, or less than twain,
  No finches were, nor nightingales,
        Nor thrushes,
  But only particles of grain,
        And earth, and air, and rain.

AN UNKINDLY MAY

A SHEPHERD stands by a gate in a white smock-frock:
He holds the gate ajar, intently counting his flock.

The sour spring wind is blurting boisterous-wise,
And bears on it dirty clouds across the skies;
Plantation timbers creak like rusty cranes,
And pigeons and rooks, dishevelled by late rains,
Are like gaunt vultures, sodden and unkempt,
And song-birds do not end what they attempt:

The buds have tried to open, but quite failing
Have pinched themselves together in their quailing.
The sun frowns whitely in eye-trying flaps
Through passing cloud-holes, mimicking audible taps.
'Nature, you're not commendable to-day!'
I think. 'Better to-morrow!' she seems to say.

That shepherd still stands in that white smock-frock,
Unnoting all things save the counting his flock.

FOUR IN THE MORNING

At four this day of June I rise:
The dawn-light strengthens steadily;
Earth is a cerule mystery,
As if not far from Paradise
   At four o'clock,

Or else near the Great Nebula,
Or where the Pleiads blink and smile:
(For though we see with eyes of guile
The grisly grin of things by day,
   At four o'clock

They show their best.) . . . In this vale's space
I am up the first, I think. Yet, no,
A whistling? and the to-and-fro
Wheezed whettings of a scythe apace
   At four o'clock? . . .

– Though pleasure spurred, I rose with irk:
Here is one at compulsion's whip
Taking his life's stern stewardship
With blithe uncare, and hard at work
   At four o'clock!

Bockhampton

AN AUGUST MIDNIGHT

I

A SHADED lamp and a waving blind,
And the beat of a clock from a distant floor:
On this scene enter – winged, horned, and spined –
A longlegs, a moth, and a dumbledore;
While 'mid my page there idly stands
A sleepy fly, that rubs its hands . . .

II

Thus meet we five, in this still place,
At this point of time, at this point in space,
– My guests besmear my new-penned line,
Or bang at the lamp and fall supine.
'God's humblest, they!' I muse. Yet why?
They know Earth-secrets that know not I.

Max Gate, 1899

SHORTENING DAYS AT THE HOMESTEAD

THE first fire since the summer is lit, and is smoking into the room:
The sun-rays thread it through, like woof-lines in a loom.
Sparrows spurt from the hedge, whom misgivings appal
That winter did not leave last year for ever, after all.
Like shock-headed urchins, spiny-haired,
Stand pollard willows, their twigs just bared.

Who is this coming with pondering pace,
Black and ruddy, with white embossed,
His eyes being black, and ruddy his face
And the marge of his hair like morning frost?
It's the cider-maker,
And appletree-shaker,
And behind him on wheels, in readiness,
His mill, and tubs, and vat, and press.

A SHEEP FAIR

THE day arrives of the autumn fair,
  And torrents fall,
Though sheep in throngs are gathered there,
  Ten thousand all,
Sodden, with hurdles round them reared:
And, lot by lot, the pens are cleared,
And the auctioneer wrings out his beard,
And wipes his book, bedrenched and smeared,
And rakes the rain from his face with the edge of his hand,
  As torrents fall.

The wool of the ewes is like a sponge
  With the daylong rain:
Jammed tight, to turn, or lie, or lunge,
  They strive in vain.
Their horns are soft as finger-nails,
Their shepherds reek against the rails,
The tied dogs soak with tucked-in tails,
The buyers' hat-brims fill like pails,
Which spill small cascades when they shift their stand
  In the daylong rain.

POSTSCRIPT

Time has trailed lengthily since met
  At Pummery Fair
Those panting thousands in their wet
  And woolly wear:
And every flock long since has bled,
And all the dripping buyers have sped,
And the hoarse auctioneer is dead,
Who 'Going–going!' so often said,
As he consigned to doom each meek, mewed band
  At Pummery Fair.

LAST WEEK IN OCTOBER

THE trees are undressing, and fling in many places –
On the gray road, the roof, the window-sill –
Their radiant robes and ribbons and yellow laces;
A leaf each second so is flung at will,
Here, there, another and another, still and still.

A spider's web has caught one while downcoming,
That stays there dangling when the rest pass on;
Like a suspended criminal hangs he, mumming
In golden garb, while one yet green, high yon,
Trembles, as fearing such a fate for himself anon.

NIGHT-TIME IN MID-FALL

IT is a storm-strid night, winds footing swift
    Through the blind profound;
  I know the happenings from their sound;
Leaves totter down still green, and spin and drift;
The tree-trunks rock to their roots, which wrench and lift
    The loam where they run onward underground.

The streams are muddy and swollen; eels migrate
    To a new abode;
  Even cross, 'tis said, the turnpike-road;
(Men's feet have felt their crawl, home-coming late):
The westward fronts of towers are saturate,
    Church-timbers crack, and witches ride abroad.

THE LATER AUTUMN

GONE are the lovers, under the bush
    Stretched at their ease;
    Gone the bees,
Tangling themselves in your hair as they rush
    On the line of your track,
    Leg-laden, back
    With a dip to their hive
    In a prepossessed dive.

Toadsmeat is mangy, frosted, and sere;
  Apples in grass
  Crunch as we pass,
And rot ere the men who make cyder appear.
  Couch-fires abound
  On fallows around,
  And shades far extend
  Like lives soon to end.

Spinning leaves join the remains shrunk and brown
  Of last year's display
  That lie wasting away,
On whose corpses they earlier as scorners gazed down
  From their aery green height:
  Now in the same plight
  They huddle; while yon
  A robin looks on.

LAST LOOK ROUND ST. MARTIN'S FAIR

THE sun is like an open furnace door,
Whose round revealed retort confines the roar
  Of fires beyond terrene;
The moon presents the lustre-lacking face
  Of a brass dial gone green,
  Whose hours no eye can trace.
The unsold heathcroppers are driven home
To the shades of the Great Forest whence they come
By men with long cord-waistcoats in brown monochrome.
The stars break out, and flicker in the breeze,
  It seems, that twitches the trees –
  From its hot idol soon
The fickle unresting earth has turned to a fresh patroon –
  The cold, now brighter, moon.
The woman in red, at the nut-stall with the gun,
  Lights up, and still goes on:
She's redder in the flare-lamp than the sun
  Showed it ere it was gone.

Her hands are black with loading all the day,
And yet she treats her labour as 'twere play,
Tosses her ear-rings, and talks ribaldry
To the young men around as natural gaiety,
And not a weary work she'd readily stay,
And never again nut-shooting see,
Though crying, 'Fire away!'

THE LAST CHRYSANTHEMUM

WHY should this flower delay so long
    To show its tremulous plumes?
Now is the time of plaintive robin-song,
    When flowers are in their tombs.

Through the slow summer, when the sun
    Called to each frond and whorl
That all he could for flowers was being done,
    Why did it not uncurl?

It must have felt that fervid call
    Although it took no heed,
Waking but now, when leaves like corpses fall,
    And saps all retrocede.

Too late its beauty, lonely thing,
    The season's shine is spent,
Nothing remains for it but shivering
    In tempests turbulent.

Had it a reason for delay,
    Dreaming in witlessness
That for a bloom so delicately gay
    Winter would stay its stress?

– I talk as if the thing were born
    With sense to work its mind;
Yet it is but one mask of many worn
    By the Great Face behind.

AT DAY-CLOSE IN NOVEMBER

THE ten hours' light is abating,
   And a late bird wings across,
Where the pines, like waltzers waiting,
   Give their black heads a toss.

Beech leaves, that yellow the noon-time,
   Float past like specks in the eye;
I set every tree in my June time,
   And now they obscure the sky.

And the children who ramble through here
   Conceive that there never has been
A time when no tall trees grew here,
   That none will in time be seen.

SNOW IN THE SUBURBS   — Imagist

EVERY branch big with it,
   Bent every twig with it;
Every fork like a white web-foot;
Every street and pavement mute:
Some flakes have lost their way, and grope back upward, when
Meeting those meandering down they turn and descend again.
   The palings are glued together like a wall,
   And there is no waft of wind with the fleecy fall.

   A sparrow enters the tree,
   Whereon immediately
A snow-lump thrice his own slight size
Descends on him and showers his head and eyes,
   And overturns him,
   And near inurns him,
   And lights on a nether twig, when its brush
Starts off a volley of other lodging lumps with a rush.

The steps are a blanched slope,
Up which, with feeble hope,
A black cat comes, wide-eyed and thin;
And we take him in.

WINTER NIGHT IN WOODLAND

(OLD TIME)

THE bark of a fox rings, sonorous and long:—
Three barks, and then silentness; 'wong, wong, wong!'
In quality horn-like, yes melancholy,
As from teachings of years; for an old one is he.
The hand of all men is against him, he knows; and yet, why?
That he knows not, – will never know, down to his death-halloo cry.

With clap-nets and lanterns off start the bird-baiters,
In trim to make raids on the roosts in the copse,
Where they beat the boughs artfully, while their awaiters
Grow heavy at home over divers warm drops.
The poachers, with swingels, and matches of brimstone, outcreep
To steal upon pheasants and drowse them a-perch and asleep.

Out there, on the verge, where a path wavers through,
Dark figures, filed singly, thrid quickly the view,
Yet heavily laden: land-carriers are they
In the hire of the smugglers from some nearest bay.
Each bears his two 'tubs,' slung across, one in front, one behind,
To a further snug hiding, which none but themselves are to find.

And then, when the night has turned twelve the air brings
From dim distance, a rhythm of voices and strings:
'Tis the quire, just afoot on their long yearly rounds,
To rouse by worn carols each house in their bounds;
Robert Penny, the Dewys, Mail, Voss, and the rest; till anon
Tired and thirsty, but cheerful, they home to their beds in the dawn.

ICE ON THE HIGHWAY

SEVEN buxom women abreast, and arm in arm,
    Trudge down the hill, tip-toed,
      And breathing warm;
They must perforce trudge thus, to keep upright
    On the glassy ice-bound road,
And they must get to market whether or no,
    Provisions running low
      With the nearing Saturday night,
While the lumbering van wherein they mostly ride
      Can nowise go:
Yet loud their laughter as they stagger and slide!

Yell'ham Hill

WINTER IN DURNOVER FIELD

SCENE. – *A wide stretch of fallow ground recently sown with wheat, and frozen to iron hardness. Three large birds walking about thereon, and wistfully eyeing the surface. Wind keen from north-east: sky a dull grey.*

(TRIOLET)

Rook. – Throughout the field I find no grain;
    The cruel frost encrusts the cornland!
Starling. – Aye: patient pecking now is vain
    Throughout the field, I find . . .
Rook. –   No grain!
Pigeon. – Nor will be, comrade, till it rain,
    Or genial thawings loose the lorn land
    Throughout the field.
Rook. –   I find no grain:
    The cruel frost encrusts the cornland!

THE FALLOW DEER AT THE LONELY HOUSE

ONE without looks in to-night
        Through the curtain-chink
From the sheet of glistening white;
One without looks in to-night
        As we sit and think
        By the fender-brink.

We do not discern those eyes
        Watching in the snow;
Lit by lamps of rosy dyes
We do not discern those eyes
        Wondering, aglow,
        Fourfooted, tiptoe.

THE DARKLING THRUSH

I LEANT upon a coppice gate
        When Frost was spectre-gray,
And Winter's dregs made desolate
        The weakening eye of day.
The tangled bine-stems scored the sky
        Like strings of broken lyres,
And all mankind that haunted nigh
        Had sought their household fires.

The land's sharp features seemed to be
        The Century's corpse outleant,
His crypt the cloudy canopy,
        The wind his death-lament.
The ancient pulse of germ and birth
        Was shrunken hard and dry,
And every spirit upon earth
        Seemed fervourless as I.

At once a voice arose among
   The bleak twigs overhead
In a full-hearted evensong
   Of joy illimited;
An aged thrush, frail, gaunt, and small,
   In blast-beruffled plume,
Had chosen thus to fling his soul
   Upon the growing gloom.

So little cause for carolings
   Of such ecstatic sound
Was written on terrestrial things
   Afar or nigh around,
That I could think there trembled through
   His happy good-night air
Some blessed Hope, whereof he knew
   And I was unaware.

31 December 1900

WEATHERS

I

THIS is the weather the cuckoo likes,
   And so do I;
When showers betumble the chestnut spikes,
   And nestlings fly:
And the little brown nightingale bills his best,
And they sit outside at 'The Travellers' Rest,'
And maids come forth sprig-muslin drest,
And citizens dream of the south and west,
   And so do I.

[Handwritten marginal annotations:]
haunts. Beyond all this, the wish to be alone
Reason for Attendance. The Trumpet's voice
Poetry of Departures.
Sometimes you hear Jh han
Coming
Naturally the Foundation will bear your expense
No Road.
Send no Money
MCMXIV
The Card Players.
going, going
The Old Fools
Solar
Next Please — (always too eager for the future)
Explosion
Age.

II

This is the weather the shepherd shuns,
    And so do I;
When beeches drip in browns and duns,
    And thresh, and ply;
And hill-hid tides throb, throe on throe,
And meadow rivulets overflow,
And drops on gate-bars hang in a row,
And rooks in families homeward go,
    And so do I.

BEFORE AND AFTER SUMMER

I

Looking forward to the spring
One puts up with anything.
On this February day
Though the winds leap down the street
Wintry scourgings seem but play,
And these later shafts of sleet
– Sharper pointed than the first –
And these later snows – the worst –
Are as a half-transparent blind
Riddled by rays from sun behind.

II

Shadows of the October pine
Reach into this room of mine:
On the pine there swings a bird;
He is shadowed with the tree.
Mutely perched he bills no word;
Blank as I am even is he.
For those happy suns are past,
Fore-discerned in winter last.
When went by their pleasure, then?
I, alas, perceived not when.

LYING AWAKE

You, Morningtide Star, now are steady-eyed, over the east,
    I know it as if I saw you;
You, Beeches, engrave on the sky your thin twigs, even the least;
    Had I paper and pencil I'd draw you.

You, Meadow, are white with your counterpane cover of dew,
    I see it as if I were there;
You, Churchyard, are lightening faint from the shade of the yew
    The names creeping out everywhere.

'I AM THE ONE'

I AM the one whom ringdoves see
    Through chinks in boughs
    When they do not rouse
    In sudden dread,
But stay on cooing, as if they said:
    'Oh; it's only he.'

I am the passer when up-eared hares,
    Stirred as they eat
    The new-sprung wheat,
    Their munch resume
As if they thought: 'He is one for whom
    Nobody cares.'

Wet-eyed mourners glance at me
    As in train they pass
    Along the grass
    To a hollowed spot,
And think: 'No matter; he quizzes not
    Our misery.'

I hear above: 'We stars must lend
    No fierce regard
    To his gaze, so hard
    Bent on us thus, –
Must scathe him not. He is one with us
    Beginning and end.'

AFTERWARDS

WHEN the Present has latched its postern behind my tremulous
    stay,
  And the May month flaps its glad green leaves like wings,
Delicate-filmed as new-spun silk, will the neighbours say,
    'He was a man who used to notice such things'?

If it be in the dusk when, like an eyelid's soundless blink,
  The dewfall-hawk comes crossing the shades to alight
Upon the wind-warped upland thorn, a gazer may think,
    'To him this must have been a familiar sight.'

If I pass during some nocturnal blackness, mothy and warm,
  When the hedgehog travels furtively over the lawn,
One may say, 'He strove that such innocent creatures should
    come to no harm,
  But he could do little for them; and now he is gone.'

If, when hearing that I have been stilled at last, they stand at
    the door,
  Watching the full-starred heavens that winter sees,
Will this thought rise on those who will meet my face no more,
    'He was one who had an eye for such mysteries'?

And will any say when my bell of quittance is heard in the
    gloom,
  And a crossing breeze cuts a pause in its outrollings,
Till they rise again, as they were a new bell's boom,
    'He hears it not now, but used to notice such things'?

COMPASSION

AN ODE

IN CELEBRATION OF THE CENTENARY OF THE ROYAL SOCIETY
FOR THE PREVENTION OF CRUELTY TO ANIMALS

I

BACKWARD among the dusky years
A lonesome lamp is seen arise,
Lit by a few fain pioneers
    Before incredulous eyes, –
We read the legend that it lights:
'Wherefore beholds this land of historied rights
Mild creatures, despot-doomed, bewildered, plead
Their often hunger, thirst, pangs, prisonment,
    In deep dumb gaze more eloquent
        Than tongues of widest heed?'

II

What was faint-written, read in a breath
In that year – ten times ten away –
A larger louder conscience saith
    More sturdily to-day. –
But still those innocents are thralls
To throbless hearts, near, far, that hear no calls
Of honour towards their too-dependent frail,
And from Columbia Cape to Ind we see
    How helplessness breeds tyranny
        In power above assail.

III

Cries still are heard in secret nooks,
　　Till hushed with gag or slit or thud;
And hideous dens whereon none looks
　　Are sprayed with needless blood.
But here, in battlings, patient, slow,
Much has been won – more, maybe, than we know –
And on we labour hopeful. 'Ailinon!'
A mighty voice calls: 'But may the good prevail!'
　　And 'Blessed are the merciful!'
　　　　Calls a yet mightier one.

22 January 1924

THROWING A TREE

NEW FOREST

The two executioners stalk along over the knolls,
Bearing two axes with heavy heads shining and wide,
And a long limp two-handled saw toothed for cutting great
　　boles,
And so they approach the proud tree that bears the death-mark on
　　its side.

Jackets doffed they swing axes and chop away just above
　　ground,
And the chips fly about and lie white on the moss and fallen
　　leaves;
Till a broad deep gash in the bark is hewn all the way round,
And one of them tries to hook upward a rope, which at last he
　　achieves.

The saw then begins, till the top of the tall giant shivers:
The shivers are seen to grow greater each cut than before:
They edge out the saw, tug the rope; but the tree only quivers,
And kneeling and sawing again, they step back to try pulling once
　　more.

Then, lastly, the living mast sways, further sways: with a
    shout
Job and Ike rush aside. Reached the end of its long staying
    powers
The tree crashes downward: it shakes all its neighbours
    throughout,
And two hundred years' steady growth has been ended in less
    than two hours.

PART II

LOVE

SECTION 1

'IN VISION I ROAMED'

TO ——

In vision I roamed the flashing Firmament,
So fierce in blazon that the Night waxed wan,
As though with awe at orbs of such ostént;
And as I thought my spirit ranged on and on

In footless traverse through ghast heights of sky,
To the last chambers of the monstrous Dome,
Where stars the brightest here are lost to the eye:
Then, any spot on our own Earth seemed Home!

And the sick grief that you were far away
Grew pleasant thankfulness that you were near,
Who might have been, set on some foreign Sphere,
Less than a Want to me, as day by day
I lived unware, uncaring all that lay
Locked in that Universe taciturn and drear.

1866

REVULSION

Though I waste watches framing words to fetter
Some unknown spirit to mine in clasp and kiss,
Out of the night there looms a sense 'twere better
To fail obtaining whom one fails to miss.

For winning love we win the risk of losing,
And losing love is as one's life were riven;
It cuts like contumely and keen ill-using
To cede what was superfluously given.

Let me then never feel the fateful thrilling
That devastates the love-worn wooer's frame,
The hot ado of fevered hopes, the chilling
That agonizes disappointed aim!
So may I live no junctive law fulfilling,
And my heart's table bear no woman's name.

1866

AT A BRIDAL

NATURE'S INDIFFERENCE

WHEN you paced forth, to await maternity,
A dream of other offspring held my mind,
Compounded of us twain as Love designed;
Rare forms, that corporate now will never be!

Should I, too, wed as slave to Mode's decree,
And each thus found apart, of false desire,
A stolid line, whom no high aims will fire
As had fired ours could ever have mingled we;

And, grieved that lives so matched should miscompose,
Each mourn the double waste; and question dare
To the Great Dame whence incarnation flows,
Why those high-purposed children never were:
What will she answer? That she does not care
If the race all such sovereign types unknows.

1866

1967

IN five-score summers! All new eyes,
New minds, new modes, new fools, new wise,
New woes to weep, new joys to prize;

With nothing left of me and you
In that live century's vivid view
Beyond a pinch of dust or two;

A century which, if not sublime,
Will show, I doubt not, at its prime,
A scope above this blinkered time.

– Yet what to me how far above?
For I would only ask thereof
That thy worm should be my worm, Love!

16 Westbourne Park Villas, 1867

NEUTRAL TONES

WE stood by a pond that winter day,
And the sun was white, as though chidden of God,
And a few leaves lay on the starving sod;
    – They had fallen from an ash, and were gray.

Your eyes on me were as eyes that rove
Over tedious riddles of years ago;
And some words played between us to and fro
    On which lost the more by our love.

The smile on your mouth was the deadest thing
Alive enough to have strength to die;
And a grin of bitterness swept thereby
    Like an ominous bird a-wing. . . .

Since then, keen lessons that love deceives,
And wrings with wrong, have shaped to me
Your face, and the God-curst sun, and a tree,
    And a pond edged with grayish leaves.

1867

THE PLACE ON THE MAP

I

I LOOK upon the map that hangs by me –
Its shires and towns and rivers lined in varnished artistry –
  And I mark a jutting height
Coloured purple, with a margin of blue sea.

II

– 'Twas a day of latter summer, hot and dry;
Ay, even the waves seemed drying as we walked on, she and I
  By this spot where, calmly quite,
She unfolded what would happen by and by.

III

This hanging map depicts the coast and place,
And re-creates therewith our unforeboded troublous case
  All distinctly to my sight,
And her tension, and the aspect of her face.

IV

Weeks and weeks we had loved beneath that blazing blue,
Which had lost the art of raining, as her eyes to-day had too,
  While she told what, as by sleight,
Shot our firmament with rays of ruddy hue.

V

For the wonder and the wormwood of the whole
Was that what in realms of reason would have joyed our double soul
  Wore a torrid tragic light
Under order-keeping's rigorous control.

VI

So, the map revives her words, the spot, the time,
And the thing we found we had to face before the next year's
    prime;
  The charted coast stares bright,
And its episode comes back in pantomime.

ON A HEATH

I COULD hear a gown-skirt rustling
   Before I could see her shape,
Rustling through the heather
   That wove the common's drape,
On that evening of dark weather
   When I hearkened, lips agape.

And the town-shine in the distance
   Did but baffle here the sight,
And then a voice flew forward:
   'Dear, is't you? I fear the night!'
And the herons flapped to norward
   In the firs upon my right.

There was another looming
   Whose life we did not see;
There was one stilly blooming
   Full nigh to where walked we;
There was a shade entombing
   All that was bright of me.

THE DAWN AFTER THE DANCE

HERE is your parents' dwelling with its curtained windows telling
Of no thought of us within it or of our arrival here;
Their slumbers have been normal after one day more of formal
Matrimonial commonplace and household life's mechanic gear.

I would be candid willingly, but dawn draws on so chillingly
As to render further cheerlessness intolerable now,
So I will not stand endeavouring to declare a day for severing,
But will clasp you just as always – just the olden love avow.

Through serene and surly weather we have walked the ways
     together,
And this long night's dance this-year's end eve now finishes the
     spell;
Yet we dreamt us but beginning a sweet sempiternal spinning
Of a cord we have spun to breaking – too intemperately, too well.

Yes; last night we danced I know, Dear, as we did that year ago,
     Dear,
When a new strange bond between our days was formed, and felt,
     and heard;
Would that dancing were the worst thing from the latest to the
     first thing
That the faded year can charge us with; but what avails a word!

That which makes man's love the lighter and the woman's burn
     no brighter
Came to pass with us inevitably while slipped the shortening
     year. . . .
And there stands your father's dwelling with its blind bleak
     windows telling
That the vows of man and maid are frail as filmy gossamere.

Weymouth, 1869

AT A SEASIDE TOWN IN 1869

(YOUNG LOVER'S REVERIE)

I WENT and stood outside myself,
     Spelled the dark sky
     And ship-lights nigh,
And grumbling winds that passed thereby.

Then next inside myself I looked,
     And there, above
     All, shone my Love,
That nothing matched the image of.

Beyond myself again I ranged;
    And saw the free
    Life by the sea,
And folk indifferent to me.

O 'twas a charm to draw within
    Thereafter, where
    But she was; care
For one thing only, her hid there!

But so it chanced, without myself
    I had to look,
    And then I took
More heed of what I had long forsook:

The boats, the sands, the esplanade,
    The laughing crowd;
    Light-hearted, loud
Greetings from some not ill-endowed;

The evening sunlit cliffs, the talk
    Hailings and halts,
    The keen sea-salts,
The band, the Morgenblätter Waltz.

Still, when at night I drew inside
    Forward she came,
    Sad, but the same
As when I first had known her name

Then rose a time when, as by force,
    Outwardly wooed
    By contacts crude,
Her image in abeyance stood. . . .

At last I said; This outside life
    Shall not endure;
    I'll seek the pure
Thought-world, and bask in her allure.

Myself again I crept within,
    Scanned with keen care
    The temple where
She'd shone, but could not find her there.

I sought and sought. But O her soul
    Has not since thrown
    Upon my own
One beam! Yea, she is gone, is gone.

From an old note

ON THE ESPLANADE

MIDSUMMER: 10 P.M.

THE broad bald moon edged up where the sea was wide,
    Mild, mellow-faced;
Beneath, a tumbling twinkle of shines, like dyed,
    A trackway traced
To the shore, as of petals fallen from a rose to waste,
    In its overblow,
And fluttering afloat on inward heaves of the tide:–
All this, so plain; yet the rest I did not know.

The horizon gets lost in a mist new-wrought by the night:
    The lamps of the Bay
That reach from behind me round to the left and right
    On the sea-wall way
For a constant mile of curve, make a long display
    As a pearl-strung row,
Under which in the waves they bore their gimlets of light:–
All this was plain; but there was a thing not so.

Inside a window, open, with undrawn blind,
    There plays and sings
A lady unseen a melody undefined:
    And where the moon flings
Its shimmer a vessel crosses, whereon to the strings
    Plucked sweetly and low
Of a harp, they dance. Yea, such did I mark. That, behind,
My Fate's masked face crept near me I did not know!

THE CONTRETEMPS

A FORWARD rush by the lamp in the gloom,
   And we clasped, and almost kissed;
But she was not the woman whom
I had promised to meet in the thawing brume
On that harbour-bridge; nor was I he of her tryst.

So loosening from me swift she said:
   'O why, why feign to be
The one I had meant! – to whom I have sped
To fly with, being so sorrily wed!'
– 'Twas thus and thus that she upbraided me.

My assignation had struck upon
   Some others' like it, I found.
And her lover rose on the night anon;
And then her husband entered on
The lamplit, snowflaked, sloppiness around.

'Take her and welcome, man!' he cried:
   'I wash my hands of her.
I'll find me twice as good a bride!'
   – All this to me, whom he had eyed,
Plainly, as his wife's planned deliverer.

And next the lover: 'Little I knew,
   Madam, you had a third!
Kissing here in my very view!'
   – Husband and lover then withdrew.
I let them; and I told them not they erred.

Why not? Well, there faced she and I –
   Two strangers who'd kissed, or near,
Chancewise. To see stand weeping by
A woman once embraced, will try
The tension of a man the most austere.

So it began; and I was young,
    She pretty, by the lamp,
As flakes came waltzing down among
    The waves of her clinging hair, that hung
Heavily on her temples, dark and damp.

And there alone still stood we two;
    She one cast off for me,
Or so it seemed; while night ondrew,
    Forcing a parley what should do
We twain hearts caught in one catastrophe.

In stranded souls a common strait
    Wakes latencies unknown,
Whose impulse may precipitate
    A life-long leap. The hour was late,
And there was the Jersey boat with its funnel agroan.

'Is wary walking worth much pother?'
    It grunted, as still it stayed.
'One pairing is as good as another
    Where all is venture! Take each other,
And scrap the oaths that you have aforetime made.'

– Of the four involved there walks but one
    On earth at this late day.
And what of the chapter so begun?
    In that odd complex what was done?
    Well; happiness comes in full to none:
Let peace lie on lulled lips: I will not say.

Weymouth

AT WAKING

WHEN night was lifting,
And dawn had crept under its shade
Amid cold clouds drifting
Dead-white as a corpse outlaid,
With a sudden scare
I seemed to behold
My Love in bare
Hard lines unfold.

Yea, in a moment,
An insight that would not die
Killed her old endowment
Of charm that had capped all nigh,
Which vanished to none
Like the gilt of a cloud,
And showed her but one
Of the common crowd.

She seemed but a sample
Of earth's poor average kind,
Lit up by no ample
Enrichments of mien or mind.
I covered my eyes
As to cover the thought,
And unrecognize
What the morn had taught.

O vision appalling
When the one believed-in thing
Is seen falling, falling,
With all to which hope can cling.
Off: it is not true;
For it cannot be
That the prize I drew
Is a blank to me!

Weymouth, 1869

THOUGHTS OF PHENA

AT NEWS OF HER DEATH

Not a line of her writing have I,
    Not a thread of her hair,
No mark of her late time as dame in her dwelling, whereby
    I may picture her there;
    And in vain do I urge my unsight
      To conceive my lost prize
At her close, whom I knew when her dreams were upbrimming
      with light,
    And with laughter her eyes.

    What scenes spread around her last days,
      Sad, shining, or dim?
Did her gifts and compassions enray and enarch her sweet ways
      With an aureate nimb?
    Or did life-light decline from her years,
      And mischances control
Her full day-star; unease, or regret, or forebodings, or fears
    Disennoble her soul?

    Thus I do but the phantom retain
      Of the maiden of yore
As my relic; yet haply the best of her – fined in my brain
      It may be the more
    That no line of her writing have I,
      Nor a thread of her hair,
No mark of her late time as dame in her dwelling, whereby
    I may picture her there.

March 1890

SECTION 2

THE WIND'S PROPHECY

I TRAVEL on by barren farms,
And gulls glint out like silver flecks
Against a cloud that speaks of wrecks,
And bellies down with black alarms.
I say: 'Thus from my lady's arms
I go; those arms I love the best!'
The wind replies from dip and rise,
'Nay; toward her arms thou journeyest.'

A distant verge morosely gray
Appears, white clots of flying foam
Break from its muddy monochrome,
And a light blinks up far away.
I sigh: 'My eyes now as all day
Behold her ebon loops of hair!'
Like bursting bonds the wind responds,
'Nay, wait for tresses flashing fair!'

From tides the lofty coastlands screen
Come smitings like the slam of doors,
Or hammerings on hollow floors,
As the swell cleaves through caves unseen.
Say I: 'Though broad this wild terrene,
Her city home is matched of none!'
From the hoarse skies the wind replies:
'Thou shouldst have said her sea-bord one.'

The all-prevailing clouds exclude
The one quick timorous transient star;
The waves outside where breakers are
Huzza like a mad multitude.

'Where the sun ups it, mist-imbued,'
I cry, 'there reigns the star for me!'
The wind outshrieks from points and peaks:
'Here, westward, where it downs, mean ye!'

Yonder the headland, vulturine,
Snores like old Skrymer in his sleep,
And every chasm and every steep
Blackens as wakes each pharos-shine
'I roam, but one is safely mine,'
I say. 'God grant she stay my own!'
Low laughs the wind as if it grinned:
'Thy Love is one thou'st not yet known.'

Rewritten from an old copy

'A MAN WAS DRAWING NEAR TO ME'

On that gray night of mournful drone,
Apart from aught to hear, to see,
I dreamt not that from shires unknown
            In gloom, alone,
            By Halworthy,
A man was drawing near to me.

I'd no concern at anything,
No sense of coming pull-heart play;
Yet, under the silent outspreading
            Of even's wing
            Where Otterham lay,
A man was riding up my way.

I thought of nobody – not of one,
But only of trifles – legends, ghosts –
Though, on the moorland dim and dun
            That travellers shun
            About these coasts,
The man had passed Tresparret Posts.

There was no light at all inland,
Only the seaward pharos-fire,
Nothing to let me understand
    That hard at hand
    By Hennett Byre
The man was getting nigh and nigher.

There was a rumble at the door,
A draught disturbed the drapery,
And but a minute passed before,
    With gaze that bore
    My destiny,
The man revealed himself to me.

'WHEN I SET OUT FOR LYONNESSE'

(1870)

When I set out for Lyonnesse,
    A hundred miles away,
    The rime was on the spray,
And starlight lit my lonesomeness
When I set out for Lyonnesse
    A hundred miles away.

What would bechance at Lyonnesse
    While I should sojourn there
    No prophet durst declare,
Nor did the wisest wizard guess
What would bechance at Lyonnesse
    While I should sojourn there.

When I came back from Lyonnesse
    With magic in my eyes,
    All marked with mute surmise
My radiance rare and fathomless,
When I came back from Lyonnesse
    With magic in my eyes!

AT THE WORD 'FAREWELL'

She looked like a bird from a cloud
    On the clammy lawn,
Moving alone, bare-browed
    In the dim of dawn.
The candles alight in the room
    For my parting meal
Made all things withoutdoors loom
    Strange, ghostly, unreal.

The hour itself was a ghost,
    And it seemed to me then
As of chances the chance furthermost
    I should see her again.
I beheld not where all was so fleet
    That a Plan of the past
Which had ruled us from birthtime to meet
    Was in working at last:

No prelude did I there perceive
    To a drama at all,
Or foreshadow what fortune might weave
    From beginnings so small;
But I rose as if quicked by a spur
    I was bound to obey,
And stepped through the casement to her
    Still alone in the gray.

'I am leaving you. . . . Farewell!' I said
    As I followed her on
By an alley bare boughs overspread;
    'I soon must be gone!'
Even then the scale might have been turned
    Against love by a feather,
— But crimson one cheek of hers burned
    When we came in together.

UNDER THE WATERFALL

'WHENEVER I plunge my arm, like this,
In a basin of water, I never miss
The sweet sharp sense of a fugitive day
Fetched back from its thickening shroud of gray.
       Hence the only prime
       And real love-rhyme
        That I know by heart,
        And that leaves no smart,
Is the purl of a little valley fall
About three spans wide and two spans tall
Over a table of solid rock,
And into a scoop of the self-same block;
The purl of a runlet that never ceases
In stir of kingdoms, in wars, in peaces;
With a hollow boiling voice it speaks
And has spoken since hills were turfless peaks.'

'And why gives this the only prime
Idea to you of a real love-rhyme?
And why does plunging your arm in a bowl
Full of spring water, bring throbs to your soul?'
'Well, under the fall, in a crease of the stone,
Though where precisely none ever has known,
Jammed darkly, nothing to show how prized,
And by now with its smoothness opalized,
       Is a drinking-glass:
       For, down that pass
        My lover and I
        Walked under a sky
Of blue with a leaf-wove awning of green,
In the burn of August, to paint the scene,
And we placed our basket of fruit and wine
By the runlet's rim, where we sat to dine;
And when we had drunk from the glass together,
Arched by the oak-copse from the weather,
I held the vessel to rinse in the fall,
Where it slipped, and sank, and was past recall,

Though we stooped and plumbed the little abyss
With long bared arms. There the glass still is.
And, as said, if I thrust my arm below
Cold water in basin or bowl, a throe
From the past awakens a sense of that time,
And the glass we used, and the cascade's rhyme.
The basin seems the pool, and its edge
The hard smooth face of the brook-side ledge,
And the leafy pattern of china-ware
The hanging plants that were bathing there.

'By night, by day, when it shines or lours,
There lies intact that chalice of ours,
And its presence adds to the rhyme of love
Persistently sung by the fall above.
No lip has touched it since his and mine
In turns therefrom sipped lovers' wine.'

NEAR LANIVET, 1872

THERE was a stunted handpost just on the crest,
　　Only a few feet high:
She was tired, and we stopped in the twilight-time for her rest,
　　At the crossways close thereby.

She leant back, being so weary, against its stem,
　　And laid her arms on its own,
Each open palm stretched out to each end of them,
　　Her sad face sideways thrown.

Her white-clothed form at this dim-lit cease of day
　　Made her look as one crucified
In my gaze at her from the midst of the dusty way,
　　And hurriedly 'Don't,' I cried.

I do not think she heard. Loosing thence she said,
　　As she stepped forth ready to go,
'I am rested now. – Something strange came into my head;
　　I wish I had not leant so!'

And wordless we moved onward down from the hill
    In the west cloud's murked obscure,
And looking back we could see the handpost still
    In the solitude of the moor.

'It struck her too,' I thought, for as if afraid
    She heavily breathed as we trailed;
Till she said, 'I did not think how 'twould look in the shade,
    When I leant there like one nailed.'

I, lightly: 'There's nothing in it. For *you*, anyhow!'
    – 'O I know there is not,' said she . . .
'Yet I wonder . . . If no one is bodily crucified now,
    In spirit one may be!'

And we dragged on and on, while we seemed to see
    In the running of Time's far glass
Her crucified, as she had wondered if she might be
    Some day. – Alas, alas!

'WE SAT AT THE WINDOW'

(BOURNEMOUTH, 1875)

WE sat at the window looking out,
    And the rain came down like silken strings
That Swithin's day. Each gutter and spout
    Babbled unchecked in the busy way
        Of witless things:
Nothing to read, nothing to see
Seemed in that room for her and me
        On Swithin's day.

We were irked by the scene, by our own selves; yes,
    For I did not know, nor did she infer
How much there was to read and guess
    By her in me, and to see and crown
        By me in her.
Wasted were two souls in their prime,
And great was the waste, that July time
        When the rain came down.

THE MUSICAL BOX

LIFELONG to be
Seemed the fair colour of the time;
That there was standing shadowed near
A spirit who sang to the gentle chime
Of the self-struck notes, I did not hear,
    I did not see.

Thus did it sing
To the mindless lyre that played indoors
As she came to listen for me without:
'O value what the nonce outpours –
This best of life – that shines about
    Your welcoming!'

I had slowed along
After the torrid hours were done,
Though still the posts and walls and road
Flung back their sense of the hot-faced sun,
And had walked by Stourside Mill, where broad
    Stream-lilies throng.

And I descried
The dusky house that stood apart,
And her, white-muslined, waiting there
In the porch with high-expectant heart,
While still the thin mechanic air
    Went on inside.

At whiles would flit
Swart bats, whose wings, be-webbed and tanned,
Whirred like the wheels of ancient clocks:
She laughed a hailing as she scanned
Me in the gloom, the tuneful box
    Intoning it.

Lifelong to be
I thought it. That there watched hard by
A spirit who sang to the indoor tune,
'O make the most of what is nigh!'
I did not hear in my dull soul-swoon –
I did not see.

'WHO'S IN THE NEXT ROOM?'

'Who's in the next room? – who?
I seemed to see
Somebody in the dawning passing through,
Unknown to me.'
'Nay: you saw nought. He passed invisibly.'

'Who's in the next room? – who?
I seem to hear
Somebody muttering firm in a language new
That chills the ear.'
'No: you catch not his tongue who has entered there.'

'Who's in the next room? – who?
I seem to feel
His breath like a clammy draught, as if it drew
From the Polar Wheel.'
'No: none who breathes at all does the door conceal.'

'Who's in the next room? – who?
A figure wan
With a message to one in there of something due?
Shall I know him anon?'
'Yea he; and he brought such; and you'll know him anon.'

THE INTERLOPER

'And I saw the figure and visage of Madness seeking for a home'

THERE are three folk driving in a quaint old chaise,
And the cliff-side track looks green and fair;
I view them talking in quiet glee
As they drop down towards the puffins' lair
    By the roughest of ways;
But another with the three rides on, I see,
    Whom I like not to be there!

No: it's not anybody you think of. Next
A dwelling appears by a slow sweet stream
Where two sit happy and half in the dark:
They read, helped out by a frail-wick'd gleam,
    Some rhythmic text;
But one sits with them whom they don't mark,
    One I'm wishing could not be there.

No: not whom you knew and name. And now
I discern gay diners in a mansion-place,
And the guests dropping wit – pert, prim, or choice,
And the hostess's tender and laughing face,
    And the host's bland brow;
But I cannot help hearing a hollow voice.
    And I'd fain not hear it there.

No: it's not from the stranger you meet once. Ah,
Yet a goodlier scene than that succeeds;
People on a lawn – quite a crowd of them. Yes,
And they chatter and ramble as fancy leads;
    And they say, 'Hurrah!'
To a blithe speech made; save one, mirthless,
    Who ought not to be there.

Nay: it's not the pale Form your imagings raise,
That waits on us all at a destined time,
It is not the Fourth Figure the Furnace showed;
O that it were such a shape sublime
    In these latter days!
It is that under which best lives corrode;
    Would, would it could not be there!

AT THE PIANO

A WOMAN was playing,
    A man looking on;
    And the mould of her face,
    And her neck, and her hair,
    Which the rays fell upon
    Of the two candles there,
Sent him mentally straying
    In some fancy-place
    Where pain had no trace.

A cowled Apparition
    Came pushing between;
    And her notes seemed to sigh;
    And the lights to burn pale,
    As a spell numbed the scene.
    But the maid saw no bale,
And the man no monition;
    And Time laughed awry,
    And the Phantom hid nigh.

A DUETTIST TO HER PIANOFORTE

SONG OF SILENCE

(E. L. H. – H. C. H.)

SINCE every sound moves memories,
    How can I play you
Just as I might if you raised no scene,
By your ivory rows, of a form between
My vision and your time-worn sheen,
    As when each day you
Answered our fingers with ecstasy?
So it's hushed, hushed, hushed, you are for me!

And as I am doomed to counterchord
    Her notes no more
In those old things I used to know,
In a fashion, when we practised so,
'Good-night! – Good-bye!' to your pleated show
    Of silk, now hoar,
Each nodding hammer, and pedal and key,
For dead, dead, dead, you are to me!

I fain would second her, strike to her stroke,
    As when she was by,
Aye, even from the ancient clamorous 'Fall
Of Paris', or 'Battle of Prague' withal,
To the 'Roving Minstrels', or 'Elfin Call'
    Sung soft as a sigh:
But upping ghosts press achefully,
And mute, mute, mute, you are for me!

Should I fling your polyphones, plaints, and quavers
    Afresh on the air,
Too quick would the small white shapes be here
Of the fellow twain of hands so dear;
And a black-tressed profile, and pale smooth ear;
    – Then how shall I bear
Such heavily-haunted harmony?
Nay: hushed, hushed, hushed, you are for me!

ALIKE AND UNLIKE

(GREAT-ORME'S HEAD)

WE watched the selfsame scene on that long drive,
Saw the magnificent purples, as one eye,
Of those near mountains; saw the storm arrive;
Laid up the sight in memory, you and I,
As if for joint recallings by and by.

But our eye-records, like in hue and line,
Had superimposed on them, that very day,
Gravings on your side deep, but slight on mine! –
Tending to sever us thenceforth alway;
Mine commonplace; yours tragic, gruesome, gray.

LOST LOVE

I PLAY my sweet old airs –
    The airs he knew
    When our love was true –
    But he does not balk
    His determined walk,
And passes up the stairs.

I sing my songs once more,
    And presently hear
    His footstep near
    As if it would stay;
    But he goes his way,
And shuts a distant door.

So I wait for another morn,
    And another night
    In this soul-sick blight;
    And I wonder much
    As I sit, why such
A woman as I was born!

Poems of 1912–13

Veteris vestigia flammae

THE GOING

Why did you give no hint that night
That quickly after the morrow's dawn,
And calmly, as if indifferent quite,
You would close your term here, up and be gone
　　Where I could not follow
　　With wing of swallow
To gain one glimpse of you ever anon!

　　Never to bid good-bye,
　　Or lip me the softest call,
Or utter a wish for a word, while I
Saw morning harden upon the wall,
　　Unmoved, unknowing
　　That your great going
Had place that moment, and altered all.

Why do you make me leave the house
And think for a breath it is you I see
At the end of the alley of bending boughs
Where so often at dusk you used to be;
　　Till in darkening dankness
　　The yawning blankness
Of the perspective sickens me!

　　You were she who abode
　　By those red-veined rocks far West,
You were the swan-necked one who rode
Along the beetling Beeny Crest,
　　And, reining nigh me,
　　Would muse and eye me,
While Life unrolled us its very best.

C

Why, then, latterly did we not speak,
Did we not think of those days long dead,
And ere your vanishing strive to seek
That time's renewal? We might have said,
        'In this bright spring weather
        We'll visit together
Those places that once we visited.'

        Well, well! All's past amend,
        Unchangeable. It must go.
I seem but a dead man held on end
To sink down soon. . . . O you could not know
        That such swift fleeing
        No soul foreseeing –
Not even I – would undo me so!

December 1912

YOUR LAST DRIVE

HERE by the moorway you returned,
And saw the borough lights ahead
That lit your face – all undiscerned
To be in a week the face of the dead,
And you told of the charm of that haloed view
That never again would beam on you.

And on your left you passed the spot
Where eight days later you were to lie,
And be spoken of as one who was not;
Beholding it with a heedless eye
As alien from you, though under its tree
You soon would halt everlastingly.

I drove not with you. . . . Yet had I sat
At your side that eve I should not have seen
That the countenance I was glancing at
Had a last-time look in the flickering sheen,
Nor have read the writing upon your face,
'I go hence soon to my resting-place;

'You may miss me then. But I shall not know
How many times you visit me there,
Or what your thoughts are, or if you go
There never at all. And I shall not care.
Should you censure me I shall take no heed,
And even your praises no more shall need.'

True: never you'll know. And you will not mind
But shall I then slight you because of such?
Dear ghost, in the past did you ever find
The thought 'What profit', move me much?
Yet abides the fact, indeed, the same, –
You are past love, praise, indifference, blame.

December 1912

THE WALK

You did not walk with me
Of late to the hill-top tree
      By the gated ways,
      As in earlier days;
      You were weak and lame,
      So you never came,
And I went alone, and I did not mind.
Not thinking of you as left behind.

I walked up there to-day
Just in the former way;
      Surveyed around
      The familiar ground
      By myself again:
      What difference, then?
Only that underlying sense
Of the look of a room on returning thence.

RAIN ON A GRAVE

CLOUDS spout upon her
  Their waters amain
  In ruthless disdain, –
Her who but lately
  Had shivered with pain
As at touch of dishonour
If there had lit on her
So coldly, so straightly
  Such arrows of rain:

One who to shelter
  Her delicate head
Would quicken and quicken
  Each tentative tread
If drops chanced to pelt her
  That summertime spills
  In dust-paven rills
When thunder-clouds thicken
  And birds close their bills.

Would that I lay there
  And she were housed here:
Or better, together
  Were folded away there
Exposed to one weather
We both, – who would stray there
When sunny the day there
  Or evening was clear
  At the prime of the year.

Soon will be growing
   Green blades from her mound,
And daisies be showing
   Like stars on the ground,
Till she form part of them –
Ay – the sweet heart of them,
Loved beyond measure
With a child's pleasure
   All her life's round.

31 January 1913

'I FOUND HER OUT THERE'

I FOUND her out there
On a slope few see,
That falls westwardly
To the salt-edged air,
Where the ocean breaks
On the purple strand,
And the hurricane shakes
The solid land.

I brought her here,
And have laid her to rest
In a noiseless nest
No sea beats near.
She will never be stirred
In her loamy cell
By the waves long heard
And loved so well.

So she does not sleep
By those haunted heights
The Atlantic smites
And the blind gales sweep,
Whence she often would gaze
At Dundagel's famed head,
While the dipping blaze
Dyed her face fire-red;

And would sigh at the tale
Of sunk Lyonnesse,
As a wind-tugged tress
Flapped her cheek like a flail;
Or listen at whiles
With a thought-bound brow
To the murmuring miles
She is far from now.

Yet her shade, maybe,
Will creep underground
Till it catch the sound
Of that western sea
As it swells and sobs
Where she once domiciled,
And joy in its throbs
With the heart of a child.

WITHOUT CEREMONY

It was your way, my dear,
To vanish without a word
When callers, friends, or kin
Had left, and I hastened in
To rejoin you, as I inferred.

And when you'd a mind to career
Off anywhere – say to town –
You were all on a sudden gone
Before I had thought thereon,
Or noticed your trunks were down.

So, now that you disappear
For ever in that swift style,
Your meaning seems to me
Just as it used to be:
'Good-bye is not worth while!'

LAMENT

How she would have loved
A party to-day! –
Bright-hatted and gloved,
With table and tray
And chairs on the lawn
Her smiles would have shone
With welcomings. . . . But
She is shut, she is shut
    From friendship's spell
    In the jailing shell
    Of her tiny cell.

Or she would have reigned
At a dinner to-night
With ardours unfeigned,
And a generous delight;
All in her abode
She'd have freely bestowed
On her guests. . . . But alas,
She is shut under grass
    Where no cups flow,
    Powerless to know
    That it might be so.

And she would have sought
With a child's eager glance
The shy snowdrops brought
By the new year's advance,
And peered in the rime
Of Candlemas-time
For crocuses . . . chanced
It that she were not tranced
    From sights she loved best;
    Wholly possessed
    By an infinite rest!

And we are here staying
Amid these stale things,
Who care not for gaying,
And those junketings
That used so to joy her,
And never to cloy her
As us they cloy! . . . But
She is shut, she is shut
    From the cheer of them, dead
    To all done and said
    In her yew-arched bed.

THE HAUNTER

He does not think that I haunt here nightly:
    How shall I let him know
That whither his fancy sets him wandering
    I, too, alertly go? –
Hover and hover a few feet from him
    Just as I used to do,
But cannot answer the words he lifts me –
    Only listen thereto!

When I could answer he did not say them:
    When I could let him know
How I would like to join in his journeys
    Seldom he wished to go.
Now that he goes and wants me with him
    More than he used to do,
Never he sees my faithful phantom
    Though he speaks thereto.

Yes, I companion him to places
    Only dreamers know,
Where the shy hares print long paces,
    Where the night rooks go;
Into old aisles where the past is all to him,
    Close as his shade can do,
Always lacking the power to call to him,
    Near as I reach thereto!

What a good haunter I am, O tell him!
    Quickly make him know
If he but sigh since my loss befell him
    Straight to his side I go.
Tell him a faithful one is doing
    All that love can do
Still that his path may be worth pursuing,
    And to bring peace thereto.

THE VOICE

WOMAN much missed, how you call to me, call to me,
Saying that now you are not as you were
When you had changed from the one who was all to me,
But as at first, when our day was fair.

Can it be you that I hear? Let me view you, then,
Standing as when I drew near to the town
Where you would wait for me: yes, as I knew you then,
Even to the original air-blue gown!

Or is it only the breeze, in its listlessness
Travelling across the wet mead to me here,
You being ever dissolved to wan wistlessness,
Heard no more again far or near?

    Thus I; faltering forward,
    Leaves around me falling,
Wind oozing thin through the thorn from norward,
    And the woman calling.

December 1912

HIS VISITOR

I COME across from Mellstock while the moon wastes weaker
To behold where I lived with you for twenty years and more:
I shall go in the gray, at the passing of the mail-train,
And need no setting open of the long familiar door
    As before.

The change I notice in my once own quarters!
A formal-fashioned border where the daisies used to be,
The rooms new painted, and the pictures altered,
And other cups and saucers, and no cosy nook for tea
        As with me.

I discern the dim faces of the sleep-wrapt servants;
They are not those who tended me through feeble hours and strong
But strangers quite, who never knew my rule here,
Who never saw me painting, never heard my softling song
        Float along.

So I don't want to linger in this re-decked dwelling,
I feel too uneasy at the contrasts I behold,
And I make again for Mellstock to return here never,
And rejoin the roomy silence, and the mute and manifold
        Souls of old.

1913

A CIRCULAR

As 'legal representative'
I read a missive not my own,
On new designs the senders give
    For clothes, in tints as shown.

Here figure blouses, gowns for tea,
And presentation-trains of state,
Charming ball-dresses, millinery,
    Warranted up to date.

And this gay-pictured, spring-time shout
Of Fashion, hails what lady proud?
Her who before last year ebbed out
    Was costumed in a shroud.

A DREAM OR NO

WHY go to Saint-Juliot? What's Juliot to me?
  Some strange necromancy
  But charmed me to fancy
That much of my life claims the spot as its key.

Yes. I have had dreams of that place in the West,
  And a maiden abiding
  Thereat as in hiding;
Fair-eyed and white-shouldered, broad-browed and brown-tressed.

And of how, coastward bound on a night long ago,
  There lonely I found her,
  The sea-birds around her,
And other than nigh things uncaring to know.

So sweet her life there (in my thought has it seemed)
  That quickly she drew me
  To take her unto me,
And lodge her long years with me. Such have I dreamed.

But nought of that maid from Saint-Juliot I see;
  Can she ever have been here,
  And shed her life's sheen here,
The woman I thought a long housemate with me?

Does there even a place like Saint-Juliot exist?
  Or a Vallency Valley
  With stream and leafed alley,
Or Beeny, or Bos with its flounce flinging mist?

February 1913

AFTER A JOURNEY

HERETO I come to view a voiceless ghost;
    Whither, O whither will its whim now draw me?
Up the cliff, down, till I'm lonely, lost,
    And the unseen waters' ejaculations awe me.
Where you will next be there's no knowing,
    Facing round about me everywhere,
        With your nut-coloured hair,
And gray eyes, and rose-flush coming and going.

Yes: I have re-entered your olden haunts at last;
    Through the years, through the dead scenes I have tracked
        you;
What have you now found to say of our past –
    Scanned across the dark space wherein I have lacked you?
Summer gave us sweets, but autumn wrought division?
    Things were not lastly as firstly well
        With us twain, you tell?
But all's closed now, despite Time's derision.

I see what you are doing: you are leading me on
    To the spots we knew when we haunted here together,
The waterfall, above which the mist-bow shone
    At the then fair hour in the then fair weather,
And the cave just under, with a voice still so hollow
    That it seems to call out to me from forty years ago,
        When you were all aglow,
And not the thin ghost that I now frailly follow!

Ignorant of what there is flitting here to see,
    The waked birds preen and the seals flop lazily;
Soon you will have, Dear, to vanish from me,
    For the stars close their shutters and the dawn whitens hazily.
Trust me, I mind not, though Life lours,
    The bringing me here; nay, bring me here again!
        I am just the same as when
Our days were a joy, and our paths through flowers.

Pentargan Bay

A DEATH-DAY RECALLED

BEENY did not quiver,
    Juliot grew not gray,
Thin Vallency's river
    Held its wonted way.
Bos seemed not to utter
    Dimmest note of dirge,
Targan mouth a mutter
    To its creamy surge.

Yet though these, unheeding,
    Listless, passed the hour
Of her spirit's speeding,
    She had, in her flower,
Sought and loved the places –
    Much and often pined
For their lonely faces
    When in towns confined.

Why did not Vallency
    In his purl deplore
One whose haunts were whence he
    Drew his limpid store?
Why did Bos not thunder,
    Targan apprehend
Body and Breath were sunder
    Of their former friend?

BEENY CLIFF

MARCH 1870–MARCH 1913

I

O THE opal and the sapphire of that wandering western sea,
And the woman riding high above with bright hair flapping
    free –
The woman whom I loved so, and who loyally loved me.

II

The pale mews plained below us, and the waves seemed far away
In a nether sky, engrossed in saying their ceaseless babbling say,
As we laughed light-heartedly aloft on that clear-sunned March
    day.

III

A little cloud then cloaked us, and there flew an irised rain,
And the Atlantic dyed its levels with a dull misfeatured stain,
And then the sun burst out again, and purples prinked the main.

IV

– Still in all its chasmal beauty bulks old Beeny to the sky,
And shall she and I not go there once again now March is nigh,
And the sweet things said in that March say anew there by and
    by?

V

What if still in chasmal beauty looms that wild weird western
    shore,
The woman now is – elsewhere – whom the ambling pony bore,
And nor knows nor cares for Beeny, and will laugh there no
    more.

AT CASTLE BOTEREL

As I drive to the junction of lane and highway,
    And the drizzle bedrenches the waggonette,
I look behind at the fading byway,
    And see on its slope, now glistening wet,
        Distinctly yet

Myself and a girlish form benighted
    In dry March weather. We climb the road
Beside a chaise. We had just alighted
    To ease the sturdy pony's load
        When he sighed and slowed.

What we did as we climbed, and what we talked of
   Matters not much, nor to what it led, –
Something that life will not be balked of
   Without rude reason till hope is dead,
      And feeling fled.

It filled but a minute. But was there ever
   A time of such quality, since or before,
In that hill's story? To one mind never,
   Though it has been climbed, foot-swift, foot-sore,
      By thousands more.

Primaeval rocks form the road's steep border,
   And much have they faced there, first and last,
Of the transitory in Earth's long order;
   But what they record in colour and cast
      Is – that we two passed.

And to me, though Time's unflinching rigour,
   In mindless rote, has ruled from sight
The substance now, one phantom figure
   Remains on the slope, as when that night
      Saw us alight.

I look and see it there, shrinking, shrinking,
   I look back at it amid the rain
For the very last time; for my sand is sinking,
   And I shall traverse old love's domain
      Never again.

    March 1913

PLACES

NOBODY says: Ah, that is the place
Where chanced, in the hollow of years ago,
What none of the Three Towns cared to know –
The birth of a little girl of grace –
The sweetest the house saw, first or last;
   Yet it was so
   On that day long past.

Nobody thinks: There, there she lay
In a room by the Hoe, like the bud of a flower,
And listened, just after the bedtime hour,
To the stammering chimes that used to play
The quaint Old Hundred-and-Thirteenth tune
    In Saint Andrew's tower
    Night, morn, and noon.

Nobody calls to mind that here
Upon Boterel Hill, where the waggoners skid,
With cheeks whose airy flush outbid
Fresh fruit in bloom, and free of fear,
She cantered down, as if she must fall
    (Though she never did),
    To the charm of all.

Nay: one there is to whom these things,
That nobody else's mind calls back,
Have a savour that scenes in being lack,
And a presence more than the actual brings;
To whom to-day is beneaped and stale,
    And its urgent clack
    But a vapid tale.

    Plymouth, March 1913

THE PHANTOM HORSEWOMAN

I

QUEER are the ways of a man I know:
    He comes and stands
    In a careworn craze,
    And looks at the sands
    And the seaward haze
    With moveless hands
    And face and gaze,
    Then turns to go . . .
And what does he see when he gazes so?

II

They say he sees as an instant thing
  More clear than to-day,
  A sweet soft scene
  That was once in play
  By that briny green;
  Yes, notes alway
  Warm, real, and keen,
  What his back years bring –
A phantom of his own figuring.

III

Of this vision of his they might say more:
  Not only there
  Does he see this sight,
  But everywhere
  In his brain – day, night,
  As if on the air
  It were drawn rose-bright –
  Yea, far from that shore
Does he carry this vision of heretofore:

IV

A ghost-girl-rider. And though, toil-tried,
  He withers daily,
  Time touches her not,
  But she still rides gaily
  In his rapt thought
  On that shagged and shaly
  Atlantic spot,
  And as when first eyed
Draws rein and sings to the swing of the tide.

1913

THE SPELL OF THE ROSE

'I MEAN to build a hall anon,
    And shape two turrets there,
    And a broad newelled stair,
And a cool well for crystal water;
    Yes; I will build a hall anon,
    Plant roses love shall feed upon,
        And apple-trees and pear.'

He set to build the manor-hall,
    And shaped the turrets there,
    And the broad newelled stair,
And the cool well for crystal water;
    He built for me that manor-hall,
    And planted many trees withal,
        But no rose anywhere.

And as he planted never a rose
    That bears the flower of love,
    Though other flowers throve
Some heart-bane moved our souls to sever
    Since he had planted never a rose;
    And misconceits raised horrid shows,
        And agonies came thereof.

'I'll mend these miseries,' then said I,
    And so, at dead of night,
    I went and, screened from sight,
That nought should keep our souls in severance,
    I set a rose-bush. 'This', said I,
    'May end divisions dire and wry,
        And long-drawn days of blight.'

But I was called from earth – yea, called
    Before my rose-bush grew;
    And would that now I knew
What feels he of the tree I planted,
    And whether, after I was called
    To be a ghost, he, as of old,
        Gave me his heart anew!

Perhaps now blooms that queen of trees
　　I set but saw not grow,
　　And he, beside its glow –
Eyes couched of the mis-vision that blurred me –
　　Ay, there beside that queen of trees
　　He sees me as I was, though sees
　　　Too late to tell me so!

ST. LAUNCE'S REVISITED

　　SLIP back, Time!
Yet again I am nearing
Castle and keep, uprearing
　　Gray, as in my prime.

　　At the inn
Smiling nigh, why is it
Not as on my visit
　　When hope and I were twin?

　　Groom and jade
Whom I found here, moulder;
Strange the tavern-holder,
　　Strange the tap-maid.

　　Here I hired
Horse and man for bearing
Me on my wayfaring
　　To the door desired.

　　Evening gloomed
As I journeyed forward
To the faces shoreward,
　　Till their dwelling loomed.

　　If again
Towards the Atlantic sea there
I should speed, they'd be there
　　Surely now as then? . . .

Why waste thought,
When I know them vanished
Under earth, yea, banished
Ever into nought!

WHERE THE PICNIC WAS

WHERE we made the fire
In the summer time
Of branch and briar
On the hill to the sea,
I slowly climb
Through winter mire,
And scan and trace
The forsaken place
Quite readily.

Now a cold wind blows,
And the grass is gray,
But the spot still shows
As a burnt circle – aye,
And stick-ends, charred,
Still strew the sward
Whereon I stand,
Last relic of the band
Who came that day!

Yes, I am here
Just as last year,
And the sea breathes brine
From its strange straight line
Up hither, the same
As when we four came.
– But two have wandered far
From this grassy rise
Into urban roar
Where no picnics are,
And one – has shut her eyes
For evermore.

[End of *Poems of 1912–13*]

'NOT ONLY I'

Not only I
Am doomed awhile to lie
In this close bin with earthen sides;
But the things I thought, and the songs I sang,
And the hopes I had, and the passioned pang
    For people I knew
    Who passed before me,
Whose memory barely abides;
    And the visions I drew
    That daily upbore me!

And the joyous springs and summers,
    And the jaunts with blithe newcomers,
And my plans and appearances; drives and rides
That fanned my face to a lively red;
    And the grays and blues
    Of the far-off views,
That nobody else discerned outspread;
And little achievements for blame or praise;
Things left undone; things left unsaid;
    In brief, my days!

Compressed here in six feet by two,
    In secrecy
    To lie with me
    Till the Call shall be,
    Are all these things I knew,
    Which cannot be handed on;
Strange happenings quite unrecorded,
Lost to the world and disregarded,
That only thinks: 'Here moulders till Doom's-dawn
    A woman's skeleton.'

THE RIFT

(SONG: MINOR MODE)

'Twas just at gnat and cobweb-time,
When yellow begins to show in the leaf,
That your old gamut changed its chime
From those true tones – of span so brief! –
That met my beats of joy, of grief,
  As rhyme meets rhyme.

So sank I from my high sublime!
We raced but chancewise after that,
And never I knew or guessed my crime. . . .
Yes; 'twas the date – or nigh thereat –
Of the yellowing leaf; at moth and gnat
  And cobweb-time.

TOLERANCE

'It is a foolish thing', said I,
'To bear with such, and pass it by;
Yet so I do, I know not why!'

And at each cross I would surmise
That if I had willed not in that wise
I might have spared me many sighs.

But now the only happiness
In looking back that I possess –
Whose lack would leave me comfortless –

Is to remember I refrained
From masteries I might have gained,
And for my tolerance was disdained;

For see, a tomb. And if it were
I had bent and broke, I should not dare
To linger in the shadows there.

HE PREFERS HER EARTHLY

THIS after-sunset is a sight for seeing,
Cliff-heads of craggy cloud surrounding it.
   – And dwell you in that glory-show?
You may; for there are strange strange things in being,
     Stranger than I know.

Yet if that chasm of splendour claim your presence
Which glows between the ash cloud and the dun,
   How changed must be your mortal mould!
Changed to a firmament-riding earthless essence
     From what you were of old:

All too unlike the fond and fragile creature
Then known to me. . . . Well, shall I say it plain?
   I would not have you thus and there,
But still would grieve on, missing you, still feature
     You as the one you were.

A NIGHT IN NOVEMBER

I MARKED when the weather changed,
  And the panes began to quake,
And the winds rose up and ranged,
  That night, lying half-awake.

Dead leaves blew into my room,
  And alighted upon my bed,
And a tree declared to the gloom
  Its sorrow that they were shed.

One leaf of them touched my hand,
  And I thought that it was you
There stood as you used to stand,
  And saying at last you knew!

    (?) *1913*

QUID HIC AGIS?

I

When I weekly knew
An ancient pew,
And murmured there
The forms of prayer
And thanks and praise
In the ancient ways,
And heard read out
During August drought
That chapter from Kings
Harvest-time brings;
– How the prophet, broken
By griefs unspoken,
Went heavily away
To fast and to pray,
And, while waiting to die.
The Lord passed by,
And a whirlwind and fire
Drew nigher and nigher,
And a small voice anon
Bade him up and be gone,
I did not apprehend
As I sat to the end
And watched for her smile
Across the sunned aisle,
That this tale of a seer
Which came once a year
Might, when sands were heaping,
Be like a sweat creeping,
Or in any degree
Bear on her or on me!

II

When later, by chance
Of circumstance,
It befel me to read
On a hot afternoon
At the lectern there
The selfsame words
As the lesson decreed,
To the gathered few
From the hamlets near –
Folk of flocks and herds
Sitting half aswoon,
Who listened thereto
As women and men
Not overmuch
Concerned as such –
So, like them then,
I did not see
What drought might be
With me, with her,
As the Kalendar
Moved on, and Time
Devoured our prime.

III

But now, at last,
When our glory has passed,
And there is no smile
From her in the aisle,
But where it once shone
A marble, men say,
With her name thereon
Is discerned to-day;
And spiritless
In the wilderness
I shrink from sight
And desire the night,
(Though, as in old wise,
I might still arise,

Go forth, and stand
And prophesy in the land),
I feel the shake
Of wind and earthquake,
And consuming fire
Nigher and nigher,
And the voice catch clear,
'What doest thou here?'

The Spectator: 1916.   During the War

SECTION 3

THE MONTH'S CALENDAR

TEAR off the calendar
Of this month past,
And all its weeks, that are
Flown, to be cast
To oblivion fast!

Darken that day
On which we met,
With its words of gay
Half-felt regret
That you'll forget!

The second day, too;
The noon I nursed
Well – thoughts; yes, through
To the thirty-first;
That was the worst.

For then it was
You let me see
There was good cause
Why you could not be
Aught ever to me!

A THUNDERSTORM IN TOWN

(A REMINISCENCE: 1893)

SHE wore a new 'terra-cotta' dress,
And we stayed, because of the pelting storm,
Within the hansom's dry recess,
Though the horse had stopped; yea, motionless
    We sat on, snug and warm.

Then the downpour ceased, to my sharp sad pain
And the glass that had screened our forms before
Flew up, and out she sprang to her door:
I should have kissed her if the rain
    Had lasted a minute more.

AT AN INN

WHEN we as strangers sought
    Their catering care,
Veiled smiles bespoke their thought
    Of what we were.
They warmed as they opined
    Us more than friends –
That we had all resigned
    For love's dear ends.

And that swift sympathy
   With living love
Which quicks the world – maybe
   The spheres above,
Made them our ministers,
   Moved them to say,
'Ah, God, that bliss like theirs
   Would flush our day!'

And we were left alone
   As Love's own pair;
Yet never the love-light shone
   Between us there!
But that which chilled the breath
   Of afternoon,
And palsied unto death
   The pane-fly's tune.

The kiss their zeal foretold,
   And now deemed come,
Came not: within his hold
   Love lingered numb.
Why cast he on our port
   A bloom not ours?
Why shaped us for his sport
   In after-hours?

As we seemed we were not
   That day afar,
And now we seem not what
   We aching are.
O severing sea and land,
   O laws of men,
Ere death, once let us stand
   As we stood then!

IN DEATH DIVIDED

I

I SHALL rot here, with those whom in their day
 You never knew,
And alien ones who, ere they chilled to clay,
 Met not my view,
Will in your distant grave-place ever neighbour you.

II

No shade of pinnacle or tree or tower,
 While earth endures,
Will fall on my mound and within the hour
 Steal on to yours;
One robin never haunt our two green covertures.

III

Some organ may resound on Sunday noons
 By where you lie,
Some other thrill the panes with other tunes
 Where moulder I;
No selfsame chords compose our common lullaby.

IV

The simply-cut memorial at my head
 Perhaps may take
A rustic form, and that above your bed
 A stately make;
No linking symbol show thereon for our tale's sake.

V

And in the monotonous moils of strained, hard-run
 Humanity,
The eternal tie which binds us twain in one
 No eye will see
Stretching across the miles that sever you from me.

189–

HE WONDERS ABOUT HIMSELF

No use hoping, or feeling vext,
Tugged by a force above or under
Like some fantocine, much I wonder
What I shall find me doing next!

Shall I be rushing where bright eyes be?
Shall I be suffering sorrows seven?
Shall I be watching the stars of heaven,
Thinking one of them looks like thee?

Part is mine of the general Will,
Cannot my share in the sum of sources
Bend a digit the poise of forces,
And a fair desire fulfil?

November 1893

THE RECALCITRANTS

LET us off and search, and find a place
Where yours and mine can be natural lives,
Where no one comes who dissects and dives
And proclaims that ours is a curious case,
Which its touch of romance can scarcely grace.

You would think it strange at first, but then
Everything has been strange in its time.
When some one said on a day of the prime
He would bow to no brazen god again
He doubtless dazed the mass of men.

None will see in us a pair whose claims
To righteous judgment we care not making;
Who have doubted if breath be worth the taking,
And have no respect for the current fames
Whence the savour has flown while abide the names.

We have found us already shunned, disdained,
And for re-acceptance have not once striven;
Whatever offence our course has given
The brunt thereof we have long sustained.
Well, let us away, scorned, unexplained.

COME NOT; YET COME!

(SONG)

IN my sage moments I can say,
        Come not near,
But far in foreign regions stay.
        So that here
A mind may grow again serene and clear.

But the thought withers. Why should I
        Have fear to earn me
Fame from your nearness, though thereby
        Old fires new burn me,
And lastly, maybe, tear and overturn me!

So I say, Come: deign again shine
        Upon this place,
Even if unslackened smart be mine
        From that sweet face,
And I faint to a phantom past all trace.

'BETWEEN US NOW'

BETWEEN us now and here –
        Two thrown together
Who are not wont to wear
        Life's flushest feather –
Who see the scenes slide past,
The daytimes dimming fast,
Let there be truth at last,
        Even if despair.

So thoroughly and long
  Have you now known me,
So real in faith and strong
  Have I now shown me,
That nothing needs disguise
Further in any wise,
Or asks or justifies
  A guarded tongue.

Face unto face, then, say,
  Eyes my own meeting,
Is your heart far away,
  Or with mine beating?
When false things are brought low,
And swift things have grown slow,
Feigning like froth shall go,
  Faith be for aye.

THE DIVISION

RAIN on the windows, creaking doors,
  With blasts that besom the green,
And I am here, and you are there,
  And a hundred miles between!

O were it but the weather, Dear,
  O were it but the miles
That summed up all our severance,
  There might be room for smiles.

But that thwart thing betwixt us twain,
  Which nothing cleaves or clears,
Is more than distance, Dear, or rain,
  And longer than the years!

1893

A BROKEN APPOINTMENT

YOU did not come,
And marching Time drew on, and wore me numb. –
Yet less for loss of your dear presence there
Than that I thus found lacking in your make
That high compassion which can overbear
Reluctance for pure lovingkindness' sake
Grieved I, when, as the hope-hour stroked its sum,
            You did not come.

You love not me,
And love alone can lend you loyalty;
– I know and knew it. But, unto the store
Of human deeds divine in all but name,
Was it not worth a little hour or more
To add yet this: Once you, a woman, came
To soothe a time-torn man; even though it be
            You love not me?

LAST LOVE-WORD

(SONG)

THIS is the last; the very, very last!
        Anon, and all is dead and dumb,
        Only a pale shroud over the past,
                That cannot be
                Of value small or vast,
                Love, then to me!

I can say no more: I have even said too much.
        I did not mean that this should come:
        I did not know 'twould swell to such –
                Nor, perhaps, you –
                When that first look and touch,
                Love, doomed us two!

189–

D

SECTION 4

AFTER THE VISIT

(TO F. E. D.)

COME again to the place
Where your presence was as a leaf that skims
Down a drouthy way whose ascent bedims
    The bloom on the farer's face.

Come again, with the feet
That were light on the green as a thistledown ball,
And those mute ministrations to one and to all
    Beyond a man's saying sweet.

Until then the faint scent
Of the bordering flowers swam unheeded away,
And I marked not the charm in the changes of day
    As the cloud-colours came and went.

Through the dark corridors
Your walk was so soundless I did not know
Your form from a phantom's of long ago
    Said to pass on the ancient floors,

Till you drew from the shade,
And I saw the large luminous living eyes
Regard me in fixed inquiring-wise
    As those of a soul that weighed,

Scarce consciously,
The eternal question of what Life was,
And why we were there, and by whose strange laws
    That which mattered most could not be.

ON THE DEPARTURE PLATFORM

WE kissed at the barrier; and passing through
She left me, and moment by moment got
Smaller and smaller, until to my view
      She was but a spot;

A wee white spot of muslin fluff
That down the diminishing platform bore
Through hustling crowds of gentle and rough
      To the carriage door.

Under the lamplight's fitful glowers,
Behind dark groups from far and near,
Whose interests were apart from ours,
      She would disappear,

Then show again, till I ceased to see
That flexible form, that nebulous white;
And she who was more than my life to me
      Had vanished quite. . . .

We have penned new plans since that fair fond day,
And in season she will appear again –
Perhaps in the same soft white array –
      But never as then!

– 'And why, young man, must eternally fly
A joy you'll repeat, if you love her well?'
– O friend, nought happens twice thus; why,
      I cannot tell!

A JOG-TROT PAIR

WHO were the twain that trod this track
      So many times together
      Hither and back,
In spells of certain and uncertain weather?

Commonplace in conduct they
    Who wandered to and fro here
        Day by day:
Two that few dwellers troubled themselves to know here.

The very gravel-path was prim
    That daily they would follow:
        Borders trim:
Never a wayward sprout, or hump, or hollow.

Trite usages in tamest style
    Had tended to their plighting.
        'It's just worth while,
Perhaps,' they had said. 'And saves much sad good-nighting.'

And petty seemed the happenings
    That ministered to their joyance:
        Simple things,
Onerous to satiate souls, increased their buoyance.

Who could those common people be,
    Of days the plainest, barest?
        They were we;
Yes; happier than the cleverest, smartest, rarest.

'WHY DO I?'

WHY do I go on doing these things?
    Why not cease?
Is it that you are yet in this world of welterings
    And unease,
And that, while so, mechanic repetitions please?

When shall I leave off doing these things? –
    When I hear
You have dropped your dusty cloak and taken your wondrous
        wings
    To another sphere,
Where no pain is: Then shall I hush this dinning gear.

'I SOMETIMES THINK'

(FOR F. E. H.)

I SOMETIMES think as here I sit
    Of things I have done,
Which seemed in doing not unfit
    To face the sun:
Yet never a soul has paused a whit
    On such – not one.

There was that eager strenuous press
    To sow good seed;
There was that saving from distress
    In the nick of need;
There were those words in the wilderness:
    Who cared to heed?

Yet can this be full true, or no?
    For one did care,
And, spiriting into my house, to, fro,
    Like wind on the stair,
Cares still, heeds all, and will, even though
    I may despair.

PART III

THE PAST AND THE PRESENT

SECTION 1

CHILDHOOD AND FAMILY

ONE WE KNEW

(M. H. 1772–1857)

She told how they used to form for the country dances –
  'The Triumph', 'The New-rigged Ship' –
To the light of the guttering wax in the panelled manses,
  And in cots to the blink of a dip.

She spoke of the wild 'poussetting' and 'allemanding'
  On carpet, on oak, and on sod;
And the two long rows of ladies and gentlemen standing,
  And the figures the couples trod.

She showed us the spot where the maypole was yearly planted,
  And where the bandsmen stood
While breeched and kerchiefed partners whirled, and panted
  To choose each other for good.

She told of that far-back day when they learnt astounded
  Of the death of the King of France:
Of the Terror; and then of Bonaparte's unbounded
  Ambition and arrogance.

Of how his threats woke warlike preparations
  Along the southern strand,
And how each night brought tremors and trepidations
  Lest morning should see him land.

She said she had often heard the gibbet creaking
    As it swayed in the lightning flash,
Had caught from the neighbouring town a small child's shrieking
    At the cart-tail under the lash. . . .

With cap-framed face and long gaze into the embers –
    We seated around her knees –
She would dwell on such dead themes, not as one who remembers,
    But rather as one who sees.

She seemed one left behind of a band gone distant
    So far that no tongue could hail:
Past things retold were to her as things existent,
    Things present but as a tale.

20 May 1902

A CHURCH ROMANCE

(MELLSTOCK: CIRCA 1835)

SHE turned in the high pew, until her sight
Swept the west gallery, and caught its row
Of music-men with viol, book, and bow
Against the sinking sad tower-window light.

She turned again; and in her pride's despite
One strenuous viol's inspirer seemed to throw
A message from his string to her below,
Which said: 'I claim thee as my own forthright!'

Thus their hearts' bond began, in due time signed.
And long years thence, when Age had scared Romance,
At some old attitude of his or glance
That gallery-scene would break upon her mind,
With him as minstrel, ardent, young, and trim,
Bowing 'New Sabbath' or 'Mount Ephraim'.

AFTER THE LAST BREATH

(J. H. 1813–1904)

THERE's no more to be done, or feared, or hoped;
None now need watch, speak low, and list, and tire;
No irksome crease outsmoothed, no pillow sloped
    Does she require.

Blankly we gaze. We are free to go or stay;
Our morrow's anxious plans have missed their aim;
Whether we leave to-night or wait till day
    Counts as the same.

The lettered vessels of medicaments
Seem asking wherefore we have set them here;
Each palliative its silly face presents
    As useless gear.

And yet we feel that something savours well;
We note a numb relief withheld before;
Our well-beloved is prisoner in the cell
    Of Time no more.

We see by littles now the deft achievement
Whereby she has escaped the Wrongers all,
In view of which our momentary bereavement
    Outshapes but small.

1904

THE SELF-UNSEEING

HERE is the ancient floor,
Footworn and hollowed and thin,
Here was the former door
Where the dead feet walked in.

She sat here in her chair,
Smiling into the fire;
He who played stood there,
Bowing it higher and higher.

Childlike, I danced in a dream;
Blessings emblazoned that day;
Everything glowed with a gleam;
Yet we were looking away!

THE OXEN

CHRISTMAS EVE, and twelve of the clock.
    'Now they are all on their knees,'
An elder said as we sat in a flock
    By the embers in hearthside ease.

We pictured the meek mild creatures where
    They dwelt in their strawy pen,
Nor did it occur to one of us there
    To doubt they were kneeling then.

So fair a fancy few would weave
    In these days! Yet, I feel,
If someone said on Christmas Eve,
    'Come; see the oxen kneel

'In the lonely barton by yonder coomb
    Our childhood used to know,'
I should go with him in the gloom,
    Hoping it might be so.

1915

THE HOUSE OF HOSPITALITIES

HERE we broached the Christmas barrel,
   Pushed up the charred log-ends;
Here we sang the Christmas carol,
   And called in friends.

Time has tired me since we met here
   When the folk now dead were young.
Since the viands were outset here
   And quaint songs sung.

And the worm has bored the viol
   That used to lead the tune,
Rust has eaten out the dial
   That struck night's noon.

Now no Christmas brings in neighbours,
   And the New Year comes unlit;
Where we sang the mole now labours,
   And spiders knit.

Yet at midnight if here walking,
   When the moon sheets wall and tree,
I see forms of old time talking,
   Who smile on me.

THE ROMAN ROAD

THE Roman Road runs straight and bare
As the pale parting-line in hair
Across the heath. And thoughtful men
Contrast its days of Now and Then,
And delve, and measure, and compare;

Visioning on the vacant air
Helmed legionaries, who proudly rear
The Eagle, as they pace again
        The Roman Road.

But no tall brass-helmed legionnaire
Haunts it for me. Uprises there
A mother's form upon my ken,
Guiding my infant steps, as when
We walked that ancient thoroughfare,
                    The Roman Road.

CHILDHOOD AMONG THE FERNS

I SAT one sprinkling day upon the lea,
Where tall-stemmed ferns spread out luxuriantly,
And nothing but those tall ferns sheltered me.

The rain gained strength, and damped each lopping frond,
Ran down their stalks beside me and beyond,
And shaped slow-creeping rivulets as I conned,

With pride, my spray-roofed house. And though anon
Some drops pierced its green rafters, I sat on,
Making pretence I was not rained upon.

The sun then burst, and brought forth a sweet breath
From the limp ferns as they dried underneath:
I said: 'I could live on here thus till death';

And queried in the green rays as I sate:
'Why should I have to grow to man's estate,
And this afar-noised World perambulate?'

AFTERNOON SERVICE AT MELLSTOCK

(CIRCA 1850)

ON afternoons of drowsy calm
We stood in the panelled pew,
Singing one-voiced a Tate-and-Brady psalm
To the tune of 'Cambridge New'.

We watched the elms, we watched the rooks,
        The clouds upon the breeze,
Between the whiles of glancing at our books,
        And swaying like the trees.

So mindless were those outpourings! –
        Though I am not aware
That I have gained by subtle thought on things
        Since we stood psalming there.

NIGHT IN THE OLD HOME

WHEN the wasting embers redden the chimney-breast,
And Life's bare pathway looms like a desert track to me,
And from hall and parlour the living have gone to their rest,
My perished people who housed them here come back to me.

They come and seat them around in their mouldy places,
Now and then bending towards me a glance of wistfulness,
A strange upbraiding smile upon all their faces,
And in the bearing of each a passive tristfulness.

'Do you uphold me, lingering and languishing here,
A pale late plant of your once strong stock?' I say to them;
'A thinker of crooked thoughts upon Life in the sere,
And on That which consigns men to night after showing the day
        to them?'

'– O let be the Wherefore! We fevered our years not thus:
Take of Life what it grants, without question!' they answer me
        seemingly.
'Enjoy, suffer, wait: spread the table here freely like us,
And, satisfied, placid, unfretting, watch Time away beamingly!'

OLD FURNITURE

I KNOW not how it may be with others
    Who sit amid relics of householdry
That date from the days of their mothers' mothers,
    But well I know how it is with me
        Continually.

I see the hands of the generations
    That owned each shiny familiar thing
In play on its knobs and indentations,
    And with its ancient fashioning
        Still dallying:

Hands behind hands, growing paler and paler,
    As in a mirror a candle-flame
Shows images of itself, each frailer
    As it recedes, though the eye may frame
        Its shape the same.

On the clock's dull dial a foggy finger,
    Moving to set the minutes right
With tentative touches that lift and linger
    In the wont of a moth on a summer night,
        Creeps to my sight.

On this old viol, too, fingers are dancing –
    As whilom – just over the strings by the nut,
The tip of a bow receding, advancing
    In airy quivers, as if it would cut
        The plaintive gut.

And I see a face by that box for tinder,
    Glowing forth in fits from the dark,
And fading again, as the linten cinder
    Kindles to red at the flinty spark,
        Or goes out stark.

Well, well. It is best to be up and doing,
 The world has no use for one to-day
Who eyes things thus – no aim pursuing!
 He should not continue in this stay,
  But sink away.

LOGS ON THE HEARTH

A MEMORY OF A SISTER

THE fire advances along the log
 Of the tree we felled,
Which bloomed and bore striped apples by the peck
 Till its last hour of bearing knelled.

The fork that first my hand would reach
 And then my foot
In climbings upward inch by inch, lies now
 Sawn, sapless, darkening with soot.

Where the bark chars is where, one year,
 It was pruned, and bled –
Then overgrew the wound. But now, at last,
 Its growings all have stagnated.

My fellow-climber rises dim
 From her chilly grave –
Just as she was, her foot near mine on the bending limb,
 Laughing, her young brown hand awave.

December 1915

'SACRED TO THE MEMORY'

(MARY H.)

THAT 'Sacred to the Memory'
Is clearly carven there I own,
And all may think that on the stone
The words have been inscribed by me
In bare conventionality.

They know not and will never know
That my full script is not confined
To that stone space, but stands deep lined
Upon the landscape high and low
Wherein she made such worthy show.

TO MY FATHER'S VIOLIN

DOES he want you down there
In the Nether Glooms where
The hours may be a dragging load upon him,
As he hears the axle grind
Round and round
Of the great world, in the blind
Still profound
Of the night-time? He might liven at the sound
Of your string, revealing you had not forgone him.

In the gallery west the nave,
But a few yards from his grave,
Did you, tucked beneath his chin, to his bowing
Guide the homely harmony
Of the quire
Who for long years strenuously –
Son and sire –
Caught the strains that at his fingering low or higher
From your four thin threads and eff-holes came outflowing.

And, too, what merry tunes
He would bow at nights or noons
That chanced to find him bent to lute a measure.
When he made you speak his heart
As in dream,
Without book or music-chart,
On some theme
Elusive as a jack-o'-lanthorn's gleam,
And the psalm of duty shelved for trill of pleasure.

Well, you can not, alas,
The barrier overpass
That screens him in those Mournful Meads hereunder,
Where no fiddling can be heard
In the glades
Of silentness, no bird
Thrills the shades;
Where no viol is touched for songs or serenades,
No bowing wakes a congregation's wonder.

He must do without you now,
Stir you no more anyhow
To yearning concords taught you in your glory;
While, your strings a tangled wreck,
Once smart drawn,
Ten worm-wounds in your neck,
Purflings wan
With dust-hoar, here alone I sadly con
Your present dumbness, shape your olden story.

1916

SINE PROLE

(MEDIAEVAL LATIN SEQUENCE-METRE)

FORTH from ages thick in mystery,
Through the morn and noon of history,
To the moment where I stand
Has my line wound: I the last one –
Outcome of each spectral past one
Of that file, so many-manned!

Nothing in its time-trail marred it:
As one long life I regard it
    Throughout all the years till now,
When it fain – the close seen coming –
After annals past all plumbing –
    Makes to Being its parting bow.

Unlike Jahveh's ancient nation,
Little in their line's cessation
    Moderns see for surge of sighs:
They have been schooled by lengthier vision,
View Life's lottery with misprision,
    And its dice that fling no prize!

SILENCES

THERE is the silence of a copse or croft
    When the wind sinks dumb,
    And of a belfry-loft
When the tenor after tolling stops its hum.

And there's the silence of a lonely pond
    Where a man was drowned,
    Nor nigh nor yond
A newt, frog, toad, to make the merest sound.

But the rapt silence of an empty house
    Where oneself was born,
    Dwelt, held carouse
With friends, is of all silences most forlorn!

Past are remembered songs and music-strains
    Once audible there:
    Roof, rafters, panes
Look absent-thoughted, tranced, or locked in prayer.

It seems no power on earth can waken it
    Or rouse its rooms,
    Or its past permit
The present to stir a torpor like a tomb's.

YULETIDE IN A YOUNGER WORLD

WE believed in highdays then,
    And could glimpse at night
      On Christmas Eve
Imminent oncomings of radiant revel –
    Doings of delight:–
    Now we have no such sight.

We had eyes for phantoms then,
    And at bridge or stile
      On Christmas Eve
Clear beheld those countless ones who had crossed it
    Cross again in file:–
    Such has ceased longwhile!

We liked divination then,
    And, as they homeward wound
      On Christmas Eve,
We could read men's dreams within them spinning
    Even as wheels spin round:–
    Now we are blinker-bound.

We heard still small voices then,
    And, in the dim serene
      Of Christmas Eve,
Caught the fartime tones of fire-filled prophets
    Long on earth unseen. . . .
    – Can such ever have been?

SECTION 2

TRAVEL

GENOA AND THE MEDITERRANEAN

(MARCH 1887)

O EPIC-FAMED, god-haunted Central Sea,
Heave careless of the deep wrong done to thee
When from Torino's track I saw thy face first flash on me.

And multimarbled Genova the Proud,
Gleam all unconscious how, wide-lipped, up-browed,
I first beheld thee clad – not as the Beauty but the Dowd.

Out from a deep-delved way my vision lit
On housebacks pink, green, ochreous – where a slit
Shoreward 'twixt row and row revealed the classic blue through it.

And thereacross waved fishwives' high-hung smocks,
Chrome kerchiefs, scarlet hose, darned underfrocks;
Often since when my dreams of thee, O Queen, that frippery
    mocks:

Whereat I grieve, Superba! . . . Afterhours
Within Palazzo Doria's orange bowers
Went far to mend these marrings of thy soul-subliming powers.

But, Queen, such squalid undress none should see,
Those dream-endangering eyewounds no more be
Where lovers first behold thy form in pilgrimage to thee.

IN THE OLD THEATRE, FIESOLE

(APRIL 1887)

I TRACED the Circus whose gray stones incline
Where Rome and dim Etruria interjoin,
Till came a child who showed an ancient coin
That bore the image of a Constantine.

She lightly passed; nor did she once opine
How, better than all books, she had raised for me
In swift perspective Europe's history
Through the vast years of Cæsar's sceptred line.

For in my distant plot of English loam
'Twas but to delve, and straightway there to find
Coins of like impress. As with one half blind
Whom common simples cure, her act flashed home
In that mute moment to my opened mind
The power, the pride, the reach of perished Rome.

ROME: ON THE PALATINE

(APRIL 1887)

WE walked where Victor Jove was shrined awhile,
And passed to Livia's rich red mural show,
Whence, thridding cave and Criptoportico,
We gained Caligula's dissolving pile.

And each ranked ruin tended to beguile
The outer sense, and shape itself as though
It wore its marble gleams, its pristine glow
Of scenic frieze and pompous peristyle.

When lo, swift hands, on strings nigh overhead,
Began to melodize a waltz by Strauss:
It stirred me as I stood, in Cæsar's house,
Raised the old routs Imperial lyres had led,

And blended pulsing life with lives long done,
Till Time seemed fiction, Past and Present one.

ROME

BUILDING A NEW STREET IN THE ANCIENT QUARTER

(APRIL 1887)

THESE umbered cliffs and gnarls of masonry
Outskeleton Time's central city, Rome;
Whereof each arch, entablature, and dome
Lies bare in all its gaunt anatomy.

And cracking frieze and rotten metope
Express, as though they were an open tome
Top-lined with caustic monitory gnome;
'Dunces, Learn here to spell Humanity!'

And yet within these ruins' very shade
The singing workmen shape and set and join
Their frail new mansion's stuccoed cove and quoin
With no apparent sense that years abrade,
Though each rent wall their feeble works invade
Once shamed all such in power of pier and groin.

ROME

THE VATICAN: SALA DELLE MUSE

(1887)

I SAT in the Muses' Hall at the mid of the day,
And it seemed to grow still, and the people to pass away,
And the chiselled shapes to combine in a haze of sun,
Till beside a Carrara column there gleamed forth One.

She looked not this nor that of those beings divine,
But each and the whole – an essence of all the Nine;
With tentative foot she neared to my halting-place,
A pensive smile on her sweet, small, marvellous face.

'Regarded so long, we render thee sad?' said she.
'Not you,' sighed I, 'but my own inconstancy!
I worship each and each; in the morning one,
And then, alas! another at sink of sun.

'To-day my soul clasps Form; but where is my troth
Of yesternight with Tune: can one cleave to both?'
– 'Be not perturbed,' said she. 'Though apart in fame,
As I and my sisters are one, those, too, are the same.'

– 'But my love goes further – to Story, and Dance, and Hymn,
The lover of all in a sun-sweep is fool to whim –
Is swayed like a river-weed as the ripples run!'
– 'Nay, wooer, thou sway'st not. These are but phases of one;

'And that one is I; and I am projected from thee,
One that out of thy brain and heart thou causest to be –
Extern to thee nothing. Grieve not, nor thyself becall,
Woo where thou wilt; and rejoice thou canst love at all!'

ROME

AT THE PYRAMID OF CESTIUS NEAR THE GRAVES OF SHELLEY AND KEATS

(1887)

Who, then, was Cestius,
And what is he to me? –
Amid thick thoughts and memories multitudinous
One thought alone brings he.

I can recall no word
Of anything he did;
For me he is a man who died and was interred
To leave a pyramid

Whose purpose was exprest
Not with its first design,
Nor till, far down in Time, beside it found their rest
Two countrymen of mine.

Cestius in life, maybe,
Slew, breathed out threatening;
I know not. This I know: in death all silently
He does a finer thing,

In beckoning pilgrim feet
With marble finger high
To where, by shadowy wall and history-haunted street,
Those matchless singers lie. . . .

– Say, then, he lived and died
That stones which bear his name
Should mark, through Time, where two immortal Shades abide;
It is an ample fame.

LAUSANNE

IN GIBBON'S OLD GARDEN: 11–12 P.M.

JUNE 27, 1897

(*The 110th anniversary of the completion of the* Decline and Fall *at the same hour and place*)

A SPIRIT seems to pass,
Formal in pose, but grave withal and grand:
He contemplates a volume in his hand,
And far lamps fleck him through the thin acacias.

Anon the book is closed,
With 'It is finished!' And at the alley's end
He turns, and when on me his glances bend
As from the Past comes speech – small, muted, yet composed.

'How fares the Truth now? – Ill?
– Do pens but slily further her advance?
May one not speed her but in phrase askance?
Do scribes aver the Comic to be Reverend still?

'Still rule those minds on earth
At whom sage Milton's wormwood words were hurled:
"Truth like a bastard comes into the world
Never without ill-fame to him who gives her birth"?'

ZERMATT

TO THE MATTERHORN

(JUNE–JULY 1897)

THIRTY-TWO years since, up against the sun,
Seven shapes, thin atomies to lower sight,
Labouringly leapt and gained thy gabled height,
And four lives paid for what the seven had won.

They were the first by whom the deed was done,
And when I look at thee, my mind takes flight
To that day's tragic feat of manly might,
As though, till then, of history thou hadst none.

Yet ages ere men topped thee, late and soon
Thou didst behold the planets lift and lower;
Saw'st, maybe, Joshua's pausing sun and moon,
And the betokening sky when Cæsar's power
Approached its bloody end; yea, even that Noon
When darkness filled the earth till the ninth hour.

THE SCHRECKHORN

(WITH THOUGHTS OF LESLIE STEPHEN)

(JUNE 1897)

ALOOF, as if a thing of mood and whim;
Now that its spare and desolate figure gleams
Upon my nearing vision, less it seems
A looming Alp-height than a guise of him
Who scaled its horn with ventured life and limb,
Drawn on by vague imaginings, maybe,
Of semblance to his personality
In its quaint glooms, keen lights, and rugged trim.

At his last change, when Life's dull coils unwind,
Will he, in old love, hitherward escape,
And the eternal essence of his mind
Enter this silent adamantine shape,
And his low voicing haunt its slipping snows
When dawn that calls the climber dyes them rose!

SECTION 3

MEMORY AND REFLECTION

THE TEMPORARY THE ALL

(SAPPHICS)

CHANGE and chancefulness in my flowering youthtime,
Set me sun by sun near to one unchosen;
Wrought us fellowlike, and despite divergence,
        Fused us in friendship.

'Cherish him can I while the true one forthcome –
Come the rich fulfiller of my prevision;
Life is roomy yet, and the odds unbounded.
          So self-communed I.

'Thwart my wistful way did a damsel saunter,
Fair, albeit unformed to be all-eclipsing;
'Maiden meet', held I, 'till arise my forefelt
          Wonder of women.'

Long a visioned hermitage deep desiring,
Tenements uncouth I was fain to house in:
'Let such lodging be for a breath-while,' thought I,
          'Soon a more seemly.

'Then high handiwork will I make my life-deed,
Truth and Light outshow; but the ripe time pending,
Intermissive aim at the thing sufficeth.'
          Thus I. . . . But lo, me!

Mistress, friend, place, aims to be bettered straightway,
Bettered not has Fate or my hand's achievement;
Sole the showance those of my onward earth-track –
          Never transcended!

A CONFESSION TO A FRIEND IN TROUBLE

Your troubles shrink not, though I feel them less
Here, far away, than when I tarried near;
I even smile old smiles – with listlessness –
Yet smiles they are, not ghastly mockeries mere.

A thought too strange to house within my brain
Haunting its outer precincts I discern:
– *That I will not show zeal again to learn
Your griefs, and, sharing them, renew my pain.* . . .

It goes, like murky bird or buccaneer
That shapes its lawless figure on the main,
And staunchness tends to banish utterly
The unseemly instinct that had lodgment here;
Yet, comrade old, can bitterer knowledge be
Than that, though banned, such instinct was in me!

1866

AT A LUNAR ECLIPSE

THY shadow, Earth, from Pole to Central Sea,
Now steals along upon the Moon's meek shine
In even monochrome and curving line
Of imperturbable serenity.

How shall I link such sun-cast symmetry
With the torn troubled form I know as thine,
That profile, placid as a brow divine,
With continents of moil and misery?

And can immense Mortality but throw
So small a shade, and Heaven's high human scheme
Be hemmed within the coasts yon arc implies?

Is such the stellar gauge of earthly show,
Nation at war with nation, brains that teem,
Heroes, and women fairer than the skies?

'I LOOK INTO MY GLASS'

I LOOK into my glass,
And view my wasting skin,
And say, 'Would God it came to pass
My heart had shrunk as thin!'

For then, I, undistrest
By hearts grown cold to me,
Could lonely wait my endless rest
With equanimity.

But Time, to make me grieve,
Part steals, lets part abide;
And shakes this fragile frame at eve
With throbbings of noontide.

MUTE OPINION

I

I TRAVERSED a dominion
Whose spokesmen spake out strong
Their purpose and opinion
Through pulpit, press, and song.
I scarce had means to note there
A large-eyed few, and dumb,
Who thought not as those thought there
That stirred the heat and hum.

II

When, grown a Shade, beholding
That land in lifetime trode,
To learn if its unfolding
Fulfilled its clamoured code,
I saw, in web unbroken,
Its history outwrought
Not as the loud had spoken,
But as the mute had thought.

TO AN UNBORN PAUPER CHILD

I

BREATHE not, hid Heart: cease silently,
And though thy birth-hour beckons thee,
    Sleep the long sleep:
    The Doomsters heap
Travails and teens around us here,
And Time-wraiths turn our songsingings to fear.

II

Hark, how the peoples surge and sigh,
And laughters fail, and greetings die:
  Hopes dwindle; yea,
  Faiths waste away,
Affections and enthusiasms numb;
Thou canst not mend these things if thou dost come.

III

Had I the ear of wombèd souls
Ere their terrestrial chart unrolls,
  And thou wert free
  To cease, or be,
Then would I tell thee all I know,
And put it to thee: Wilt thou take Life so?

IV

Vain vow! No hint of mine may hence
To theeward fly: to thy locked sense
  Explain none can
  Life's pending plan:
Thou wilt thy ignorant entry make
Though skies spout fire and blood and nations quake.

V

Fain would I, dear, find some shut plot
Of earth's wide wold for thee, where not
  On tear, one qualm,
  Should break the calm.
But I am weak as thou and bare;
No man can change the common lot to rare.

VI

Must come and bide. And such are we –
Unreasoning, sanguine, visionary –
  That I can hope
  Health, love, friends, scope
In full for thee; can dream thou'lt find
Joys seldom yet attained by humankind!

A WASTED ILLNESS

THROUGH vaults of pain,
Enribbed and wrought with groins of ghastliness.
I passed, and garish spectres moved my brain
              To dire distress.

And hammerings,
And quakes, and shoots, and stifling hotness, blent
With webby waxing things and waning things
              As on I went.

'Where lies the end
To this foul way?' I asked with weakening breath.
Thereon ahead I saw a door extend –
              The door to Death.

It loomed more clear:
'At last!' I cried. 'The all-delivering door!'
And then, I knew not how, it grew less near
              Than theretofore.

And back slid I
Along the galleries by which I came,
And tediously the day returned, and sky,
              And life – the same.

And all was well:
Old circumstance resumed its former show,
And on my head the dews of comfort fell
              As ere my woe.

I roam anew,
Scarce conscious of my late distress. . . . And yet
Those backward steps to strength I cannot view
              Without regret.

For that dire train
Of waxing shapes and waning, passed before,
And those grim chambers, must be ranged again
              To reach that door.

HE ABJURES LOVE

At last I put off love,
    For twice ten years
The daysman of my thought,
    And hope, and doing;
Being ashamed thereof,
    And faint of fears
And desolations, wrought
    In his pursuing,

Since first in youthtime those
    Disquietings
That heart-enslavement brings
    To hale and hoary,
Became my housefellows.
    And, fool and blind,
I turned from kith and kind
    To give him glory.

I was as children be
    Who have no care;
I did not shrink or sigh,
    I did not sicken;
But lo, Love beckoned me
    And I was bare,
And poor, and starved, and dry,
    And fever-stricken.

Too many times ablaze
    With fatuous fires,
Enkindled by his wiles
    To new embraces,
Did I, by wilful ways
    And baseless ires,
Return the anxious smiles
    Of friendly faces.

E

No more will now rate I
  The common rare,
The midnight drizzle dew,
  The gray hour golden,
The wind a yearning cry,
  The faulty fair,
Things dreamt, of comelier hue
  Than things beholden! . . .

– I speak as one who plumbs
  Life's dim profound,
One who at length can sound
  Clear views and certain.
But – after love what comes?
  A scene that lours,
A few sad vacant hours,
  And then, the Curtain.

A COUNTENANCE

HER laugh was not in the middle of her face quite,
  As a gay laugh springs,
It was plain she was anxious about some things
  I could not trace quite.
Her curls were like fir-cones – piled up, brown –
  Or rather like tight-tied sheaves:
It seemed they could never be taken down. . . .

And her lips were too full, some might say:
I did not think so. Anyway,
The shadow her lower one would cast
Was green in hue whenever she passed
  Bright sun on midsummer leaves.
Alas, I knew not much of her,
And lost all sight and touch of her!

If otherwise, should I have minded
The shy laugh not in the middle of her mouth quite,
And would my kisses have died of drouth quite
    As love became unblinded?

1884

THE LAST SIGNAL

(OCT. 11, 1886)

A MEMORY OF WILLIAM BARNES

SILENTLY I footed by an uphill road
That led from my abode to a spot yew-boughed;
Yellowly the sun sloped low down to westward,
    And dark was the east with cloud.

Then, amid the shadow of that livid sad east,
    Where the light was least, and a gate stood wide,
Something flashed the fire of the sun that was facing it,
    Like a brief blaze on that side.

Looking hard and harder I knew what it meant –
    The sudden shine sent from the livid east scene;
It meant the west mirrored by the coffin of my friend there,
    Turning to the road from his green,

To take his last journey forth – he who in his prime
    Trudged so many a time from that gate athwart the land!
Thus a farewell to me he signalled on his grave-way,
    As with a wave of his hand.

Winterborne-Came Path

IN TENEBRIS

I

'Percussus sum sicut foenum, et aruit cor meum.' – Psalm ci

WINTERTIME nighs;
But my bereavement-pain
It cannot bring again:
        Twice no one dies.

Flower-petals flee;
But, since it once hath been,
No more that severing scene
        Can harrow me.

Birds faint in dread:
I shall not lose old strength
In the lone frost's black length:
        Strength long since fled!

Leaves freeze to dun;
But friends can not turn cold
This season as of old
        For him with none.

Tempests may scath;
But love can not make smart
Again this year his heart
        Who no heart hath.

Black is night's cope;
Buth death will not appal
One who, past doubtings all,
        Waits in unhope.

IN TENEBRIS

II

*'Considerabam ad dexteram, et videbam; et non erat qui cognosceret me....
Non est qui requirat animam meam.' – Psalm cxli*

WHEN the clouds' swoln bosoms echo back the shouts of the
    many and strong
That things are all as they best may be, save a few to be right
    ere long,
And my eyes have not the vision in them to discern what to these
    is so clear,
The blot seems straightway in me alone; one better he were not
    here.

The stout upstanders say, All's well with us: ruers have nought
    to rue!
And what the potent say so oft, can it fail to be somewhat true?
Breezily go they, breezily come; their dust smokes around their
    career,
Till I think I am one born out of due time, who has no calling
    here.

Their dawns bring lusty joys, it seems; their evenings all that is
    sweet;
Our times are blessed times, they cry; Life shapes it as is most
    meet,
And nothing is much the matter; there are many smiles to a tear;
Then what is the matter is I, I say. Why should such an one be
    here? . . .

Let him in whose ears the low-voiced Best is killed by the clash
    of the First,
Who holds that if way to the Better there be, it exacts a full look
    at the Worst,
Who feels that delight is a delicate growth cramped by crooked-
    ness, custom, and fear,
Get him up and be gone as one shaped awry; he disturbs the
    order here.

1895–96

IN TENEBRIS

III

'Heu mihi, quia incolatus meus prolongatus est! Habitavi cum habitantibus
Cedar; multum incola fuit anima mea.' – Psalm cxix

THERE have been times when I well might have passed and the
ending have come –
Points in my path when the dark might have stolen on me, artless,
unrueing –
Ere I had learnt that the world was a welter of futile doing:
Such had been times when I well might have passed, and the ending
have come!

Say, on the noon when the half-sunny hours told that April was nigh,
And I upgathered and cast forth the snow from the crocus-border,
Fashioned and furbished the soil into a summer-seeming order,
Glowing in gladsome faith that I quickened the year thereby.

Or on that loneliest of eves when afar and benighted we stood,
She who upheld me and I, in the midmost of Egdon together,
Confident I in her watching and ward through the blackening
heather,
Deeming her matchless in might and with measureless scope endued.

Or on that winter-wild night when, reclined by the chimney-nook
quoin,
Slowly a drowse overgat me, the smallest and feeblest of folk there,
Weak from my baptism of pain; when at times and anon I awoke
there –
Heard of a world wheeling on, with no listing or longing to join.

Even then! while unweeting that vision could vex or that knowledge
could numb,
That sweets to the mouth in the belly are bitter, and tart, and
untoward,
Then, on some dim-coloured scene should my briefly raised curtain
have lowered,
Then might the Voice that is law have said 'Cease!' and the ending
have come.

1896

WESSEX HEIGHTS

(1896)

THERE are some heights in Wessex, shaped as if by a kindly hand
For thinking, dreaming, dying on, and at crises when I stand,
Say, on Ingpen Beacon eastward, or on Wylls-Neck westwardly,
I seem where I was before my birth, and after death may be.

In the lowlands I have no comrade, not even the lone man's friend –
Her who suffereth long and is kind; accepts what he is too weak to
    mend:
Down there they are dubious and askance; there nobody thinks as I,
But mind-chains do not clank where one's next neighbour is the sky.

In the towns I am tracked by phantoms having weird detective
    ways –
Shadows of beings who fellowed with myself of earlier days:
They hang about at places, and they say harsh heavy things –
Men with a wintry sneer, and women with tart disparagings.

Down there I seem to be false to myself, my simple self that was,
And is not now, and I see him watching, wondering what crass
    cause
Can have merged him into such a strange continuator as this,
Who yet has something in common with himself, my chrysalis.

I cannot go to the great grey Plain; there's a figure against the
    moon,
Nobody sees it but I, and it makes my breast beat out of tune;
I cannot go to the tall-spired town, being barred by the forms now
    passed
For everybody but me, in whose long vision they stand there fast.

There's a ghost at Yell'ham Bottom chiding loud at the fall of the
    night,
There's a ghost in Froom-side Vale, thin-lipped and vague, in a
    shroud of white,
There is one in the railway train whenever I do not want it near,
I see its profile against the pane, saying what I would not hear.

As for one rare fair woman, I am now but a thought of hers,
I enter her mind and another thought succeeds me that she prefers;
Yet my love for her in its fulness she herself even did not know;
Well, time cures hearts of tenderness, and now I can let her go.

So I am found on Ingpen Beacon, or on Wylls-Neck to the west,
Or else on homely Bulbarrow, or little Pilsdon Crest,
Where men have never cared to haunt, nor women have walked
    with me,
And ghosts then keep their distance; and I know some liberty.

IN FRONT OF THE LANDSCAPE

PLUNGING and labouring on in a tide of visions,
    Dolorous and dear,
Forward I pushed my way as amid waste waters
    Stretching around,
Through whose eddies there glimmered the customed landscape
    Yonder and near.

Blotted to feeble mist. And the coomb and the upland
    Coppice-crowned,
Ancient chalk-pit, milestone, rills in the grass-flat
    Stroked by the light,
Seemed but a ghost-like gauze, and no substantial
    Meadow or mound.

What were the infinite spectacles featuring foremost
    Under my sight,
Hindering me to discern my paced advancement
    Lengthening to miles;
What were the re-creations killing the daytime
    As by the night?

O they were speechful faces, gazing insistent,
    Some as with smiles,
Some as with slow-born, tears that brinily trundled
    Over the wrecked
Cheeks that were fair in their flush-time, ash now with anguish,
    Harrowed by wiles.

Yes, I could see them, feel them, hear them, address them –
    Halo-bedecked –
And, alas, onwards, shaken by fierce unreason,
    Rigid in hate,
Smitten by years-long wryness born of misprision,
    Dreaded, suspect.

Then there would breast me shining sights, sweet seasons
    Further in date;
Instruments of strings with the tenderest passion
    Vibrant, beside
Lamps long extinguished, robes, cheeks, eyes with the earth's crust
    Now corporate.

Also there rose a headland of hoary aspect
    Gnawed by the tide,
Frilled by the nimb of the morning as two friends stood there
    Guilelessly glad –
Wherefore they knew not – touched by the fringe of an ecstasy
    Scantly descried.

Later images too did the day unfurl me,
    Shadowed and sad,
Clay cadavers of those who had shared in the dramas,
    Laid now at ease,
Passions all spent, chiefest the one of the broad brow
    Sepulture-clad.

So did beset me scenes, miscalled of the bygone,
    Over the leaze,
Past the clump, and down to where lay the beheld ones;
    – Yea, as the rhyme
Sung by the sea-swell, so in their pleading dumbness
    Captured me these.

For, their lost revisiting manifestations
    In their live time
Much had I slighted, caring not for their purport,
    Seeing behind
Things more coveted, reckoned the better worth calling
    Sweet, sad, sublime.

Thus do they now show hourly before the intenser
  Stare of the mind
As they were ghosts avenging their slights by my bypast
  Body-borne eyes,
Show, too, with fuller translation than rested upon them
  As living kind.

Hence wag the tongues of the passing people, saying
  In their surmise,
'Ah – whose is this dull form that perambulates, seeing nought
  Round him that looms
Whithersoever his footsteps turn in his farings,
  Save a few tombs?'

SHUT OUT THAT MOON

CLOSE up the casement, draw the blind,
  Shut out that stealing moon,
She wears too much the guise she wore
  Before our lutes were strewn
With years-deep dust, and names we read
  On a white stone were hewn.

Step not forth on the dew-dashed lawn
  To view the Lady's Chair,
Immense Orion's glittering form,
  The Less and Greater Bear:
Stay in; to such sights we were drawn
  When faded ones were fair.

Brush not the bough for midnight scents
  That come forth lingeringly,
And wake the same sweet sentiments
  They breathed to you and me
When living seemed a laugh, and love
  All it was said to be.

Within the common lamp-lit room
        Prison my eyes and thought;
Let dingy details crudely loom,
        Mechanic speech be wrought:
Too fragrant was Life's early bloom,
        Too tart the fruit it brought!

1904

LAST WORDS TO A DUMB FRIEND

PET was never mourned as you,
Purrer of the spotless hue,
Plumy tail, and wistful gaze
While you humoured our queer ways,
Or outshrilled your morning call
Up the stairs and through the hall –
Foot suspended in its fall –
While, expectant, you would stand
Arched, to meet the stroking hand;
Till your way you chose to wend
Yonder, to your tragic end.

Never another pet for me!
Let your place all vacant be;
Better blankness day by day
Than companion torn away.
Better bid his memory fade,
Better blot each mark he made,
Selfishly escape distress
By contrived forgetfulness,
Than preserve his prints to make
Every morn and eve an ache.

From the chair whereon he sat
Sweep his fur, nor wince thereat;
Rake his little pathways out
Mid the bushes roundabout;
Smooth away his talons' mark
From the claw-worn pine-tree bark,
Where he climbed as dusk embrowned,
Waiting us who loitered round.

Strange it is this speechless thing,
Subject to our mastering,
Subject for his life and food
To our gift, and time, and mood
Timid pensioner of us Powers,
His existence ruled by ours,
Should – by crossing at a breath
Into safe and shielded death,
By the merely taking hence
Of his insignificance –
Loom as largened to the sense,
Shape as part, above man's will,
Of the Imperturbable.

As a prisoner, flight debarred,
Exercising in a yard,
Still retain I, troubled, shaken,
Mean estate, by him forsaken;
And this home, which scarcely took
Impress from his little look,
By his faring to the Dim
Grows all eloquent of him.

Housemate, I can think you still
Bounding to the window-sill,
Over which I vaguely see
Your small mound beneath the tree,
Showing in the autumn shade
That you moulder where you played.

2 October 1904

GEORGE MEREDITH

(1828–1909)

FORTY years back, when much had place
That since has perished out of mind,
I heard that voice and saw that face.

He spoke as one afoot will wind
A morning horn ere men awake;
His note was trenchant, turning kind.

He was of those whose wit can shake
And riddle to the very core
The counterfeits that Time will break.

Of late, when we two met once more,
The luminous countenance and rare
Shone just as forty years before.

So that, when now all tongues declare
His shape unseen by his green hill,
I scarce believe he sits not there.

No matter. Further and further still
Through the world's vaporous vitiate air
His words wing on – as live words will.

May 1909

A SINGER ASLEEP

(ALGERNON CHARLES SWINBURNE, 1837–1909)

I

IN this fair niche above the unslumbering sea,
That sentrys up and down all night, all day,
From cove to promontory, from ness to bay,
The Fates have fitly bidden that he should be
    Pillowed eternally.

II

– It was as though a garland of red roses
Had fallen about the hood of some smug nun
When irresponsibly dropped as from the sun,
In fulth of numbers freaked with musical closes,
Upon Victoria's formal middle time
      His leaves of rhythm and rhyme.

III

O that far morning of a summer day
When, down a terraced street whose pavements lay
Glassing the sunshine into my bent eyes,
I walked and read with a quick glad surprise
      New words, in classic guise, –

IV

The passionate pages of his earlier years,
Fraught with hot sighs, sad laughters, kisses, tears;
Fresh-fluted notes, yet from a minstrel who
Blew them not naïvely, but as one who knew
      Full well why thus he blew.

V

I still can hear the brabble and the roar
At those thy tunes, O still one, now passed through
That fitful fire of tongues then entered new!
Their power is spent like spindrift on this shore;
      Thine swells yet more and more.

VI

– His singing-mistress verily was no other
Than she the Lesbian, she the music-mother
Of all the tribe that feel in melodies;
Who leapt, love-anguished, from the Leucadian steep
Into the rambling world-encircling deep
      Which hides her where none sees.

VII

And one can hold in thought that nightly here
His phantom may draw down to the water's brim,
And hers come up to meet it, as a dim
Lone shine upon the heaving hydrosphere,
And mariners wonder as they traverse near,
        Unknowing of her and him.

VIII

One dreams him sighing to her spectral form:
'O teacher, where lies hid thy burning line;
Where are those songs, O poetess divine
Whose very orts are love incarnadine?'
And her smile back: 'Disciple true and warm,
        Sufficient now are thine.' . . .

IX

So here, beneath the waking constellations,
Where the waves peal their everlasting strains,
And their dull subterrene reverberations
Shake him when storms make mountains of their plains –
Him once their peer in sad improvisations,
And deft as wind to cleave their frothy manes –
I leave him, while the daylight gleam declines
        Upon the capes and chines.

Bonchurch, 1910

EXEUNT OMNES

I

EVERYBODY else, then, going,
And I still left where the fair was? . . .
Much have I seen of neighbour loungers
    Making a lusty showing,
    Each now past all knowing.

II

There is an air of blankness
In the street and the littered spaces;
Thoroughfare, steeple, bridge and highway
Wizen themselves to lankness;
Kennels dribble dankness.

III

Folk all fade. And whither,
As I wait alone where the fair was?
Into the clammy and numbing night-fog
Whence they entered hither.
Soon one more goes thither!

2 June 1913

THE PHOTOGRAPH

THE flame crept up the portrait line by line
As it lay on the coals in the silence of night's profound,
 And over the arm's incline,
And along the marge of the silkwork superfine,
And gnawed at the delicate bosom's defenceless round.

Then I vented a cry of hurt, and averted my eyes;
The spectacle was one that I could not bear,
 To my deep and sad surprise;
But, compelled to heed, I again looked furtivewise
Till the flame had eaten her breasts, and mouth, and hair.

'Thank God, she is out of it now!' I said at last,
In a great relief of heart when the thing was done
 That had set my soul aghast,
And nothing was left of the picture unsheathed from the past
But the ashen ghost of the card it had figured on.

She was a woman long hid amid packs of years,
She might have been living or dead; she was lost to my sight,
   And the deed that had nigh drawn tears
Was done in a casual clearance of life's arrears;
But I felt as if I had put her to death that night! . . .

     .   .   .   .   .   .

– Well; she knew nothing thereof did she survive,
And suffered nothing if numbered among the dead;
   Yet – yet – if on earth alive
Did she feel a smart, and with vague strange anguish strive?
If in heaven, did she smile at me sadly and shake her head?

AT A COUNTRY FAIR

   At a bygone Western country fair
I saw a giant led by a dwarf
With a red string like a long thin scarf;
How much he was the stronger there
     The giant seemed unaware.

And then I saw that the giant was blind,
  And the dwarf a shrewd-eyed little thing;
The giant, mild, timid, obeyed the string
As if he had no independent mind,
     Or will of any kind.

Wherever the dwarf decided to go
At his heels the other trotted meekly,
(Perhaps – I know not – reproaching weakly)
Like one Fate bade that it must be so,
     Whether he wished or no.

Various sights in various climes
I have seen, and more I may see yet,
But that sight never shall I forget,
And have thought it the sorriest of pantomimes,
     If once, a hundred times!

GREAT THINGS

Sweet cyder is a great thing,
  A great thing to me,
Spinning down to Weymouth town
  By Ridgway thirstily,
And maid and mistress summoning
  Who tend the hostelry:
O cyder is a great thing,
  A great thing to me!

The dance it is a great thing,
  A great thing to me,
With candles lit and partners fit
  For night-long revelry;
And going home when day-dawning
  Peeps pale upon the lea:
O dancing is a great thing,
  A great thing to me!

Love is, yea, a great thing,
  A great thing to me,
When, having drawn across the lawn
  In darkness silently,
A figure flits like one a-wing
  Out from the nearest tree:
O love is, yes, a great thing,
  A great thing to me!

Will these be always great things,
  Great things to me? . . .
Let it befall that One will call,
  'Soul, I have need of thee:'
What then? Joy-jaunts, impassioned flings
  Love, and its ecstasy,
Will always have been great things,
  Great things to me!

THE SOMETHING THAT SAVED HIM

IT was when
Whirls of thick waters laved me
　　Again and again,
That something arose and saved me;
　　Yea, it was then.

In that day
Unseeing the azure went I
　　On my way,
And to white winter bent I,
　　Knowing no May.

Reft of renown,
Under the night clouds beating
　　Up and down,
In my needfulness greeting
　　Cit and clown.

Long there had been
Much of a murky colour
　　In the scene,
Dull prospects meeting duller;
　　Nought between.

Last, there loomed
A closing-in blind alley,
　　Though there boomed
A feeble summons to rally
　　Where it gloomed.

The clock rang;
The hour brought a hand to deliver;
　　I upsprang,
And looked back at den, ditch and river,
　　And sang.

FAINTHEART IN A RAILWAY TRAIN

At nine in the morning there passed a church,
At ten there passed me by the sea,
At twelve a town of smoke and smirch,
At two a forest of oak and birch,
    And then, on a platform, she:

A radiant stranger, who saw not me.
I said, 'Get out to her do I dare?'
But I kept my seat in my search for a plea,
And the wheels moved on. O could it but be
    That I had alighted there!

THE OPPORTUNITY

(FOR H. P.)

Forty springs back, I recall,
    We met at this phase of the Maytime:
We might have clung close through all,
    But we parted when died that daytime.

We parted with smallest regret;
    Perhaps should have cared but slightly,
Just then, if we never had met:
    Strange, strange that we lived so lightly!

Had we mused a little space
    At that critical date in the Maytime.
One life had been ours, one place,
    Perhaps, till our long cold claytime.

– This is a bitter thing
    For thee, O man: what ails it?
The tide of chance may bring
    Its offer; but nought avails it!

THE LITTLE OLD TABLE

CREAK, little wood thing, creak,
When I touch you with elbow or knee;
That is the way you speak
Of one who gave you to me!

You, little table, she brought –
Brought me with her own hand,
As she looked at me with a thought
That I did not understand.

– Whoever owns it anon,
And hears it, will never know
What a history hangs upon
This creak from long ago.

'ANY LITTLE OLD SONG'

ANY little old song
    Will do for me,
Tell it of joys gone long,
    Or joys to be,
Or friendly faces best
    Loved to see.

Newest themes I want not
    On subtle strings,
And for thrillings pant not
    That new song brings:
I only need the homeliest
    Of heartstirrings.

WAITING BOTH

A STAR looks down at me,
And says: 'Here I and you
Stand, each in our degree:
What do you mean to do, –
       Mean to do?'

I say: 'For all I know,
Wait, and let Time go by,
Till my change come.' – 'just so,'
The star says: 'So mean I:–
       So mean I.'

IN ST. PAUL'S A WHILE AGO

SUMMER and winter close commune
On this July afternoon
As I enter chilly Paul's,
With its chasmal classic walls.
– Drifts of gray illumination
From the lofty fenestration
Slant them down in bristling spines that spread
Fan-like upon the vast dust-moted shade.

Moveless here, no whit allied
To the daemonian din outside,
Statues stand, cadaverous, wan,
Round the loiterers looking on
Under the yawning dome and nave,
Pondering whatnot, giddy or grave.
Here a verger moves a chair,
Or a red rope fixes there:–
A brimming Hebe, rapt in her adorning,
Brushes an Artemisia craped in mourning;
Beatrice Benedick piques, coquetting;
All unknowing or forgetting
That strange Jew, Damascus-bound,
Whose name, thereafter travelling round

To this precinct of the world,
    Spread here like a flag unfurled:
Anon inspiring architectural sages
To frame this pile, writ his throughout the ages:
    Whence also the encircling mart
    Assumed his name, of him no part,
    And to his vision-seeing mind
    Charmless, blank in every kind;
And whose displays, even had they called his eye,
No gold or silver had been his to buy;
    Whose haunters, had they seen him stand
    On his own steps here, lift his hand
    In stress of eager, stammering speech,
    And his meaning chanced to reach,
    Would have proclaimed him as they passed
    An epilept enthusiast.

NOBODY COMES

Tree-leaves labour up and down,
    And through them the fainting light
    Succumbs to the crawl of night.
Outside in the road the telegraph wire
    To the town from the darkening land
Intones to travellers like a spectral lyre
    Swept by a spectral hand.

A car comes up, with lamps full-glare,
    That flash upon a tree:
    It has nothing to do with me,
And whangs along in a world of its own,
    Leaving a blacker air;
And mute by the gate I stand again alone,
    And nobody pulls up there.

9 October 1924

A NIGHTMARE, AND THE NEXT THING

On this decline of Christmas Day
The empty street is fogged and blurred:
The house-fronts all seem backwise turned
As if the outer world were spurned:
Voices and songs within are heard,
Whence red rays gleam when fires are stirred,
Upon this nightmare Christmas Day.

The lamps, just lit, begin to outloom
Like dandelion-globes in the gloom;
The stonework, shop-signs, doors, look bald;
Curious crude details seem installed,
And show themselves in their degrees
As they were personalities
Never discerned when the street was bustling
With vehicles, and farmers hustling.
Three clammy casuals wend their way
To the Union House. I hear one say:
'Jimmy, this is a treat! Hay-hay!'

Six laughing mouths, six rows of teeth,
Six radiant pairs of eyes, beneath
Six yellow hats, looking out at the back
Of a waggonette on its slowed-down track
Up the steep street to some gay dance,
Suddenly interrupt my glance.

They do not see a gray nightmare
Astride the day, or anywhere.

SO VARIOUS

You may have met a man – quite young –
A brisk-eyed youth, and highly strung:
        One whose desires
        And inner fires
        Moved him as wires.

And you may have met one stiff and old,
If not in years; of manner cold;
   Who seemed as stone,
   And never had known
   Of mirth or moan.

And there may have crossed your path a lover,
In whose clear depths you could discover
   A staunch, robust,
   And tender trust,
   Through storm and gust.

And you may have also known one fickle,
Whose fancies changed as the silver sickle
   Of yonder moon,
   Which shapes so soon
   To demilune!

You entertained a person once
Whom you internally deemed a dunce:-
   As he sat in view
   Just facing you
   You saw him through.

You came to know a learned seer
Of whom you read the surface mere:
   Your soul quite sank;
   Brain of such rank
   Dubbed yours a blank.

Anon you quizzed a man of sadness,
Who never could have known true gladness:
   Just for a whim
   You pitied him
   In his sore trim.

You journeyed with a man so glad
You never could conceive him sad:
   He proved to be
   Indubitably
   Good company.

You lit on an unadventurous slow man,
Who, said you, need be feared by no man;
  That his slack deeds
  And sloth must needs
  Produce but weeds.

A man of enterprise, shrewd and swift,
Who never suffered affairs to drift,
  You eyed for a time
  Just in his prime,
  And judged he might climb.

You smoked beside one who forgot
All that you said, or grasped it not.
  Quite a poor thing,
  Not worth a sting
  By satirizing!

Next year you nearly lost for ever
Goodwill from one who forgot slights never;
  And, with unease,
  Felt you must seize
  Occasion to please . . .

Now. . . . All these specimens of man,
So various in their pith and plan,
  Curious to say
  Were *one* man. Yea,
  I was all they.

NOT KNOWN

THEY know the wilings of the world,
  The latest flippancy;
They know each jest at hazard hurled,
  But know not me.

They know a phasm they name as me,
    In whom I should not find
A single self-held quality
    Of body or mind.

A NECESSITARIAN'S EPITAPH

A WORLD I did not wish to enter
Took me and poised me on my centre,
Made me grimace, and foot, and prance,
As cats on hot bricks have to dance
Strange jigs to keep them from the floor,
Till they sink down and feel no more.

CHRISTMAS: 1924

'PEACE upon earth!' was said. We sing it,
And pay a million priests to bring it.
After two thousand years of mass
We've got as far as poison-gas.

1924

HE NEVER EXPECTED MUCH

[or]

A CONSIDERATION
[*A reflection*] ON MY EIGHTY-SIXTH BIRTHDAY

WELL, World, you have kept faith with me,
    Kept faith with me;
Upon the whole you have proved to be
    Much as you said you were.
Since as a child I used to lie
Upon the leaze and watch the sky,
Never, I own, expected I
    That life would all be fair.

'Twas then you said, and since have said,
    Times since have said,
In that mysterious voice you shed
    From clouds and hills around:
'Many have loved me desperately,
Many with smooth serenity,
While some have shown contempt of me
    Till they dropped underground.

'I do not promise overmuch,
    Child; overmuch;
Just neutral-tinted haps and such,'
    You said to minds like mine.
Wise warning for your credit's sake!
Which I for one failed not to take,
And hence could stem such strain and ache
    As each year might assign.

A PRIVATE MAN ON PUBLIC MEN

WHEN my contemporaries were driving
Their coach through Life with strain and striving,
And raking riches into heaps,
And ably pleading in the Courts
With smart rejoinders and retorts,
Or where the Senate nightly keeps
Its vigils, till their fames were fanned
By rumour's tongue throughout the land,
I lived in quiet, screened, unknown,
Pondering upon some stick or stone,
Or news of some rare book or bird
Latterly bought, or seen, or heard,
Not wishing ever to set eyes on
The surging crowd beyond the horizon,
Tasting years of moderate gladness
Mellowed by sundry days of sadness,
Shut from the noise of the world without,
Hearing but dimly its rush and rout,
Unenvying those amid its roar,
Little endowed, not wanting more.

HE RESOLVES TO SAY NO MORE

O MY soul, keep the rest unknown!
It is too like a sound of moan
    When the charnel-eyed
    Pale Horse has nighed:
Yea, none shall gather what I hide!

Why load men's minds with more to bear
That bear already ails to spare?
    From now alway
    Till my last day
What I discern I will not say.

Let Time roll backward if it will;
(Magians who drive the midnight quill
    With brain aglow
    Can see it so,)
What I have learnt no man shall know.

And if my vision range beyond
The blinkered sight of souls in bond,
    – By truth made free –
    I'll let all be,
And show to no man what I see.

SECTION 4

BELIEF AND UNBELIEF

HAP

IF but some vengeful god would call to me
From up the sky, and laugh: 'Thou suffering thing,
Know that thy sorrow is my ecstasy,
That thy love's loss is my hate's profiting!'

Then would I bear it, clench myself, and die,
Steeled by the sense of ire unmerited;
Half-eased in that a Powerfuller than I
Had willed and meted me the tears I shed.

But not so. How arrives it joy lies slain,
And why unblooms the best hope ever sown?
– Crass Casualty obstructs the sun and rain,
And dicing Time for gladness casts a moan. . . .
These purblind Doomsters had as readily strown
Blisses about my pilgrimage as pain.

1866

A YOUNG MAN'S EPIGRAM ON EXISTENCE

A SENSELESS school, where we must give
Our lives that we may learn to live!
A dolt is he who memorizes
Lessons that leave no time for prizes.

16 W. P. V., 1866

A SIGN-SEEKER

I MARK the months in liveries dank and dry,
   The noontides many-shaped and hued;
   I see the nightfall shades subtrude,
And hear the monotonous hours clang negligently by.

I view the evening bonfires of the sun
   On hills where morning rains have hissed;
   The eyeless countenance of the mist
Pallidly rising when the summer droughts are done.

I have seen the lightning-blade, the leaping star,
   The cauldrons of the sea in storm,
   Have felt the earthquake's lifting arm,
And trodden where abysmal fires and snow-cones are.

I learn to prophesy the hid eclipse,
   The coming of eccentric orbs;
   To mete the dust the sky absorbs,
To weigh the sun, and fix the hour each planet dips.

I witness fellow earth-men surge and strive;
   Assemblies meet, and throb, and part;
   Death's sudden finger, sorrow's smart;
– All the vast various moils that mean a world alive.

But that I fain would wot of shuns my sense –
   Those sights of which old prophets tell,
   Those signs the general word so well
As vouchsafed their unheed, denied my long suspense.

In graveyard green, where his pale dust lies pent
   To glimpse a phantom parent, friend,
   Wearing his smile, and 'Not the end!'
Outbreathing softly: that were blest enlightenment;

Or, if a dead Love's lips, whom dreams reveal
   When midnight imps of King Decay
   Delve sly to solve me back to clay,
Should leave some print to prove her spirit-kisses real;

Or, when Earth's Frail lie bleeding of her Strong,
   If some Recorder, as in Writ,
   Near to the weary scene should flit
And drop one plume as pledge that Heaven inscrolls the wrong.

– There are who, rapt to heights of trancelike trust,
   These tokens claim to feel and see,
   Read radiant hints of times to be –
Of heart to heart returning after dust to dust.

Such scope is granted not to lives like mine . . .
   I have lain in dead men's beds, have walked
   The tombs of those with whom I had talked,
Called many a gone and goodly one to shape a sign,

And panted for response. But none replies;
    No warnings loom, nor whisperings
    To open out my limitings,
And Nescience mutely muses: When a man falls he lies.

THE IMPERCIPIENT

(AT A CATHEDRAL SERVICE)

THAT with this bright believing band
        I have no claim to be,
That faiths by which my comrades stand
        Seem fantasies to me,
And mirage-mists their Shining Land,
        Is a strange destiny.

Why thus my soul should be consigned
        To infelicity,
Why always I must feel as blind
        To sights my brethren see,
Why joys, they've found I cannot find
        Abides a mystery.

Since heart of mine knows not that ease
        Which they know; since it be
That He who breathes All's Well to these
        Breathes no All's-Well to me,
My lack might move their sympathies
        And Christian charity!

I am like a gazer who should mark
        An inland company
Standing upfingered, with, 'Hark! hark!
        The glorious distant sea!'
And feel, 'Alas, 'tis but yon dark
        And wind-swept pine to me!'

Yet I would bear my shortcomings
    With meet tranquillity,
But for the charge that blessed things
    I'd liefer not have be.
O, doth a bird deprived of wings
    Go earth-bound wilfully!

.   .   .   .   .

Enough. As yet disquiet clings
    About us. Rest shall we.

HER IMMORTALITY

Upon a noon I pilgrimed through
    A pasture, mile by mile,
Unto the place where last I saw
    My dead Love's living smile.

And sorrowing I lay me down
    Upon the heated sod:
It seemed as if my body pressed
    The very ground she trod.

I lay, and thought; and in a trance
    She came and stood thereby –
The same, even to the marvellous ray
    That used to light her eye.

'You draw me, and I come to you,
    My faithful one,' she said,
In voice that had the moving tone
    It bore ere she was wed.

'Seven years have circled since I died:
    Few now remember me;
My husband clasps another bride:
    My children's love has she.

F

'My brethren, sisters, and my friends
    Care not to meet my sprite:
Who prized me most I did not know
    Till I passed down from sight.'

I said: 'My days are lonely here;
    I need thy smile alway:
I'll use this night my ball or blade,
    And join thee ere the day.'

A tremor stirred her tender lips,
    Which parted to dissuade:
'That cannot be, O friend,' she cried;
    'Think, I am but a Shade!

'A Shade but in its mindful ones
    Has immortality;
By living, me you keep alive,
    By dying you slay me.

'In you resides my single power
    Of sweet continuance here;
On your fidelity I count
    Through many a coming year.'

– I started through me at her plight,
    So suddenly confessed:
Dismissing late distaste for life,
    I craved its bleak unrest.

'I will not die, my One of all! –
    To lengthen out thy days
I'll guard me from minutest harms
    That may invest my ways!'

She smiled and went. Since then she comes
    Oft when her birth-moon climbs,
Or at the seasons' ingresses,
    Or anniversary times;

But grows my grief. When I surcease,
  Through whom alone lives she,
Her spirit ends its living lease,
  Never again to be!

NATURE'S QUESTIONING

When I look forth at dawning, pool,
    Field, flock, and lonely tree,
    All seem to gaze at me
Like chastened children sitting silent in a school;

  Their faces dulled, constrained, and worn,
    As though the master's ways
    Through the long teaching days
Had cowed them till their early zest was overborne.

  Upon them stirs in lippings mere
    (As if once clear in call,
    But now scarce breathed at all) –
'We wonder, ever wonder, why we find us here!

  'Has some Vast Imbecility,
    Mighty to build and blend,
    But impotent to tend,
Framed us in jest, and left us now to hazardry?

  'Or come we of an Automaton
    Unconscious of our pains? . . .
    Or are we live remains
Of Godhead dying downwards, brain and eye now gone?

  'Or is it that some high Plan betides,
    As yet not understood,
    Of Evil stormed by Good,
We the Forlorn Hope over which Achievement strides?'

Thus things around. No answerer I. . . .
    Meanwhile the winds, and rains,
    And Earth's old glooms and pains
Are still the same, and Life and Death are neighbours nigh.

THE SUBALTERNS

I

'Poor wanderer,' said the leaden sky,
    'I fain would lighten thee,
But there are laws in force on high
    Which say it must not be.'

II

– 'I would not freeze thee, shorn one,' cried
    The North, 'knew I but how
To warm my breath, to slack my stride;
    But I am ruled as thou.'

III

– 'To-morrow I attack thee, wight,'
    Said Sickness. 'Yet I swear
I bear thy little ark no spite,
    But am bid enter there.'

IV

– 'Come hither, Son,' I heard Death say;
    'I did not will a grave
Should end thy pilgrimage to-day,
    But I, too, am a slave!'

V

We smiled upon each other then,
    And life to me had less
Of that fell look it wore ere when
    They owned their passiveness.

GOD-FORGOTTEN

I TOWERED far, and lo! I stood within
The presence of the Lord Most High,
Sent thither by the sons of Earth, to win
    Some answer to their cry.

– 'The Earth, sayest thou? The Human race?
By Me created? Sad its lot?
Nay: I have no remembrance of such place:
    Such world I fashioned not.' –

– 'O Lord, forgive me when I say
Thou spakest the word that made it all.' –
'The Earth of men – let me bethink me. . . . Yea!
    I dimly do recall

'Some tiny sphere I built long back
(Mid millions of such shapes of mine)
So named . . . It perished, surely – not a wrack
    Remaining, or a sign?

'It lost my interest from the first,
My aims therefor succeeding ill;
Haply it died of doing as it durst?' –
    'Lord, it existeth still.' –

'Dark, then, its life! For not a cry
Of aught it bears do I now hear;
Of its own act the threads were snapt whereby
    Its plaints had reached mine ear.

'It used to ask for gifts of good,
Till came its severance, self-entailed,
When sudden silence on that side ensued,
    And has till now prevailed.

'All other orbs have kept in touch;
Their voicings reach me speedily:
Thy people took upon them overmuch
    In sundering them from me!

'And it is strange – though sad enough –
Earth's race should think that one whose call
Frames, daily, shining spheres of flawless stuff
        Must heed their tainted ball! ...

'But sayest it is by pangs distraught,
And strife, and silent suffering? –
Sore grieved am I that injury should be wrought
        Even on so poor a thing!

'Thou shouldst have learnt that *Not to Mend*
For Me could mean but *Not to Know*:
Hence, Messengers! and straightway put an end
        To what men undergo.' ...

Homing at dawn, I thought to see
One of the Messengers standing by.
– Oh, childish thought! ... Yet often it comes to me
        When trouble hovers nigh.

THE BEDRIDDEN PEASANT

TO AN UNKNOWING GOD

MUCH wonder I – here long low-laid –
        That this dead wall should be
Betwixt the Maker and the made,
        Between Thyself and me!

For, say one puts a child to nurse,
        He eyes it now and then
To know if better it is, or worse,
        And if it mourn, and when.

But Thou, Lord, giv'st us men our day
        In helpless bondage thus
To Time and Chance, and seem'st straightway
        To think no more of us!

That some disaster cleft Thy scheme
　　And tore us wide apart,
So that no cry can cross, I deem;
　　For Thou art mild of heart,

And wouldst not shape and shut us in
　　Where voice can not be heard:
Plainly Thou meant'st that we should win
　　Thy succour by a word.

Might but Thy sense flash down the skies
　　Like man's from clime to clime,
Thou wouldst not let me agonize
　　Through my remaining time;

But, seeing how much Thy creatures bear –
　　Lame, starved, or maimed, or blind –
Wouldst heal the ills with quickest care
　　Of me and all my kind.

Then, since Thou mak'st not these things be,
　　But these things dost not know,
I'll praise Thee as were shown to me
　　The mercies Thou wouldst show!

BY THE EARTH'S CORPSE

I

'O LORD, why grievest Thou? –
　　Since Life has ceased to be
Upon this globe, now cold
　　As lunar land and sea,
And humankind, and fowl, and fur
　　Are gone eternally,
All is the same to Thee as ere
　　They knew mortality.'

II

'O Time,' replied the Lord,
    'Thou readest me ill, I ween;
Were all *the same*, I should not grieve
    At that late earthly scene,
Now blestly past – though planned by me
    With interest close and keen! –
Nay, nay: things now are *not* the same
    As they have earlier been.

III

    'Written indelibly
    On my eternal mind
    Are all the wrongs endured
    By Earth's poor patient kind,
Which my too oft unconscious hand
    Let enter undesigned.
No god can cancel deeds foredone,
    Or thy old coils unwind!

IV

    'As when, in Noë's days,
    I whelmed the plains with sea,
    So at this last, when flesh
    And herb but fossils be,
And, all extinct, their piteous dust
    Revolves obliviously,
That I made Earth, and life, and man,
    It still repenteth me!'

HIS IMMORTALITY

I

I SAW a dead man's finer part
Shining within each faithful heart
Of those bereft. Then said I: 'This must be
    His immortality.'

II

I looked there as the seasons wore,
And still his soul continuously bore
A life in theirs. But less its shine excelled
    Than when I first beheld.

III

His fellow-yearsmen passed, and then
In later hearts I looked for him again;
And found him – shrunk, alas! into a thin
    And spectral mannikin.

IV

Lastly I ask – now old and chill –
If aught of him remain unperished still;
And find, in me alone, a feeble spark,
    Dying amid the dark.

February 1899

THE TO-BE-FORGOTTEN

I

I HEARD a small sad sound,
And stood awhile among the tombs around:
'Wherefore, old friends,' said I, 'are you distrest,
    Now, screened from life's unrest?'

II

– 'O not at being here;
But that our future second death is near;
When, with the living, memory of us numbs,
    And blank oblivion comes!

III

'These, our sped ancestry,
Lie here embraced by deeper death than we;
Nor shape nor thought of theirs can you descry
    With keenest backward eye.

IV

'They count as quite forgot;
They are as men who have existed not;
Theirs is a loss past loss of fitful breath;
        It is the second death.

V

'We here, as yet, each day
Are blest with dear recall; as yet, can say
We hold in some soul loved continuance
        Of shape and voice and glance.

VI

'But what has been will be –
First memory, then oblivion's swallowing sea;
Like men foregone, shall we merge into those
        Whose story no one knows.

VII

'For which of us could hope
To show in life that world-awakening scope
Granted the few whose memory none lets die,
        But all men magnify?

VIII

'We were but Fortune's sport;
Things true, things lovely, things of good report
We neither shunned nor sought ... We see our bourne,
        And seeing it we mourn.'

YELL'HAM-WOOD'S STORY

Coomb-Firtrees say that Life is a moan,
        And Clyffe-hill Clump says 'Yea!'
But Yell'ham says a thing of its own:

It's not 'Gray, gray
Is Life alway!'
That Yell'ham says,
Nor that Life is for ends unknown.

It says that Life would signify
A thwarted purposing:
That we come to live, and are called to die.
Yes, that's the thing
In fall, in spring,
That Yell'ham says:–
'Life offers – to deny!'

1902

᾽ΑΓΝΩΣΤΩι ΘΕΩι

Long have I framed weak phantasies of Thee,
O Willer masked and dumb!
Who makest Life become, –
As though by labouring all-unknowingly,
Like one whom reveries numb.

How much of consciousness informs Thy will,
Thy biddings, as if blind,
Of death-inducing kind,
Nought shows to us ephemeral ones who fill
But moments in Thy mind.

Perhaps Thy ancient rote-restricted ways
Thy ripening rule transcends;
That listless effort tends
To grow percipient with advance of days,
And with percipience mends.

For, in unwonted purlieus, far and nigh,
At whiles or short or long,
May be discerned a wrong
Dying as of self-slaughter; whereat I
Would raise my voice in song.

BEFORE LIFE AND AFTER

A TIME there was – as one may guess
And as, indeed, earth's testimonies tell –
Before the birth of consciousness,
  When all went well.

None suffered sickness, love, or loss,
None knew regret, starved hope, or heart-burnings;
None cared whatever crash or cross
  Brought wrack to things.

If something ceased, no tongue bewailed,
If something winced and waned, no heart was wrung;
If brightness dimmed, and dark prevailed,
  No sense was stung.

But the disease of feeling germed,
And primal rightness took the tinct of wrong;
Ere nescience shall be reaffirmed
  How long, how long?

THE UNBORN

I ROSE at night, and visited
  The Cave of the Unborn:
And crowding shapes surrounded me
For tidings of the life to be,
Who long had prayed the silent Head
  To haste its advent morn.

Their eyes were lit with artless trust,
  Hope thrilled their every tone;
'A scene the loveliest, is it not?
A pure delight, a beauty-spot
Where all is gentle, true and just,
  And darkness is unknown?'

My heart was anguished for their sake,
    I could not frame a word;
And they descried my sunken face,
And seemed to read therein, and trace
The news that pity would not break,
    Nor truth leave unaverred.

And as I silently retired
    I turned and watched them still,
And they came helter-skelter out,
Driven forward like a rabble rout
Into the world they had so desired,
    By the all-immanent Will.

1905

NEW YEAR'S EVE

'I HAVE finished another year,' said God,
    'In grey, green, white, and brown;
I have strewn the leaf upon the sod,
Sealed up the worm within the clod,
    And let the last sun down.'

'And what's the good of it?' I said,
    'What reasons made you call
From formless void this earth we tread,
When nine-and-ninety can be read
    Why nought should be at all?

'Yea, Sire; why shaped you us, "who in
    This tabernacle groan" –
If ever a joy be found herein,
Such joy no man had wished to win
    If he had never known!'

Then he: 'My labours – logicless –
    You may explain; not I:
Sense-sealed I have wrought, without a guess
That I evolved a Consciousness
    To ask for reasons why.

'Strange that ephemeral creatures who
    By my own ordering are,
Should see the shortness of my view,
Use ethic tests I never knew,
    Or made provision for!'

He sank to raptness as of yore,
    And opening New Year's Day
Wove it by rote as theretofore,
And went on working evermore
    In his unweeting way.

1906

GOD'S EDUCATION

I saw him steal the light away
    That haunted in her eye:
It went so gently none could say
More than that it was there one day
    And missing by-and-by.

I watched her longer, and he stole
    Her lily tincts and rose;
All her young sprightliness of soul
Next fell beneath his cold control,
    And disappeared like those.

I asked: 'Why do you serve her so?
    Do you, for some glad day,
Hoard these her sweets –?' He said, 'O no,
They charm not me; I bid Time throw
    Them carelessly away.'

Said I: 'We call that cruelty –
    We, your poor mortal kind.'
He mused. 'The thought is new to me.
Forsooth, though I men's master be,
    Theirs is the teaching mind!'

A PLAINT TO MAN

WHEN you slowly emerged from the den of Time,
And gained percipience as you grew,
And fleshed you fair out of shapeless slime,

Wherefore, O Man, did there come to you
The unhappy need of creating me –
A form like your own – for praying to?

My virtue, power, utility,
Within my maker must all abide,
Since none in myself can ever be,

One thin as a phasm on a lantern-slide
Shown forth in the dark upon some dim sheet,
And by none but its showman vivified.

'Such a forced device', you may say, 'is meet
For easing a loaded heart at whiles:
Man needs to conceive of a mercy-seat.

Somewhere above the gloomy aisles
Of this wailful world, or he could not bear
The irk no local hope beguiles.'

– But since I was framed in your first despair
The doing without me has had no play
In the minds of men when shadows scare;

And now that I dwindle day by day
Beneath the deicide eyes of seers
In a light that will not let me stay,

And to-morrow the whole of me disappears,
The truth should be told, and the fact be faced
That had best been faced in earlier years:

The fact of life with dependence placed
On the human heart's resource alone,
In brotherhood bonded close and graced

With loving-kindness fully blown,
And visioned help unsought, unknown.

1909–10

GOD'S FUNERAL

I

I SAW a slowly-stepping train –
Lined on the brows, scoop-eyed and bent and hoar –
Following in files across a twilit plain
A strange and mystic form the foremost bore.

II

And by contagious throbs of thought
Or latent knowledge that within me lay
And had already stirred me, I was wrought
To consciousness of sorrow even as they.

III

The fore-borne shape, to my blurred eyes,
At first seemed man-like, and anon to change
To an amorphous cloud of marvellous size,
At times endowed with wings of glorious range.

IV

And this phantasmal variousness
Ever possessed it as they drew along:
Yet throughout all it symboled none the less
Potency vast and loving-kindness strong.

V

Almost before I knew I bent
Towards the moving columns without a word;
They, growing in bulk and numbers as they went,
Struck out sick thoughts that could be overheard:–

VI

'O man-projected Figure, of late
Imaged as we, thy knell who shall survive?
Whence came it we were tempted to create
One whom we can no longer keep alive?

VII

'Framing him jealous, fierce, at first,
We gave him justice as the ages rolled,
Will to bless those by circumstance accurst,
And longsuffering, and mercies manifold.

VIII

'And, tricked by our own early dream
And need of solace, we grew self-deceived,
Our making soon our maker did we deem,
And what we had imagined we believed.

IX

'Till, in Time's stayless stealthy swing,
Uncompromising rude reality
Mangled the Monarch of our fashioning,
Who quavered, sank; and now has ceased to be.

X

'So, toward our myth's oblivion,
Darkling, and languid-lipped, we creep and grope
Sadlier than those who wept in Babylon,
Whose Zion was a still abiding hope.

XI

'How sweet it was in years far hied
To start the wheels of day with trustful prayer,
To lie down liegely at the eventide
And feel a blest assurance he was there!

XII

'And who or what shall fill his place?
Whither will wanderers turn distracted eyes
For some fixed star to stimulate their pace
Towards the goal of their enterprise?' . . .

XIII

Some in the background then I saw,
Sweet women, youths, men, all incredulous,
Who chimed: 'This is a counterfeit of straw,
This requiem mockery! Still he lives to us!'

XIV

I could not buoy their faith: and yet
Many I had known: with all I sympathized;
And though struck speechless, I did not forget
That what was mourned for, I, too, long had prized.

XV

Still, how to bear such loss I deemed
The insistent question for each animate mind,
And gazing, to my growing sight there seemed
A pale yet positive gleam low down behind,

XVI

Whereof, to lift the general night,
A certain few who stood aloof had said,
'See you upon the horizon that small light –
Swelling somewhat?' Each mourner shook his head.

XVII

And they composed a crowd of whom
Some were right good, and many nigh the best. . . .
Thus dazed and puzzled 'twixt the gleam and gloom
Mechanically I followed with the rest.

1908–10

HEREDITY

I AM the family face;
Flesh perishes, I live on,
Projecting trait and trace
Through time to times anon,
And leaping from place to place
Over oblivion.

The years-heired feature that can
In curve and voice and eye
Despise the human span
Of durance – that is I;
The eternal thing in man,
That heeds no call to die.

FRAGMENT

AT last I entered a long dark gallery,
   Catacomb-lined; and ranged at the side
   Were the bodies of men from far and wide
Who, motion past, were nevertheless not dead.

   'The sense of waiting here strikes strong;
Everyone's waiting, waiting, it seems to me;
   What are you waiting for so long? –
      What is to happen?' I said.

'O we are waiting for one called God,' said they,
   '(Though by some the Will, or Force, or Laws;
   And, vaguely, by some, the Ultimate Cause;)
Waiting for him to see us before we are clay.
   Yes; waiting, waiting, for God *to know it.*' . . .

      'To know what?' questioned I.
'To know how things have been going on earth and below it:
   It is clear he must know some day.'
   I thereon asked them why.

'Since he made us humble pioneers
Of himself in consciousness of Life's tears,
   It needs no mighty prophecy
To tell that what he could mindlessly show
His creatures, he himself will know.

'By some still close-cowled mystery
We have reached feeling faster than he,
But he will overtake us anon,
   If the world goes on.'

'ACCORDING TO THE MIGHTY WORKING'

I

WHEN moiling seems at cease
    In the vague void of night-time,
    And heaven's wide roomage stormless
    Between the dusk and light-time,
    And fear at last is formless,
We call the allurement Peace.

II

Peace, this hid riot, Change,
    This revel of quick-cued mumming,
    This never truly being,
    This evermore becoming,
    This spinner's wheel onfleeing
Outside perception's range.

1917

A DRIZZLING EASTER MORNING

AND he is risen? Well, be it so. . . .
And still the pensive lands complain,
And dead men wait as long ago,
As if, much doubting, they would know
What they are ransomed from, before
They pass again their sheltering door.

I stand amid them in the rain,
While blusters vex the yew and vane;
And on the road the weary wain
Plods forward, laden heavily;
And toilers with their aches are fain
For endless rest – though risen is he.

THE GRAVEYARD OF DEAD CREEDS

I LIT upon the graveyard of dead creeds
In wistful wanderings through old wastes of thought,
Where bristled fennish fungi, fruiting nought,
Amid the sepulchres begirt with weeds,

Which stone by stone recorded sanct, deceased
Catholicons that had, in centuries flown,
Physicked created man through his long groan,
Ere they went under, all their potence ceased.

When in a breath-while, lo, their spectres rose
Like wakened winds that autumn summons up:–
'Out of us cometh an heir, that shall disclose
New promise!' cried they. 'And the caustic cup

'We ignorantly upheld to men, be filled
With draughts more pure than those we ever distilled,
That shall make tolerable to sentient seers
The melancholy marching of the years.'

A CATHEDRAL FAÇADE AT MIDNIGHT

ALONG the sculptures of the western wall
    I watched the moonlight creeping:
It moved as if it hardly moved at all
    Inch by inch thinly peeping.
Round on the pious figures of freestone, brought
And poised there when the Universe was wrought
To serve its centre, Earth, in mankind's thought.

The lunar look skimmed scantly toe, breast, arm,
    Then edged on slowly, slightly,
To shoulder, hand, face; till each austere form
    Was blanched its whole length brightly
Of prophet, king, queen, cardinal in state,
That dead men's tools had striven to simulate;
And the stiff images stood irradiate.

A frail moan from the martyred saints there set
    Mid others of the erection
Against the breeze, seemed sighings of regret
    At the ancient faith's rejection
Under the sure, unhasting, steady stress
Of Reason's movement, making meaningless
The coded creeds of old-time godliness.

OUR OLD FRIEND DUALISM

ALL hail to him, the Protean! A tough old chap is he:
Spinoza and the Monists cannot make him cease to be.
We pound him with our 'Truth, Sir, please!' and quite appear to
    still him:
He laughs; holds Bergson up, and James; and swears we cannot
    kill him.
We argue them pragmatic cheats. 'Aye,' says he. 'They're de-
    ceiving:
But I must live; for flamens plead I am all that's worth believing!'

1920

THE ABSOLUTE EXPLAINS

I

'O NO,' said It: her lifedoings
    Time's touch hath not destroyed:
They lie their length, with the throbbing things
    Akin them, down the Void,
        Live, unalloyed.

II

'Know, Time is toothless, seen all through;
    The Present, that men but see,
Is phasmal: since in a sane purview
    All things are shaped to be
        Eternally.

III

'Your "Now" is just a gleam, a glide
    Across your gazing sense:
With me, "Past", "Future", ever abide:
    They come not, go not, whence
        They are never hence.

IV

'As one upon a dark highway,
    Plodding by lantern-light,
Finds but the reach of its frail ray
    Uncovered to his sight,
        Though mid the night

V

'The road lies all its length the same,
    Forwardly as at rear,
So, outside what you "Present" name,
    Future and Past stand sheer,
        Cognate and clear.'

VI

– Thus It: who straightway opened then
    The vista called the Past,
Wherein were seen, as fair as when
    They seemed they could not last,
        Small things and vast.

VII

There were those songs, a score times sung,
    With all their tripping tunes,
There were the laughters once that rung,
    There those unmatched full moons,
        Those idle noons!

VIII

There fadeless, fixed, were dust-dead flowers
    Remaining still in blow;
Elsewhere, wild love-makings in bowers;
    Hard by, that irised bow
        Of years ago.

IX

There were my ever memorable
Glad days of pilgrimage,
Coiled like a precious parchment fell,
Illumined page by page,
Unhurt by age.

X

'– Here you see spread those mortal ails
So powerless to restrain
Your young life's eager hot assails,
With hazards then not plain
Till past their pain.

XI

'Here you see her who, by these laws
You learn of, still shines on,
As pleasing-pure as erst she was,
Though you think she lies yon,
Graved, glow all gone.

XII

'Here are those others you used to prize. –
But why go further we?
The Future? – Well, I would advise
You let the future be,
Unshown by me!

XIII

' 'Twould harrow you to see undraped
The scenes in ripe array
That wait your globe – all worked and shaped;
And I'll not, as I say,
Bare them to-day.

XIV

'In fine, Time is a mock, – yea, such! –
As he might well confess:
Yet hath he been believed in much,
Though lately, under stress
Of science, less.

XV

'And hence, of her you asked about
At your first speaking: she
Hath, I assure you, not passed out
Of continuity,
          But is in me.

XVI

'So thus doth Being's length transcend
          Time's ancient regal claim
To see all lengths begin and end.
          "The Fourth Dimension" fame
          Bruits as its name.'

New Year's Eve, 1922

'SO, TIME'

(THE SAME THOUGHT RESUMED)

So, Time,
          Royal, sublime;
Heretofore held to be
Master and enemy,
Thief of my Love's adornings,
Despoiling her to scornings:–
The sound philosopher
Now sets him to aver
          You are nought
          But a thought
Without reality.

            Young, old,
              Passioned, cold,
        All the loved-lost thus
        Are beings continuous,
        In dateless dure abiding,
        Over the present striding
        With placid permanence
        That knows not transience:
              Firm in the Vast,
              First, last;
        Afar, yet close to us.

AN INQUIRY

A PHANTASY

'Circumdederunt me dolores mortis.' – Psalm xviii

I SAID to It: 'We grasp not what you meant,
(Dwelling down here, so narrowly pinched and pent)
By crowning Death the King of the Firmament:
        – The query I admit to be
        One of unwonted size,
        But it is put you sorrowingly,
        And not in idle-wise.'

'Sooth, since you ask me gravely,' It replied,
'Though too incisive questions I have decried,
This shows some thought, and may be justified.
        I'll gauge its value as I go
        Across the Universe,
        And bear me back in a moment or so
        And say, for better or worse.'

Many years later, when It came again,
'That matter an instant back which brought you pain',
It said, 'and you besought me to explain:
        Well, my forethoughtless modes to you
        May seem a shameful thing,
        But – I'd no meaning, that I knew,
        In crowning Death as King!'

THE AËROLITE

I THOUGHT a germ of Consciousness
Escaped on an aërolite
      Aions ago
From some far globe, where no distress
Had means to mar supreme delight;

But only things abode that made
The power to feel a gift uncloyed
      Of gladsome glow,
And life unendingly displayed
Emotions loved, desired, enjoyed.

And that this stray, exotic germ
Fell wanderingly upon our sphere,
      After its wingings,
Quickened, and showed to us the worm
That gnaws vitalities native here,

And operated to unblind
Earth's old-established ignorance
      Of stains and stingings,
Which grin no griefs while not opined,
But cruelly tax intelligence.

'How shall we', then the seers said,
'Oust this awareness, this disease
      Called sense, here sown,
Though good, no doubt, where it was bred,
And wherein all things work to please?'

Others cried: 'Nay, we rather would,
Since this untoward gift is sent
      For ends unknown,
Limit its registerings to good,
And hide from it all anguishment.'

I left them pondering. This was how
(Or so I dreamed) was waked on earth
  The mortal moan
Begot of sentience. Maybe now
Normal unwareness waits rebirth.

A PHILOSOPHICAL FANTASY

'Milton . . . made God argue.' – WALTER BAGEHOT

 'WELL, if thou wilt, then, ask me;
 To answer will not task me:
 I've a response, I doubt not,
 And quite agree to flout not
 Thy question, if of reason,
 Albeit not quite in season:
 A universe to marshal,
 What god can give but partial
 Eye to frail Earth – life-shotten
 Ere long, extinct, forgotten! –
 But seeing indications
 That thou read'st my limitations,
 And since my lack of forethought
 Aggrieves thy more and more thought,
 I'll hearken to thy pleading:
 Some lore may lie in heeding
 Thy irregular proceeding.'

 ' 'Tis this *unfulfilled intention*,
 O Causer, I would mention:–
 Will you, in condescension
 This evening, ere we've parted,
 Say why you felt fainthearted,
 And let your aim be thwarted,
 Its glory be diminished,
 Its concept stand unfinished? –
 Such I ask you, Sir or Madam,
 (I know no more than Adam,
 Even vaguely, what your sex is, –

Though feminine I had thought you
Till seers as "Sire" besought you; –
And this my ignorance vexes
Some people not a little,
And, though not me one tittle,
It makes me sometimes choose me
Call you "It", if you'll excuse me?')

'Call me "It" with a good conscience,
And be sure it is all nonsense
That I mind a fault of manner
In a pigmy towards his planner!
Be I, be not I, sexless,
I am in nature vexless.
– How vain must clay-carved man be
To deem such folly can be
As that freaks of my own framing
Can set my visage flaming –
Start me volleying interjections
Against my own confections,
As the Jews and others limned me,
And in fear and trembling hymned me!
Call me "but dream-projected",
I shall not be affected;
Call me "blind force persisting",
I shall remain unlisting;
(A few have done it lately,
And, maybe, err not greatly.)
– Another such a vanity
In witless weak humanity
Is thinking that of those all
Through space at my disposal,
Man's shape must needs resemble
Mine, that makes zodiacs tremble!

'Continuing where we started:–
As for my aims being thwarted,
Wherefore I feel fainthearted,
Aimless am I, revealing
No heart-scope for faint feeling.
– But thy mistake I'll pardon,
And, as Adam's mentioned to me,
(Though in timeless truth there never
Was a man like him whatever)
I'll meet thee in thy garden,
As I did not him, beshrew me!
In the sun of so-called daytime –
Say, just about the Maytime
Of my next, or next, Creation?
(I love procrastination,
To use the words in thy sense,
Which have no hold on my sense)
Or at any future stray-time. –
One of thy representatives
In some later incarnation
I mean, of course, well knowing
Thy present conformation
But a unit of my tentatives,
Whereof such heaps lie blowing
As dust, where thou art going;
Yea, passed to where suns glow not,
Begrieved of those that go not
(Though what grief is, I know not.)

'Perhaps I may inform thee,
In case I should alarm thee,
That no dramatic stories
Like ancient ones whose core is
A mass of superstition
And monkish imposition
Will mark my explanation
Of the world's sore situation
(As thou tell'st), with woes that shatter;
Though from former aions to latter
To me 'tis malleable matter

For treatment scientific
More than sensitive and specific –
Stuff without moral features,
Which I've no sense of ever,
Or of ethical endeavour,
Or of justice to Earth's creatures,
Or how Right from Wrong to sever:
Let these be as men learn such;
For me, I don't discern such,
And – real enough I daresay –
I know them but by hearsay
As something Time hath rendered
Out of substance I engendered,
Time, too, being a condition
Beyond my recognition.
– I would add that, while unknowing
Of this justice earthward owing,
Nor explanation offering
Of what is meant by suffering,
Thereof I'm not a spurner,
Or averse to be a learner.

'To return from wordy wandering
To the question we are pondering;
Though, viewing the world in *my* mode,
I fail to see it in *thy* mode
As "unfulfilled intention",
Which is past my comprehension
Being unconscious in my doings
So largely, (whence thy rueings); –
Aye, to human tribes nor kindlessness
Nor love I've given, but mindlessness,
Which state, though far from ending,
May nevertheless be mending.

'However, I'll advise him –
Him thy scion, who will walk here
When Death hath dumbed thy talk here –
In phrase that may surprise him,
What thing it was befel me,
(A thing that my confessing
Lack of forethought helps thy guessing),
And acted to compel me
By that *purposeless propension*
Which is mine, and not intention,
Along lines of least resistance,
Or, in brief, unsensed persistence,
That saddens thy existence
To think my so-called scheming
Not that of my first dreaming.'

1920 and 1926

DRINKING SONG

ONCE on a time when thought began
    Lived Thales: he
    Was said to see
Vast truths that mortals seldom can;
    It seems without
    A moment's doubt
That everything was made for man.

Chorus
  Fill full your cups: feel no distress
    That thoughts so great should now be less!

Earth mid the sky stood firm and flat,
    He held, till came
    A sage by name
Copernicus, and righted that.
    We trod, he told,
    A globe that rolled
Around a sun it warmed it at.

Chorus
Fill full your cups: feel no distress;
'Tis only one great thought the less!

But still we held, as Time flew by
    And wit increased,
    Ours was, at least,
The only world whose rank was high:
    Till rumours flew
    From folk who knew
Of globes galore about the sky.

Chorus
Fill full your cups: feel no distress;
'Tis only one great thought the less!

And that this earth, our one estate,
    Was no prime ball,
    The best of all,
But common, mean; indeed, tenth-rate:
    And men, so proud,
    A feeble crowd,
Unworthy any special fate.

Chorus
Fill full your cups: feel no distress;
'Tis only one great thought the less!

Then rose one Hume, who could not see,
    If earth were such,
    Required were much
To prove no miracles could be:
    'Better believe
    The eyes deceive
Than that God's clockwork jolts,' said he.

Chorus
Fill full your cups: feel no distress;
'Tis only one great thought the less!

G

Next this strange message Darwin brings,
     (Though saying his say
     In a quiet way);
We all are one with creeping things;
     And apes and men
     Blood-brethren,
And likewise reptile forms with stings.

Chorus
Fill full your cups: feel no distress;
'Tis only one great thought the less!

And when this philosoph had done
     Came Doctor Cheyne:
     Speaking plain he
Proved no virgin bore a son.
     'Such tale, indeed,
     Helps not our creed,'
He said. 'A tale long known to none.'

Chorus
Fill full your cups: feel no distress;
'Tis only one great thought the less!

And now comes Einstein with a notion –
     Not yet quite clear
     To many here –
That's there's no time, no space, no motion,
     Nor rathe nor late,
     Nor square nor straight,
But just a sort of bending-ocean.

Chorus
Fill full your cups: feel no distress;
'Tis only one great thought the less!

So here we are, in piteous case:
  Like butterflies
  Of many dyes
Upon an Alpine glacier's face:
  To fly and cower
  In some warm bower
Our chief concern in such a place.

Chorus
  Fill full your cups: feel no distress
  At all our great thoughts shrinking less:
  We'll do a good deed nevertheless!

'WE ARE GETTING TO THE END'

We are getting to the end of visioning
The impossible within this universe,
Such as that better whiles may follow worse,
And that our race may mend by reasoning.

We know that even as larks in cages sing
Unthoughtful of deliverance from the curse
That holds them lifelong in a latticed hearse,
We ply spasmodically our pleasuring.

And that when nations set them to lay waste
Their neighbours' heritage by foot and horse,
And hack their pleasant plains in festering seams,
They may again, – not warely, or from taste,
But tickled mad by some demonic force. –
Yes. We are getting to the end of dreams!

SECTION 5
WAR

DRUMMER HODGE

I

THEY throw in Drummer Hodge, to rest
    Uncoffined – just as found:
His landmark is a kopje-crest
    That breaks the veldt around;
And foreign constellations west
    Each night above his mound.

II

Young Hodge the Drummer never knew –
    Fresh from his Wessex home –
The meaning of the broad Karoo,
    The Bush, the dusty loam,
And why uprose to nightly view
    Strange stars amid the gloam.

III

Yet portion of that unknown plain
    Will Hodge for ever be;
His homely Northern breast and brain
    Grow to some Southern tree,
And strange-eyed constellations reign
    His stars eternally.

THE SOULS OF THE SLAIN

I

THE thick lids of Night closed upon me
    Alone at the Bill
    Of the Isle by the Race[1] –
Many-caverned, bald, wrinkled of face –
And with darkness and silence the spirit was on me
    To brood and be still.

[1] The 'Race' is the turbulent sea-area off the Bill of Portland, where contrary tides meet.

II

No wind fanned the flats of the ocean,
    Or promontory sides,
    Or the ooze by the strand,
  Or the bent-bearded slope of the land,
Whose base took its rest amid everlong motion
    Of criss-crossing tides.

III

Soon from out of the Southward seemed nearing
    A whirr, as of wings
    Waved by mighty-vanned flies,
  Or by night-moths of measureless size,
And in softness and smoothness well-nigh beyond hearing
    Of corporal things.

IV

And they bore to the bluff, and alighted –
    A dim-discerned train
    Of sprites without mould,
  Frameless souls none might touch or might hold –
On the ledge by the turreted lantern, far-sighted
    By men of the main.

V

And I heard them say 'Home!' and I knew them
    For souls of the felled
    On the earth's nether bord
  Under Capricorn, whither they'd warred,
And I neared in my awe, and gave heedfulness to them
    With breathings inheld.

VI

Then, it seemed, there approached from the northward
    A senior soul-flame
    Of the like filmy hue:
  And he met them and spake: 'Is it you,
O my men?' Said they, 'Aye! We bear homeward and hearth-
      ward
    To feast on our fame!'

VII

'I've flown there before you,' he said then:
 'Your households are well;
 But – your kin linger less
On your glory and war-mightiness
Than on dearer things.' – 'Dearer?' cried these from the dead
  then,
 'Of what do they tell?'

VIII

'Some mothers muse sadly, and murmur
 Your doings as boys –
 Recall the quaint ways
Of your babyhood's innocent days.
Some pray that, ere dying, your faith had grown firmer,
 And higher your joys.

IX

'A father broods: "Would I had set him
 To some humble trade,
 And so slacked his high fire,
And his passionate martial desire;
And told him no stories to woo him and whet him
 To this dire crusade!" '

X

'And, General, how hold out our sweethearts,
 Sworn loyal as doves?'
 – 'Many mourn; many think
It is not unattractive to prink
Them in sables for heroes. Some fickle and fleet hearts
 Have found them new loves.'

XI

'And our wives?' quoth another resignedly,
 'Dwell they on our deeds?'
 – 'Deeds of home; that live yet
Fresh as new – deeds of fondness or fret;
Ancient words that were kindly expressed or unkindly,
 These, these have their heeds.'

XII

– 'Alas! then it seems that our glory
  Weighs less in their thought
  Than our old homely acts,
 And the long-ago commonplace facts
Of our lives – held by us as scarce part of our story,
  And rated as nought!'

XIII

Then bitterly some: 'Was it wise now
  To raise the tomb-door
  For such knowledge? Away!'
 But the rest: 'Fame we prized till to-day;
Yet that hearts keep us green for old kindness we prize now
  A thousand times more!'

XIV

Thus speaking, the trooped apparitions
  Began to disband
  And resolve them in two:
 Those whose record was lovely and true
Bore to northward for home: those of bitter traditions
  Again left the land,

XV

And, towering to seaward in legions,
  They paused at a spot
  Overbending the Race –
 That engulphing, ghast, sinister place –
Whither headlong they plunged, to the fathomless regions
  Of myriads forgot.

XVI

And the spirits of those who were homing
  Passed on, rushingly,
  Like the Pentecost Wind;
 And the whirr of their wayfaring thinned
And surceased on the sky, and but left in the gloaming
  Sea-mutterings and me.

December 1899

THE MAN HE KILLED

'HAD he and I but met
    By some old ancient inn,
We should have sat us down to wet
    Right many a nipperkin!

'But ranged as infantry,
    And staring face to face,
I shot at him as he at me,
    And killed him in his place.

'I shot him dead because –
    Because he was my foe,
Just so: my foe of course he was;
    That's clear enough; although

'He thought he'd 'list, perhaps,
    Of-hand like – just as I –
Was out of work – had sold his traps –
    No other reason why.

'Yes; quaint and curious war is!
    You shoot a fellow down
You'd treat if met where any bar is,
    Or help to half-a-crown.'

1902

IN TIME OF 'THE BREAKING OF NATIONS'[1]

I

ONLY a man harrowing clods
    In a slow silent walk
With an old horse that stumbles and nods
    Half asleep as they stalk.

[1] Jeremiah li. 20

II

Only thin smoke without flame
　　From the heaps of couch-grass;
Yet this will go onward the same
　　Though Dynasties pass.

III

Yonder a maid and her wight
　　Come whispering by:
War's annals will cloud into night
　　Ere their story die.

1915

A NEW YEAR'S EVE IN WAR TIME

I

PHANTASMAL fears,
And the flap of the flame,
And the throb of the clock,
And a loosened slate,
And the blind night's drone,
Which tiredly the spectral pines intone.

II

And the blood in my ears
Strumming always the same,
And the gable-cock
With its fitful grate,
And myself, alone.

III

The twelfth hour nears
Hand-hid, as in shame;
I undo the lock,
And listen, and wait
For the Young Unknown.

IV

In the dark there careers –
As if Death astride came
To numb all with his knock –
A horse at mad rate
Over rut and stone.

V

No figure appears,
No call of my name,
No sound but 'Tic-toc'
Without check. Past the gate
It clatters – is gone.

VI

What rider it bears
There is none to proclaim;
And the Old Year has struck,
And, scarce animate,
The New makes moan.

VII

Maybe that 'More Tears! –
More Famine and Flame –
More Severance and Shock!'
Is the order from Fate
That the Rider speeds on
To pale Europe; and tiredly the pines intone.

1915–1916

'I MET A MAN'

I MET a man when night was nigh,
Who said, with shining face and eye
Like Moses' after Sinai:–

'I have seen the Moulder of Monarchies,
      Realms, peoples, plains and hills,
   Sitting upon the sunlit seas! –
   And, as He sat, soliloquies
Fell from Him like an antiphonic breeze
      That pricks the waves to thrills.

'Meseemed that of the maimed and dead
      Mown down upon the globe, –
   Their plenteous blooms of promise shed
   Ere fruiting-time – His words were said,
Sitting against the western web of red
      Wrapt in His crimson robe.

'And I could catch them now and then:
      – "Why let these gambling clans
   Of human Cockers, pit liege men
   From mart and city, dale and glen,
In death-mains, but to swell and swell again
      Their swollen All-Empery plans,

' "When a mere nod (if my malign
      Compeer but passive keep)
   Would mend that old mistake of mine
   I made with Saul, and ever consign
All Lords of War whose sanctuaries enshrine
      Liberticide, to sleep?

' "With violence the lands are spread
      Even as in Israel's day,
   And it repenteth me I bred
   Chartered armipotents lust-led
To feuds. . . . Yea, grieves my heart, as then I said,
      To see their evil way!"

   – 'The utterance grew, and flapped like flame,
      And further speech I feared;
   But no Celestial tongued acclaim,
   And no huzzas from earthlings came,
And the heavens mutely masked as 'twere in shame
      Till daylight disappeared.'

Thus ended he as night rode high –
The man of shining face and eye,
Like Moses' after Sinai.

1916

'I LOOKED UP FROM MY WRITING'

I LOOKED up from my writing,
    And gave a start to see,
As if rapt in my inditing,
    The moon's full gaze on me.

Her meditative misty head
    Was spectral in its air,
And I involuntarily said,
    'What are you doing there?'

'Oh, I've been scanning pond and hole
    And waterway hereabout
For the body of one with a sunken soul
    Who has put his life-light out.

'Did you hear his frenzied tattle?
    It was sorrow for his son
Who is slain in brutish battle,
    Though he has injured none.

'And now I am curious to look
    Into the blinkered mind
Of one who wants to write a book
    In a world of such a kind.'

Her temper overwrought me,
    And I edged to shun her view,
For I felt assured she thought me
    One who should drown him too.

'AND THERE WAS A GREAT CALM'

(ON THE SIGNING OF THE ARMISTICE, NOV. 11, 1918)

I

THERE had been years of Passion – scorching, cold,
And much Despair, and Anger heaving high,
Care whitely watching, Sorrows manifold,
Among the young, among the weak and old,
And the pensive Spirit of Pity whispered, 'Why?'

II

Men had not paused to answer. Foes distraught
Pierced the thinned peoples in a brute-like blindness,
Philosophies that sages long had taught,
And Selflessness, were as an unknown thought,
And 'Hell!' and 'Shell!' were yapped at Lovingkindness.

III

The feeble folk at home had grown full-used
To 'dug-outs', 'snipers', 'Huns', from the war adept
In the mornings heard, and at evetides perused;
To day-dreamt men in millions, when they mused –
To nightmare-men in millions when they slept.

IV

Waking to wish existence timeless, null,
Sirius they watched above where armies fell;
He seemed to check his flapping when, in the lull
Of night a boom came thencewise, like the dull
Plunge of a stone dropped into some deep well.

V

So, when old hopes that earth was bettering slowly
Were dead and damned, there sounded 'War is done!'
One morrow. Said the bereft, and meek, and lowly,
'Will men some day be given to grace? yea, wholly,
And in good sooth, as our dreams used to run?'

VI

Breathless they paused. Out there men raised their glance
To where had stood those poplars lank and lopped,
As they had raised it through the four years' dance
Of Death in the now familiar flats of France;
And murmured, 'Strange, this! How? All firing stopped?'

VII

Aye; all was hushed. The about-to-fire fired not,
The aimed-at moved away in trance-lipped song.
One checkless regiment slung a clinching shot
And turned. The Spirit of Irony smirked out, 'What?
Spoil peradventures woven of Rage and Wrong?'

VIII

Thenceforth no flying fires inflamed the gray,
No hurtlings shook the dewdrop from the thorn,
No moan perplexed the mute bird on the spray;
Worn horses mused: 'We are not whipped to-day';
No weft-winged engines blurred the moon's thin horn.

IX

Calm fell. From Heaven distilled a clemency;
There was peace on earth, and silence in the sky;
Some could, some could not, shake off misery:
The Sinister Spirit sneered: 'It had to be!'
And again the Spirit of Pity whispered, 'Why?'

PART IV

POEMS DRAMATIC AND PERSONATIVE

DREAM OF THE CITY SHOPWOMAN

'TWERE sweet to have a comrade here,
Who'd vow to love this garreteer,
By city people's snap and sneer
  Tried oft and hard!

We'd rove a truant cock and hen
To some snug solitary glen,
And never be seen to haunt again
  This teeming yard.

Within a cot of thatch and clay
We'd list the flitting pipers play,
Our lives a twine of good and gay
  Enwreathed discreetly;

Our blithest deeds so neighbouring wise
That doves should coo in soft surprise,
'These must belong to Paradise
  Who live so sweetly.'

Our clock should be the closing flowers,
Our sprinkle-bath the passing showers,
Our church the alleyed willow bowers,
  The truth our theme;

And infant shapes might soon abound:
Their shining heads would dot us round
Like mushroom balls on grassy ground. . . .
  – But all is dream!

O God, that creatures framed to feel
A yearning nature's strong appeal
Should writhe on this eternal wheel
  In rayless grime;

And vainly note, with wan regret,
Each star of early promise set;
Till Death relieves, and they forget
Their one Life's time!

Westbourne Park Villas, 1866

HER DILEMMA

(IN ——— CHURCH)

THE two were silent in a sunless church,
Whose mildewed walls, uneven paving-stones,
And wasted carvings passed antique research;
And nothing broke the clock's dull monotones.

Leaning against a wormy poppy-head,
So wan and worn that he could scarcely stand,
– For he was soon to die – he softly said,
'Tell me you love me!' – holding long her hand.

She would have given a world to breathe 'yes' truly,
So much his life seemed hanging on her mind,
And hence she lied, her heart persuaded throughly
'Twas worth her soul to be a moment kind.

But the sad need thereof, his nearing death,
So mocked humanity that she shamed to prize
A world conditioned thus, or care for breath
Where Nature such dilemmas could devise.

1866

THE RUINED MAID

'O 'MELIA, my dear, this does everything crown!
Who could have supposed I should meet you in Town?
And whence such fair garments, such prosperi-ty?' –
'O didn't you know I'd been ruined?' said she.

– 'You left us in tatters, without shoes or socks,
Tired of digging potatoes, and spudding up docks;
And now you've gay bracelets and bright feathers three!' –
'Yes: that's how we dress when we're ruined,' said she.

– 'At home in the barton you said "thee" and "thou",
And "thik oon", and "theäs oon", and "t'other"; but now
Your talking quite fits 'ee for high compa-ny!' –
'Some polish is gained with one's ruin,' said she.

– 'Your hands were like paws then, your face blue and bleak
But now I'm bewitched by your delicate cheek,
And your little gloves fit as on any la-dy!' –
'We never do work when we're ruined,' said she.

– 'You used to call home-life a hag-ridden dream,
And you'd sigh, and you'd sock; but at present you seem
To know not of megrims or melancho-ly!' –
'True. One's pretty lively when ruined,' said she.

– 'I wish I had feathers, a fine sweeping gown,
And a delicate face, and could strut about Town!' –
'My dear – a raw country girl, such as you be,
Cannot quite expect that. You ain't ruined,' said she.

Westbourne Park Villas, 1866

THE LEVELLED CHURCHYARD

'O PASSENGER, pray list and catch
        Our sighs and piteous groans,
Half stifled in this jumbled patch
        Of wretched memorial stones!

'We late-lamented, resting here,
        Are mixed to human jam,
And each to each exclaims in fear,
        "I know not which I am!"

'The wicked people have annexed
                The verses on the good;
A roaring drunkard sports the text
                Teetotal Tommy should!

'Where we are huddled none can trace,
                And if our names remain,
They pave some path or porch or place
                Where we have never lain!

'Here's not a modest maiden elf
                But dreads the final Trumpet,
Lest half of her should rise herself,
                And half some sturdy strumpet!

'From restorations of Thy fane,
                From smoothings of Thy sward,
From zealous Churchmen's pick and plane
                Deliver us O Lord! Amen!'

1882

A BEAUTY'S SOLILOQUY DURING HER HONEYMOON

Too late, too late! I did not know my fairness
                Would catch the world's keen eyes so!
How the men look at me! My radiant rareness
                I deemed not they would prize so!

That I was a peach for any man's possession
                Why did not some one say
Before I leased myself in an hour's obsession
                To this dull mate for aye!

His days are mine. I am one who cannot steal her
                Ahead of his plodding pace:
As he is, so am I. One doomed to feel her
                A wasted form and face!

I was so blind! It did sometimes just strike me
　　　All girls were not as I,
But, dwelling much alone, how few were like me
　　　I could not well descry;

Till, at this Grand Hotel, all looks bend on me
　　　In homage as I pass
To take my seat at breakfast, dinner, – con me
　　　As poorly spoused, alas!

I was too young. I dwelt too much on duty:
　　　If I had guessed my powers
Where might have sailed this cargo of choice beauty
　　　In its unanchored hours!

Well, husband, poor plain man; I've lost life's battle! –
　　　Come – let them look at me.
O damn, don't show in your looks that I'm your chattel
　　　Quite so emphatically!

　　　In a London Hotel, 1892

FRIENDS BEYOND

WILLIAM DEWY, Tranter Reuben, Farmer Ledlow late at plough,
　　　Robert's kin, and John's, and Ned's,
And the Squire, and Lady Susan, lie in Mellstock churchyard now!

'Gone,' I call them, gone for good, that group of local hearts and
　　　　　heads;
　　　Yet at mothy curfew-tide,
And at midnight when the noon-heat breathes it back from walls
　　　and leads,

They've a way of whispering to me – fellow-wight who yet abide –
　　　In the muted, measured note
Of a ripple under archways, or a lone cave's stillicide:

'We have triumphed: this achievement turns the bane to antidote,
 Unsuccesses to success,
Many thought-worn eves and morrows to a morrow free of
 thought.

'No more need we corn and clothing, feel of old terrestrial stress;
 Chill detraction stirs no sigh;
Fear of death has even bygone us: death gave all that we possess.'

W. D. – 'Ye mid burn the old bass-viol that I set such value by.'
Squire. – 'You may hold the manse in fee,
 You may wed my spouse, may let my children's memory of
 me die.'

Lady S. – 'You may have my rich brocades, my laces; take each
 household key;
 Ransack coffer, desk, bureau;
 Quiz the few poor treasures hid there, con the letters kept by
 me.'

Far. – 'Ye mid zell my favourite heifer, ye mid let the charlock
 grow,
 Foul the grinterns, give up thrift.'
Far. Wife. – 'If ye break my best blue china, children, I shan't care
 or ho.'

All. – 'We've no wish to hear the tidings, how the people's fortunes
 shift;
 What your daily doings are;
 Who are wedded, born, divided; if your lives beat slow or
 swift.

'Curious not the least are we if our intents you make or mar,
 If you quire to our old tune,
If the City stage still passes, if the weirs still roar afar.'

– Thus, with very gods' composure, freed those crosses late and soon
 Which, in life, the Trine allow
(Why, none witteth), and ignoring all that haps beneath the moon,

William Dewy, Tranter Reuben, Farmer Ledlow late at plough,
    Robert's kin, and John's, and Ned's,
And the Squire, and Lady Susan, murmur mildly to me now.

THE MILKMAID

UNDER a daisied bank
There stands a rich red ruminating cow,
    And hard against her flank
A cotton-hooded milkmaid bends her brow.

The flowery river-ooze
Upheaves and falls; the milk purrs in the pail;
    Few pilgrims but would choose
The peace of such a life in such a vale.

The maid breathes words – to vent,
It seems, her sense of Nature's scenery,
    Of whose life, sentiment,
And essence, very part itself is she.

She bends a glance of pain,
And, at a moment, lets escape a tear;
    Is it that passing train,
Whose alien whirr offends her country ear? –

Nay! Phyllis does not dwell
On visual and familiar things like these;
    What moves her is the spell
Of inner themes and inner poetries:

Could but by Sunday morn
Her gay new gown come, meads might dry to dun,
    Trains shriek till ears were torn,
If Fred would not prefer that Other One.

THE RESPECTABLE BURGHER

ON 'THE HIGHER CRITICISM'

SINCE Reverend Doctors now declare
That clerks and people must prepare
To doubt if Adam ever were;
To hold the flood a local scare;
To argue, though the stolid stare,
That everything had happened ere
The prophets to its happening sware;
That David was no giant-slayer,
Nor one to call a God-obeyer
In certain details we could spare,
But rather was a debonair
Shrewd bandit, skilled as banjo-player:
That Solomon sang the fleshly Fair,
And gave the Church no thought whate'er,
That Esther with her royal wear,
And Mordecai, the son of Jair,
And Joshua's triumphs, Job's despair,
And Balaam's ass's bitter blare;
Nebuchadnezzar's furnace-flare,
And Daniel and the den affair,
And other stories rich and rare,
Were writ to make old doctrine wear
Something of a romantic air:
That the Nain widow's only heir,
And Lazarus with cadaverous glare
(As done in oils by Piombo's care)
Did not return from Sheol's lair:
That Jael set a fiendish snare,
That Pontius Pilate acted square,
That never a sword cut Malchus' ear;
And (but for shame I must forbear)
That —— —— did not reappear! . . .
– Since thus they hint, nor turn a hair
All churchgoing will I forswear,
And sit on Sundays in my chair,
And read that moderate man Voltaire.

THE CURATE'S KINDNESS

A WORKHOUSE IRONY

I

I THOUGHT they'd be strangers aroun' me,
  But she's to be there!
Let me jump out o' waggon and go back and drown me
  At Pummery or Ten-Hatches Weir.

II

I thought: 'Well, I've come to the Union –
  The workhouse at last –
After honest hard work all the week, and Communion
  O' Zundays, these fifty years past.

III

' 'Tis hard; but,' I thought, 'never mind it:
  There's gain in the end:
And when I get used to the place I shall find it
  A home, and may find there a friend.

IV

'Life there will be better than t'other,
  For peace is assured.
The men in one wing and their wives in another
  Is strictly the rule of the Board.'

V

Just then one young Pa'son arriving
  Steps up out of breath
To the side o' the waggon wherein we were driving
  To Union; and calls out and saith:

VI

'Old folks, that harsh order is altered,
  Be not sick of heart!
The Guardians they poohed and they pished and they paltered
  When urged not to keep you apart.

VII

‘ "It is wrong", I maintained, "to divide them,
      Near forty years wed."
"Very well, sir. We promise, then, they shall abide them
      In one wing together," they said.’

VIII

Then I sank – knew 'twas quite a foredone thing
      That misery should be
To the end! . . . To get freed of her there was the one thing
      Had made the change welcome to me.

IX

To go there was ending but badly;
      'Twas shame and 'twas pain;
‘But anyhow', thought I, ‘thereby I shall gladly
      Get free of this forty years' chain.’

X

I thought they'd be strangers aroun' me,
      But she's to be there!
Let me jump out o' waggon and go back and drown me
      At Pummery or Ten-Hatches Weir.

REMINISCENCES OF A DANCING MAN

I

Who now remembers Almack's balls –
      Willis's sometime named –
In those two smooth-floored upper halls
      For faded ones so famed?
Where as we trod to trilling sound
The fancied phantoms stood around,
      Or joined us in the maze,
Of the powdered Dears from Georgian years,
Whose dust lay in sightless sealed-up biers,
      The fairest of former days.

II

Who now remembers gay Cremorne,
        And all its jaunty jills,
And those wild whirling figures born
        Of Jullien's grand quadrilles?
With hats on head and morning coats
There footed to his prancing notes
        Our partner-girls and we;
And the gas-jets winked, and the lustres clinked,
And the platform throbbed as with arms enlinked
        We moved to the minstrelsy.

III

Who now recalls those crowded rooms
        Of old yclept 'The Argyle',
Where to the deep Drum-polka's booms
        We hopped in standard style?
Whither have danced those damsels now!
Is Death the partner who doth moue
        Their wormy chaps and bare?
Do their spectres spin like sparks within
The smoky halls of the Prince of Sin
        To a thunderous Jullien air?

ONE RALPH BLOSSOM SOLILOQUIZES

('It being deposed that vij women who were mayds before he knew them
have been brought upon the towne [rates?] by the fornicacions of one
Ralph Blossom, Mr. Maior inquired why he should not contribute xiv
pence weekly toward their mayntenance. But it being shewn that the
sayd R. B. was dying of a purple feaver, no order was made.' – *Budmouth
Borough Minutes*: 16—.)

WHEN I am in hell or some such place,
A-groaning over my sorry case,
What will those seven women say to me
Who, when I coaxed them, answered 'Aye' to me?

'I did not understand your sign!'
Will be the words of Caroline;
While Jane will cry, 'If I'd had proof of you,
I should have learnt to hold aloof of you!'

'I won't reproach: it was to be!'
Will dryly murmur Cicely;
And Rosa: 'I feel no hostility,
For I must own I lent facility.'

Lizzy says: 'Sharp was my regret,
And sometimes it is now! But yet
I joy that, though it brought notoriousness,
I knew Love once and all its gloriousness!'

Says Patience: 'Why are we apart?
Small harm did you, my poor Sweet Heart!
A manchild born, now tall and beautiful,
Was worth the ache of days undutiful.'

And Anne cries: 'O the time was fair,
So wherefore should you burn down there?
There is a deed under the sun, my Love,
And that was ours. What's done is done, my Love.
These trumpets here in Heaven are dumb to me
With you away. Dear, come, O come to me!'

LIDDELL AND SCOTT

ON THE COMPLETION OF THEIR LEXICON

*(Written after the death of Liddell in 1898. Scott had
died some ten years earlier.)*

'WELL, though it seems
Beyond our dreams,'
Said Liddell to Scott,
'We've really got
To the very end,
All inked and penned
Blotless and fair
Without turning a hair,
This sultry summer day, A.D.
Eighteen hundred and forty-three.

'I've often, I own,
Belched many a moan
At undertaking it,
And dreamt forsaking it.
– Yes, on to Pi,
When the end loomed nigh,
And friends said: "You've as good as done,"
I almost wished we'd not begun.
Even now, if people only knew
My sinkings, as we slowly drew
Along through Kappa, Lambda, Mu,
They'd be concerned at my misgiving,
And how I mused on a College living
    Right down to Sigma,
    But feared a stigma
If I succumbed, and left old Donnegan
For weary freshmen's eyes to con again:
And how I often, often wondered
What could have led me to have blundered
So far away from sound theology
To dialects and etymology;
Words, accents not to be breathed by men
Of any country ever again!'

    'My heart most failed,
    Indeed, quite quailed,'
    Said Scott to Liddell,
    'Long ere the middle! . . .
    'Twas one wet dawn
    When, slippers on,
    And a cold in the head anew,
    Gazing at Delta
    I turned and felt a
    Wish for bed anew,
    And to let supersedings
    Of Passow's readings
    In dialects go.
    "That German has read
    More than we!" I said;
Yea, several times did I feel so! . . .

'O that first morning, smiling bland,
With sheets of foolscap, quills in hand,
To write ἀάατος and ἀαγής,
Followed by fifteen hundred pages,
    What nerve was ours
    So to back our powers,
Assured that we should reach ὠῴδης
While there was breath left in our bodies!'

Liddell replied: 'Well, that's past now;
The job's done, thank God, anyhow.'
    'And yet it's not,'
    Considered Scott,
    'For we've to get
    Subscribers yet
    We must remember;
    Yes; by September.'

'O Lord; dismiss that. We'll succeed.
Dinner is my immediate need.
I feel as hollow as a fiddle,
Working so many hours,' said Liddell.

AT CASTERBRIDGE FAIR

FORMER BEAUTIES

THESE market-dames, mid-aged, with lips thin-drawn,
    And tissues sere,
Are they the ones we loved in years agone,
    And courted here?

Are these the muslined pink young things to whom
    We vowed and swore
In nooks on summer Sundays by the Froom,
    Or Budmouth shore?

Do they remember those gay tunes we trod
　　Clasped on the green;
Aye; trod till moonlight set on the beaten sod
　　A satin sheen?

They must forget, forget! They cannot know
　　What once they were,
Or memory would transfigure them, and show
　　Them always fair.

THE MARKET-GIRL

NOBODY took any notice of her as she stood on the causey kerb,
All eager to sell her honey and apples and bunches of garden
　　herb;
And if she had offered to give her wares and herself with them
　　too that day,
I doubt if a soul would have cared to take a bargain so choice
　　away.

But chancing to trace her sunburnt grace that morning as I
　　passed nigh,
I went and I said 'Poor maidy dear! – and will none of the
　　people buy?'
And so it began; and soon we knew what the end of it all
　　must be,
And I found that though no others had bid, a prize had been
　　won by me.

AFTER THE FAIR

THE singers are gone from the Cornmarket-place
　　With their broadsheets of rhymes,
The street rings no longer in treble and bass
　　With their skits on the times,
And the Cross, lately thronged, is a dim naked space
　　That but echoes the stammering chimes.

From Clock-corner steps, as each quarter ding-dongs,
    Away the folk roam
By the 'Hart' and Grey's Bridge into byways and 'drongs',
    Or across the ridged loam;
The younger ones shrilling the lately heard songs,
    The old saying, 'Would we were home.'

The shy-seeming maiden so mute in the fair
    Now rattles and talks,
And that one who looked the most swaggering there
    Grows sad as she walks,
And she who seemed eaten by cankering care
    In statuesque sturdiness stalks.

And midnight clears High Street of all but the ghosts
    Of its buried burghees,
From the latest far back to those old Roman hosts
    Whose remains one yet sees,
Who loved, laughed, and fought, hailed their friends, drank
    their toasts
    At their meeting-times here, just as these!

1902

NOTE – *The chimes* (line 6) will be listened for in vain here at midnight
now, having been abolished some years ago.

JULIE-JANE

SING; how 'a would sing!
How 'a would raise the tune
When we rode in the waggon from harvesting
    By the light o' the moon!

Dance; how 'a would dance!
If a fiddlestring did but sound
She would hold out her coats, give a slanting glance,
    And go round and round.

Laugh; how 'a would laugh!
Her peony lips would part
As if none such a place for a lover to quaff
At the deeps of a heart.

Julie, O girl of joy,
Soon, soon that lover he came.
Ah, yes; and gave thee a baby-boy,
But never his name. . . .

– Tolling for her, as you guess;
And the baby too. . . . 'Tis well.
You knew her in maidhood likewise? – Yes,
That's her burial bell.

'I suppose,' with a laugh, she said,
'I should blush that I'm not a wife;
But how can it matter, so soon to be dead,
What one does in life!'

When we sat making the mourning
By her death-bed side, said she,
'Dears, how can you keep from your lovers, adorning
In honour of me!'

Bubbling and brightsome eyed!
But now – O never again.
She chose her bearers before she died
From her fancy-men.

NOTE – It is, or was, a common custom in Wessex, and probably other
country places, to prepare the mourning beside the death-bed, the dying
person sometimes assisting, who also selects his or her bearers on such
occasions.
    Coats (line 7), old name for petticoats.

AUTUMN IN KING'S HINTOCK PARK

HERE by the baring bough
    Raking up leaves,
Often I ponder how
    Springtime deceives, –
I, an old woman now,
    Raking up leaves.

Here in the avenue
    Raking up leaves,
Lords' ladies pass in view,
    Until one heaves
Sighs at life's russet hue,
    Raking up leaves!

Just as my shape you see
    Raking up leaves,
I saw, when fresh and free,
    Those memory weaves
Into grey ghosts by me,
    Raking up leaves.

Yet, Dear, though one may sigh,
    Raking up leaves,
New leaves will dance on high –
    Earth never grieves! –
Will not, when missed am I,
    Raking up leaves.

1901

H

BEREFT

In the black winter morning
No light will be struck near my eyes
While the clock in the stairway is warning
For five, when he used to rise.
   Leave the door unbarred,
   The clock unwound.
   Make my lone bed hard –
   Would 'twere underground!

When the summer dawns clearly,
And the appletree-tops seem alight,
Who will undraw the curtain and cheerly
Call out that the morning is bright?

When I tarry at market
No form will cross Durnover Lea
In the gathering darkness, to hark at
Grey's Bridge for the pit-pat o' me.

When the supper crock's steaming,
And the time is the time of his tread,
I shall sit by the fire and wait dreaming
In a silence as of the dead.
   Leave the door unbarred,
   The clock unwound,
   Make my lone bed hard –
   Would 'twere underground!

1901

SHE HEARS THE STORM

There was a time in former years –
 While my roof-tree was his –
When I should have been distressed by fears
 At such a night as this!

I should have murmured anxiously,
    'The pricking rain strikes cold;
His road is bare of hedge or tree,
    And he is getting old.'

But now the fitful chimney-roar,
    The drone of Thorncombe trees,
The Froom in flood upon the moor,
    The mud of Mellstock Leaze,

The candle slanting sooty-wick'd,
    The thuds upon the thatch,
The eaves-drops on the window flicked,
    The clacking garden-hatch,

And what they mean to wayfarers,
    I scarcely heed or mind;
He has won that storm-tight roof of hers
    Which Earth grants all her kind.

WAGTAIL AND BABY

A BABY watched a ford, whereto
    A wagtail came for drinking;
A blaring bull went wading through,
    The wagtail showed no shrinking.

A stallion splashed his way across,
    The birdie nearly sinking;
He gave his plumes a twitch and toss,
    And held his own unblinking.

Next saw the baby round the spot
    A mongrel slowly slinking;
The wagtail gazed, but faltered not
    In dip and sip and prinking.

A perfect gentleman then neared;
    The wagtail, in a winking,
With terror rose and disappeared;
    The baby fell a-thinking.

BEYOND THE LAST LAMP

(NEAR TOOTING COMMON)

I

While rain, with eve in partnership,
Descended darkly, drip, drip, drip,
Beyond the last lone lamp I passed
    Walking slowly, whispering sadly,
      Two linked loiterers, wan, downcast:
Some heavy thought constrained each face,
And blinded them to time and place.

II

The pair seemed lovers, yet absorbed
In mental scenes no longer orbed
By love's young rays. Each countenance
    As it slowly, as it sadly
      Caught the lamplight's yellow glance,
Held in suspense a misery
At things which had been or might be.

III

When I retrod that watery way
Some hours beyond the droop of day,
Still I found pacing there the twain
    Just as slowly, just as sadly,
      Heedless of the night and rain.
One could but wonder who they were
And what wild woe detained them there.

IV

Though thirty years of blur and blot
Have slid since I beheld that spot,
And saw in curious converse there
    Moving slowly, moving sadly
      That mysterious tragic pair,
Its olden look may linger on –
All but the couple; they have gone.

V

Whither? Who knows, indeed. . . . And yet
To me, when nights are weird and wet,
Without those comrades there at tryst
    Creeping slowly, creeping sadly,
    That lone lane does not exist.
There they seem brooding on their pain,
And will, while such a lane remain.

A KING'S SOLILOQUY

ON THE NIGHT OF HIS FUNERAL

FROM the slow march and muffled drum,
        And crowds distrest,
And book and bell, at length I have come
        To my full rest.

A ten years' rule beneath the sun
        Is wound up here,
And what I have done, what left undone,
        Figures out clear.

Yet in the estimate of such
        It grieves me more
That I by some was loved so much
        Than that I bore,

From others, judgment of that hue
        Which over-hope
Breeds from a theoretic view
        Of regal scope.

For kingly opportunities
        Right many have sighed;
How best to bear its devilries
        Those learn who have tried!

I have eaten the fat and drunk the sweet.
    Lived the life out
From the first greeting glad drum-beat
    To the last shout.

What pleasure earth affords to kings
    I have enjoyed
Through its long vivid pulse-stirrings
    Even till it cloyed.

What days of drudgery, nights of stress
    Can cark a throne,
Even one maintained in peacefulness,
    I too have known.

And so, I think, could I step back
    To life again,
I should prefer the average track
    Of average men,

Since, as with them, what kingship would
    It cannot do,
Nor to first thoughts however good
    Hold itself true.

Something binds hard the royal hand,
    As all that be,
And it is That has shaped, has planned
    My acts and me.

May 1910

THE CORONATION

At Westminster, hid from the light of day,
Many who once had shone as monarchs lay.

Edward the Pious, and two Edwards more
The second Richard, Henrys three or four;

That is to say, those who were called the Third,
Fifth, Seventh, and Eighth (the much self-widowered);

And James the Scot, and near him Charles the Second,
And, too, the second George could there be reckoned.

Of women, Mary and Queen Elizabeth,
And Anne, all silent in a musing death;

And William's Mary, and Mary, Queen of Scots,
And consort-queens whose names oblivion blots;

And several more whose chronicle one sees
Adorning ancient royal pedigrees.

– Now, as they drowsed on, freed from Life's old thrall,
And heedless, save of things exceptional,

Said one: 'What means this throbbing thudding sound
That reaches to us here from overground;

'A sound of chisels, augers, planes, and saws,
Infringing all ecclesiastic laws?

'And these tons-weight of timber on us pressed,
Unfelt here since we entered into rest?

'Surely, at least to us, being corpses royal,
A meet repose is owing by the loyal?'

'– Perhaps a scaffold!' Mary Stuart sighed,
'If such still be. It was that way I died.'

'– Ods! Far more like,' said he the many-wived,
'That for a wedding 'tis this work's contrived.

'Ha-ha! I never would bow down to Rimmon,
But I had a rare time with those six women!'

'Not all at once?' gasped he who loved confession.
'Nay, nay!' said Hal. 'That would have been transgression.'

'– They build a catafalque here, black and tall,
Perhaps', mused Richard, 'for some funeral?'

And Anne chimed in: 'Ah, yes: it may be so!'
'Nay!' squeaked Eliza. 'Little you seem to know –

'Clearly 'tis for some crowning here in state,
As they crowned us at our long bygone date;

'Though we'd no such a power of carpentry,
But let the ancient architecture be;

'If I were up there where the parsons sit,
In one of my gold robes, I'd see to it!'

'But you are not,' Charles chuckled. 'You are here,
And never will know the sun again, my dear!'

'Yea,' whispered those whom no one had addressed;
'With slow, sad march, amid a folk distressed,
We were brought here, to take our dusty rest.

'And here, alas, in darkness laid below,
We'll wait and listen, and endure the show. . . .
Clamour dogs kingship; afterwards not so!'

1911

THE CONVERGENCE OF THE TWAIN

(*Lines on the loss of the* Titanic)

I

IN a solitude of the sea
Deep from human vanity,
And the Pride of Life that planned her, stilly couches she.

II

Steel chambers, late the pyres
Of her salamandrine fires,
Cold currents thrid, and turn to rhythmic tidal lyres.

III

Over the mirrors meant
To glass the opulent
The sea-worm crawls – grotesque, slimed, dumb, indifferent.

IV

Jewels in joy designed
To ravish the sensuous mind
Lie lightless, all their sparkles bleared and black and blind.

V

Dim moon-eyed fishes near
Gaze at the gilded gear
And query: 'What does this vaingloriousness down here?'

VI

Well: while was fashioning
This creature of cleaving wing,
The Immanent Will that stirs and urges everything

VII

Prepared a sinister mate
For her – so gaily great –
A Shape of Ice, for the time far and dissociate.

VIII

And as the smart ship grew
In stature, grace, and hue,
In shadowy silent distance grew the Iceberg too.

IX

Alien they seemed to be:
No mortal eye could see
The intimate welding of their later history,

X

Or sign that they were bent
By paths coincident
On being anon twin halves of one august event,

XI

Till the Spinner of the Years
Said 'Now!' And each one hears,
And consummation comes, and jars two hemispheres.

CHANNEL FIRING

THAT night your great guns, unawares,
Shook all our coffins as we lay,
And broke the chancel window-squares,
We thought it was the Judgment-day

And sat upright. While drearisome
Arose the howl of wakened hounds:
The mouse let fall the altar-crumb,
The worms drew back into the mounds,

The glebe cow drooled. Till God called, 'No;
It's gunnery practice out at sea
Just as before you went below;
The world is as it used to be:

'All nations striving strong to make
Red war yet redder. Mad as hatters
They do no more for Christés sake
Than you who are helpless in such matters.

'That this is not the judgment-hour
For some of them's a blessed thing,
For if it were they'd have to scour
Hell's floor for so much threatening. . . .

'Ha, ha. It will be warmer when
I blow the trumpet (if indeed
I ever do; for you are men,
And rest eternal sorely need).'

So down we lay again. 'I wonder,
Will the world ever saner be',
Said one, 'than when He sent us under
In our indifferent century!'

And many a skeleton shook his head.
'Instead of preaching forty year,'
My neighbour Parson Thirdly said,
'I wish I had stuck to pipes and beer.'

Again the guns disturbed the hour,
Roaring their readiness to avenge,
As far inland as Stourton Tower,
And Camelot, and starlit Stonehenge.

April 1914

IN CHURCH

'AND now to God the Father,' he ends,
And his voice thrills up to the topmost tiles:
Each listener chokes as he bows and bends,
And emotion pervades the crowded aisles.
Then the preacher glides to the vestry-door,
And shuts it, and thinks he is seen no more.

The door swings softly ajar meanwhile,
And a pupil of his in the Bible class,
Who adores him as one without gloss or guile,
Sees her idol stand with a satisfied smile
And re-enact at the vestry-glass
Each pulpit gesture in deft dumb-show
That had moved the congregation so.

IN THE CEMETERY

'You see those mothers squabbling there?'
Remarks the man of the cemetery.
'One says in tears, " '*Tis mine lies here !*"
Another, "*Nay, mine, you Pharisee !*"
Another, "*How dare you move my flowers*
And put your own on this grave of ours !"
But all their children were laid therein
At different times, like sprats in a tin.

'And then the main drain had to cross,
And we moved the lot some nights ago,
And packed them away in the general foss
With hundreds more. But their folks don't know,
And as well cry over a new-laid drain
As anything else, to ease your pain!'

IN THE STUDY

He enters, and mute on the edge of a chair
Sits a thin-faced lady, a stranger there,
A type of decayed gentility;
And by some small signs he well can guess
That she comes to him almost breakfastless.

'I have called – I hope I do not err –
I am looking for a purchaser
Of some score volumes of the works
Of eminent divines I own, –
Left by my father – though it irks
My patience to offer them.' And she smiles

As if necessity were unknown;
'But the truth of it is that oftenwhiles
I have wished, as I am fond of art,
To make my rooms a little smart,
And these old books are so in the way.'
And lightly still she laughs to him,
As if to sell were a mere gay whim,
And that, to be frank, Life were indeed
To her not vinegar and gall,
But fresh and honey-like; and Need
No household skeleton at all.

OVER THE COFFIN

THEY stand confronting, the coffin between,
His wife of old, and his wife of late,
And the dead man whose they both had been
Seems listening aloof, as to things past date.
– 'I have called,' says the first. 'Do you marvel or not?'
'In truth', says the second, 'I do – somewhat.'

'Well, there was a word to be said by me! . . .
I divorced that man because of you –
It seemed I must do it, boundenly;
But now I am older, and tell you true,
For life is little, and dead lies he;
I would I had let alone you two!
And both of us, scorning parochial ways,
Had lived like the wives in the patriarchs' days.'

'SHE CHARGED ME'

SHE charged me with having said this and that
To another woman long years before,
In the very parlour where we sat, –

Sat on a night when the endless pour
Of rain on the roof and the road below
Bent the spring of the spirit more and more. . . .

– So charged she me; and the Cupid's bow
Of her mouth was hard, and her eyes, and her face,
And her white forefinger lifted slow.

Had she done it gently, or shown a trace
That not too curiously would she view
A folly flown ere her reign had place,

A kiss might have closed it. But I knew
From the fall of each word, and the pause between,
That the curtain would drop upon us two
Ere long, in our play of slave and queen.

IN THE SERVANTS' QUARTERS

'MAN, you too, aren't you, one of these rough followers of the
        criminal?
All hanging hereabout to gather how he's going to bear
Examination in the hall.' She flung disdainful glances on
The shabby figure standing at the fire with others there,
        Who warmed them by its flare.

'No indeed, my skipping maiden: I know nothing of the trial
        here,
Or criminal, if so he be. – I chanced to come this way,
And the fire shone out into the dawn, and morning airs are cold
        now;
I, too, was drawn in part by charms I see before me play,
        That I see not every day.'

'Ha, ha!' then laughed the constables who also stood to warm
      themselves,
The while another maiden scrutinized his features hard,
As the blaze threw into contrast every line and knot that
      wrinkled them,
Exclaiming, 'Why, last night when he was brought in by the
      guard,
      You were with him in the yard!'

'Nay, nay, you teasing wench, I say! You know you speak
      mistakenly.
Cannot a tired pedestrian who has legged it long and far
Here on his way from northern parts, engrossed in humble
      marketings,
Come in and rest awhile, although judicial doings are
      Afoot by morning star?'

'O, come, come!' laughed the constables. 'Why, man, you speak
      the dialect
He uses in his answers; you can hear him up the stairs.
So own it. We sha'n't hurt ye. There he's speaking now!
      His syllables
Are those you sound yourself when you are talking unawares,
      As this pretty girl declares.'

'And you shudder when his chain clinks!' she rejoined. 'O yes,
      I noticed it.
And you winced, too, when those cuffs they gave him echoed
      to us here.
They'll soon be coming down, and you may then have to defend
      yourself
Unless you hold your tongue, or go away and keep you clear
      When he's led to judgment near!'

'No! I'll be damned in hell if I know anything about the man!
No single thing about him more than everybody knows!
Must not I even warm my hands but I am charged with
      blasphemies?' . . .
– His face convulses as the morning cock that moment crows,
      And he droops, and turns, and goes.

AQUAE SULIS

THE chimes called midnight, just at interlune,
And the daytime parle on the Roman investigations
Was shut to silence, save for the husky tune
The bubbling waters played near the excavations.

And a warm air came up from underground,
And the flutter of a filmy shape unsepulchred,
That collected itself, and waited, and looked around:
Nothing was seen, but utterances could be heard:

Those of the Goddess whose shrine was beneath the pile
Of the God with the baldachined altar overhead:
'And what did you win by raising this nave and aisle
Close on the site of the temple I tenanted?

'The notes of your organ have thrilled down out of view
To the earth-clogged wrecks of my edifice many a year,
Though stately and shining once – ay, long ere you
Had set up crucifix and candle here.

'Your priests have trampled the dust of mine without rueing,
Despising the joys of man whom I so much loved,
Though my springs boil on by your Gothic arcades and pewing,
And sculptures crude. . . . Would Jove they could be removed!'

'Repress, O lady proud, your traditional ires;
You know not by what a frail thread we equally hang;
It is said we are images both – twitched by people's desires;
And that I, like you, fail as a song men yesterday sang!'

'What – a Jumping-jack you, and myself but a poor Jumping-jill,
Now worm-eaten, times agone twitched at Humanity's bid?
O I cannot endure it! – But, chance to us whatso there will,
Let us kiss and be friends! Come, agree you?' – None heard if
    he did. . . .

And the olden dark hid the cavities late laid bare,
And all was suspended and soundless as before,
Except for a gossamery noise fading off in the air,
And the boiling voice of the waters' medicinal pour.

Bath

THE CHOIRMASTER'S BURIAL

HE often would ask us
That, when he died,
After playing so many
To their last rest,
If out of us any
Should here abide,
And it would not task us,
We would with our lutes
Play over him
By his grave-brim
The psalm he liked best –
The one whose sense suits
'Mount Ephraim' –
And perhaps we should seem
To him, in Death's dream,
Like the seraphim.

As soon as I knew
That his spirit was gone
I thought this his due,
And spoke thereupon.
'I think', said the vicar,
'A read service quicker
Than viols out-of-doors
In these frosts and hoars.
That old-fashioned way
Requires a fine day,
And it seems to me
It had better not be.'

Hence, that afternoon,
Though never knew he
That his wish could not be,
To get through it faster
They buried the master
Without any tune.

But 'twas said that, when
At the dead of next night
The vicar looked out,
There struck on his ken
Thronged roundabout,
Where the frost was graying
The headstoned grass,
A band all in white
Like the saints in church-glass,
Singing and playing
The ancient stave
By the choirmaster's grave.

Such the tenor man told
When he had grown old.

DURING WIND AND RAIN

THEY sing their dearest songs –
He, she, all of them – yea,
Treble and tenor and bass,
　　And one to play;
With the candles mooning each face. . . .
　　Ah, no; the years O!
How the sick leaves reel down in throngs!

They clear the creeping moss –
Elders and juniors – aye,
Making the pathways neat
　　And the garden gay;
And they build a shady seat. . . .
　　Ah, no; the years, the years;
See, the white storm-birds wing across!

They are blithely breakfasting all –
Men and maidens – yea,
Under the summer tree,
    With a glimpse of the bay,
While pet fowl come to the knee. . . .
        Ah, no; the years O!
And the rotten rose is ript from the wall.

They change to a high new house,
He, she, all of them – aye,
Clocks and carpets and chairs
    On the lawn all day,
And brightest things that are theirs. . . .
        Ah, no; the years, the years;
Down their carved names the rain-drop ploughs.

THE CAGED GOLDFINCH

WITHIN a churchyard, on a recent grave,
    I saw a little cage
That jailed a goldfinch. All was silence save
    Its hops from stage to stage.

There was inquiry in its wistful eye,
    And once it tried to sing;
Of him or her who placed it there, and why,
    No one knew anything.

THE SUNSHADE

AH – it's the skeleton of a lady's sunshade,
    Here at my feet in the hard rock's chink,
    Merely a naked sheaf of wires! –
    Twenty years have gone with their livers and diers
    Since it was silked in its white or pink.

Noonshine riddles the ribs of the sunshade,
   No more a screen from the weakest ray;
   Nothing to tell us the hue of its dyes,
   Nothing but rusty bones as it lies
   In its coffin of stone, unseen till to-day.

Where is the woman who carried that sunshade
   Up and down this seaside place? –
   Little thumb standing against its stem,
   Thoughts perhaps bent on a love-stratagem.
   Softening yet more the already soft face!

Is the fair woman who carried that sunshade
   A skeleton just as her property is,
   Laid in the chink that none may scan?
   And does she regret – if regret dust can –
   The vain things thought when she flourished this?

   Swanage Cliffs

MIDNIGHT ON THE GREAT WESTERN

In the third-class seat sat the journeying boy,
   And the roof-lamp's oily flame
Played down on his listless form and face,
Bewrapt past knowing to what he was going,
   Or whence he came.

In the band of his hat the journeying boy
   Had a ticket stuck; and a string
Around his neck bore the key of his box,
That twinkled gleams of the lamp's sad beams
   Like a living thing.

What past can be yours, O journeying boy
   Towards a world unknown,
Who calmly, as if incurious quite
On all at stake, can undertake
   This plunge alone?

Knows your soul a sphere, O journeying boy,
    Our rude realms far above,
Whence with spacious vision you mark and mete
This region of sin that you find you in,
    But are not of?

IN A WAITING-ROOM

On a morning sick as the day of doom
    With the drizzling gray
    Of an English May,
There were few in the railway waiting-room.
About its walls were framed and varnished
Pictures of liners, fly-blown, tarnished.
The table bore a Testament
For travellers' reading, if suchwise bent.

    I read it on and on,
And, thronging the Gospel of Saint John,
Were figures – additions, multiplications –
By some one scrawled, with sundry emendations;
    Not scoffingly designed,
    But with an absent mind, –
Plainly a bagman's counts of cost,
What he had profited, what lost;
And whilst I wondered if there could have been
    Any particle of a soul
    In that poor man at all,
    To cypher rates of wage
    Upon that printed page,
    There joined in the charmless scene
And stood over me and the scribbled book
    (To lend the hour's mean hue
    A smear of tragedy too)
A soldier and wife, with haggard look
Subdued to stone by strong endeavour;
    And then I heard
    From a casual word
They were parting as they believed for ever.

But next there came
Like the eastern flame
Of some high altar, children – a pair –
Who laughed at the fly-blown pictures there.
'Here are the lovely ships that we,
Mother, are by and by going to see!
When we get there it's 'most sure to be fine,
And the band will play, and the sun will shine!'

It rained on the skylight with a din
As we waited and still no train came in;
But the words of the child in the squalid room
Had spread a glory through the gloom.

THE CLOCK-WINDER

It is dark as a cave,
Or a vault in the nave
When the iron door
Is closed, and the floor
Of the church relaid
With trowel and spade.

But the parish-clerk
Cares not for the dark
As he winds in the tower
At a regular hour
The rheumatic clock
Whose dilatory knock
You can hear when praying
At the day's decaying,
Or at any lone while
From a pew in the aisle.

Up, up from the ground
Around and around
In the turret stair
He clambers, to where
The wheelwork is,
With its tick, click, whizz,
Reposefully measuring
Each day to its end
That mortal men spend
In sorrowing and pleasuring.
Nightly thus does he climb
To the trackway of Time.

Him I followed one night
To this place without light,
And, ere I spoke, heard
Him say, word by word,
At the end of his winding,
The darkness unminding:–

'So I wipe out one more,
My Dear, of the sore
Sad days that still be,
Like a drying Dead Sea,
Between you and me!'

Who she was no man knew:
He had long borne him blind
To all womankind;
And was ever one who
Kept his past out of view.

TO SHAKESPEARE

AFTER THREE HUNDRED YEARS

BRIGHT baffling Soul, least capturable of themes,
Thou, who display'dst a life of commonplace,
Leaving no intimate word or personal trace
Of high design outside the artistry
    Of thy penned dreams,
Still shalt remain at heart unread eternally.

Through human orbits thy discourse to-day,
Despite thy formal pilgrimage, throbs on
In harmonies that cow Oblivion,
And, like the wind, with all-uncared effect
    Maintain a sway
Not fore-desired, in tracks unchosen and unchecked.

And yet, at thy last breath, with mindless note
The borough clocks but samely tongued the hour
The Avon just as always glassed the tower,
Thy age was published on thy passing-bell
    But in due rote
With other dwellers' deaths accorded a like knell.

And at the strokes some townsman (met, maybe,
And thereon queried by some squire's good dame
Driving in shopward) may have given thy name,
With, 'Yes, a worthy man and well-to-do;
    Though, as for me,
I knew him but by just a neighbour's nod, 'tis true.

'I' faith, few knew him much here, save by word,
He having elsewhere led his busier life;
Though to be sure he left with us his wife.'
– 'Ah, one of the tradesmen's sons, I now recall. . . .
    Witty, I've heard. . . .
We did not know him. . . . Well, good-day. Death comes
    to all.'

So, like a strange bright bird we sometimes find
To mingle with the barn-door brood awhile,
Then vanish from their homely domicile –
Into man's poesy, we wot not whence,
    Flew thy strange mind,
Lodged there a radiant guest, and sped for ever thence.

1916

AT LULWORTH COVE A CENTURY BACK

HAD I but lived a hundred years ago
I might have gone, as I have gone this year,
By Warmwell Cross on to a Cove I know,
And Time have placed his finger on me there:

'*You see that man?*' – I might have looked, and said,
'O yes: I see him. One that boat has brought
Which dropped down Channel round Saint Alban's Head.
So commonplace a youth calls not my thought.'

'*You see that man?*' – 'Why yes; I told you; yes:
Of an idling town-sort; thin; hair brown in hue;
And as the evening light scants less and less
He looks up at a star, as many do.'

'*You see that man?*' – 'Nay, leave me!' then I plead,
'I have fifteen miles to vamp across the lea,
And it grows dark, and I am weary-kneed:
I have said the third time; yes, that man I see!'

'Good. That man goes to Rome – to death, despair;
And no one notes him now but you and I:
A hundred years, and the world will follow him there,
And bend with reverence where his ashes lie.'

September 1920

NOTE – In September 1820 Keats, on his way to Rome, landed one day
on the Dorset coast, and composed the sonnet, 'Bright star! would I were
steadfast as thou art.' The spot of his landing is judged to have been
Lulworth Cove.

BARTHÉLÉMON AT VAUXHALL

François Hippolite Barthélémon, first-fiddler at Vauxhall Gardens, com-
posed what was probably the most popular morning hymn-tune ever
written. It was formerly sung, full-voiced, every Sunday in most churches,
to Bishop Ken's words, but is now seldom heard.

He said: 'Awake my soul, and with the sun,' . . .
And paused upon the bridge, his eyes due east,
Where was emerging like a full-robed priest
The irradiate globe that vouched the dark as done.

It lit his face – the weary face of one
Who in the adjacent gardens charged his string,
Nightly, with many a tuneful tender thing,
Till stars were weak, and dancing hours outrun.

And then were threads of matin music spun
In trial tones as he pursued his way:
'This is a morn', he murmured, 'well begun:
This strain to Ken will count when I am clay!'

And count it did; till, caught by echoing lyres,
It spread to galleried naves and mighty quires.

HAUNTING FINGERS

A PHANTASY IN A MUSEUM OF MUSICAL INSTRUMENTS

'Are you awake,
    Comrades, this silent night?
Well 'twere if all of our glossy gluey make
Lay in the damp without, and fell to fragments quite!'

'O viol, my friend,
    I watch, though Phosphor nears,
And I fain would drowse away to its utter end
This dumb dark stowage after our loud melodious years!'

And they felt past handlers clutch them,
   Though none was in the room,
Old players' dead fingers touch them,
    Shrunk in the tomb.

  ' 'Cello, good mate,
    You speak my mind as yours:
Doomed to this voiceless, crippled, corpselike state,
Who, dear to famed Amphion, trapped here, long endures?'

   'Once I could thrill
    The populace through and through,
Wake them to passioned pulsings past their will.'. . .
(A contra-basso spake so, and the rest sighed anew.)

And they felt old muscles travel
    Over their tense contours,
And with long skill unravel
    Cunningest scores.

   'The tender pat
    Of her aery finger-tips
Upon me daily – I rejoiced thereat!'
(Thuswise a harpsichord, as 'twere from dampered lips.)

    'My keys' white shine,
    Now sallow, met a hand
Even whiter. . . . Tones of hers fell forth with mine
In sowings of sound so sweet no lover could withstand!'

And its clavier was filmed with fingers
    Like tapering flames – wan, cold –
Or the nebulous light that lingers
    In charnel mould.

   'Gayer than most
    Was I,' reverbed a drum;
'The regiments, marchings, throngs, hurrahs! What a host I
stirred – even when crape mufflings gagged me well-nigh dumb!'

Trilled an aged viol:
'Much tune have I set free
To spur the dance, since my first timid trial
Where I had birth – far hence, in sun-swept Italy!'

And he feels apt touches on him
From those that pressed him then;
Who seem with their glance to con him,
Saying, 'Not again!'

A holy calm,'
Mourned a shawm's voice subdued,
'Steeped my Cecilian rhythms when hymn and psalm
Poured from devout souls met in Sabbath sanctitude.'

'I faced the sock
Nightly,' twanged a sick lyre,
'Over ranked lights! O charm of life in mock,
O scenes that fed love, hope, wit, rapture, mirth, desire!'

Thus they, till each past player
Stroked thinner and more thin,
And the morning sky grew grayer
And day crawled in.

VOICES FROM THINGS GROWING IN A CHURCHYARD

THESE flowers are I, poor Fanny Hurd,
Sir or Madam,
A little girl here sepultured.
Once I flit-fluttered like a bird
Above the grass, as now I wave
In daisy shapes above my grave,
All day cheerily,
All night eerily!

      – I am one Bachelor Bowring, 'Gent',
             Sir or Madam;
In shingled oak my bones were pent;
Hence more than a hundred years I spent
In my feat of change from a coffin-thrall
To a dancer in green as leaves on a wall,
          All day cheerily,
          All night eerily!

      – I, these berries of juice and gloss,
             Sir or Madam,
Am clean forgotten as Thomas Voss;
Thin-urned, I have burrowed away from the moss
That covers my sod, and have entered this yew,
And turned to clusters ruddy of view,
          All day cheerily,
          All night eerily!

      – The Lady Gertrude, proud, high-bred,
             Sir or Madam,
Am I – this laurel that shades your head;
Into its veins I have stilly sped,
And made them of me; and my leaves now shine,
As did my satins superfine,
          All day cheerily,
          All night eerily!

      – I, who as innocent withwind climb,
             Sir or Madam,
Am one Eve Greensleeves, in olden time
Kissed by men from many a clime,
Beneath sun, stars, in blaze, in breeze,
As now by glowworms and by bees,
          All day cheerily,
          All night eerily![1]

---

[1] It was said her real name was Eve Trevillian or Trevelyan; and that she was the handsome mother of two or three illegitimate children, *circa* 1784–95.

– I'm old Squire Audeley Grey, who grew,
            Sir or Madam,
Aweary of life, and in scorn withdrew;
Till anon I clambered up anew
As ivy-green, when my ache was stayed,
And in that attire I have longtime gayed
            All day cheerily,
            All night eerily!

– And so these maskers breathe to each,
            Sir or Madam
Who lingers there, and their lively speech
Affords an interpreter much to teach,
As their murmurous accents seem to come
Thence hitheraround in a radiant hum,
            All day cheerily,
            All night eerily!

THE CHILDREN AND SIR NAMELESS

SIR NAMELESS, once of Athelhall, declared:
'These wretched children romping in my park
Trample the herbage till the soil is bared,
And yap and yell from early morn till dark!
Go keep them harnessed to their set routines:
Thank God I've none to hasten my decay;
For green remembrance there are better means
Than offspring, who but wish their sires away.'

Sir Nameless of that mansion said anon:
'To be perpetuate for my mightiness
Sculpture must image me when I am gone.'
– He forthwith summoned carvers there express
To shape a figure stretching seven-odd feet
(For he was tall) in alabaster stone,
With shield, and crest, and casque, and sword complete:
When done a statelier work was never known.

Three hundred years hied; Church-restorers came,
And, no one of his lineage being traced,
They thought an effigy so large in frame
Best fitted for the floor. There it was placed,
Under the seats for schoolchildren. And they
Kicked out his name, and hobnailed off his nose;
And, as they yawn through sermon-time, they say,
'Who was this old stone man beneath our toes?'

AT THE RAILWAY STATION, UPWAY

'THERE is not much that I can do,
    For I've no money that's quite my own!'
    Spoke up the pitying child –
A little boy with a violin
At the station before the train came in, –
'But I can play my fiddle to you,
And a nice one 'tis, and good in tone!'

    The man in the handcuffs smiled;
The constable looked, and he smiled, too,
    As the fiddle began to twang;
And the man in the handcuffs suddenly sang
            With grimful glee:
            'This life so free
            Is the thing for me!'
And the constable smiled, and said no word,
As if unconscious of what he heard;
And so they went on till the train came in –
The convict, and boy with the violin.

AN ANCIENT TO ANCIENTS

Where once we danced, where once we sang,
  Gentlemen,
The floors are sunken, cobwebs hang,
And cracks creep; worms have fed upon
The doors. Yea, sprightlier times were then
Than now, with harps and tabrets gone,
  Gentlemen!

Where once we rowed, where once we sailed,
  Gentlemen,
And damsels took the tiller, veiled
Against too strong a stare (God wot
Their fancy, then or anywhen!)
Upon that shore we are clean forgot,
  Gentlemen!

We have lost somewhat, afar and near,
  Gentlemen!
The thinning of our ranks each year
Affords a hint we are nigh undone,
That we shall not be ever again
The marked of many, loved of one,
  Gentlemen.

In dance the polka hit our wish,
  Gentlemen,
The paced quadrille, the spry schottische,
'Sir Roger'. – And in opera spheres
The 'Girl' (the famed 'Bohemian'),
And 'Trovatore', held the ears,
  Gentlemen.

This season's paintings do not please,
  Gentlemen,
Like Etty, Mulready, Maclise;
Throbbing romance has waned and wanned;
No wizard wields the witching pen
Of Bulwer, Scott, Dumas, and Sand,
  Gentlemen.

The bower we shrined to Tennyson,
        Gentlemen,
Is roof-wrecked; damps there drip upon
Sagged seats, the creeper-nails are rust,
The spider is sole denizen;
Even she who voiced those rhymes is dust,
        Gentlemen!

We who met sunrise sanguine-souled,
        Gentlemen,
Are wearing weary. We are old;
These younger press; we feel our rout
Is imminent to Aïdes' den, –
That evening shades are stretching out,
        Gentlemen!

And yet, though ours be failing frames,
        Gentlemen,
So were some others' history names,
Who trode their track light-limbed and fast
As these youth, and not alien
From enterprise, to their long last,
        Gentlemen.

Sophocles, Plato, Socrates,
        Gentlemen,
Pythagoras, Thucydides,
Herodotus, and Homer, – yea,
Clement, Augustin, Origen,
Burnt brightlier towards their setting-day,
        Gentlemen.

And ye, red-lipped and smooth-browed; list,
        Gentlemen;
Much is there waits you we have missed;
Much lore we leave you worth the knowing,
Much, much has lain outside our ken:
Nay, rush not: time serves: we are going,
        Gentlemen.

I

THE NEW TOY

SHE cannot leave it alone,
    The new toy;
She pats it, smooths it, rights it, to show it's her own,
As the other train-passengers muse on its temper and tone,
    Till she draws from it cries of annoy:–
She feigns to appear as if thinking it nothing so rare
    Or worthy of pride, to achieve
This wonder a child, though with reason the rest of them there
    May so be inclined to believe.

A LAST JOURNEY

'FATHER, you seem to have been sleeping fair?'
The child uncovered the dimity-curtained window-square
    And looked out at the dawn,
    And back at the dying man nigh gone,
    And propped up in his chair,
Whose breathing a robin's 'chink' took up in antiphon.

    The open fireplace spread
  Like a vast weary yawn above his head,
Its thin blue blower waved against his whitening crown,
    For he could not lie down:
  He raised him on his arms so emaciated:–

  'Yes; I've slept long, my child. But as for rest,
    Well, that I cannot say.
The whole night have I footed field and turnpike way –
    A regular pilgrimage – as at my best
    And very briskest day!

  ' 'Twas first to Weatherb'ry, to see them there,
    And thence to King's-Stag, where
I joined in a jolly trip to Weydon-Priors Fair:
  I shot for nuts, bought gingerbreads, cream-cheese;
    And, not content with these,
I went to London: heard the watchmen cry the hours.

'I soon was off again, and found me in the bowers
  Of father's apple-trees,
 And he shook the apples down: they fell in showers,
Whereon he turned, smiled strange at me, as ill at ease;
  And then you pulled the curtain; and, ah me,
  I found me back where I wished not to be!'

 'Twas told the child next day: 'Your father's dead.'
  And, struck, she questioned, 'O,
 That journey, then, did father really go? –
Buy nuts, and cakes, and travel at night till dawn was red,
  And tire himself with journeying, as he said,
  To see those old friends that he cared for so?'

LIFE AND DEATH AT SUNRISE

(NEAR DOGBURY GATE, 1867)

THE hills uncap their tops
 Of woodland, pasture, copse,
 And look on the layers of mist
 At their foot that still persist:
They are like awakened sleepers on one elbow lifted,
Who gaze around to learn if things during night have shifted.

A waggon creaks up from the fog
 With a laboured leisurely jog;
 Then a horseman from off the hill-tip
 Comes clapping down into the dip;
While woodlarks, finches, sparrows, try to entune at one time,
And cocks and hens and cows and bulls take up the chime.

With a shouldered basket and flagon
 A man meets the one with the waggon,
 And both the men halt of long use.
 'Well,' the waggoner says, 'what's the news?'
' – 'Tis a boy this time. You've just met the doctor trotting back.
She's doing very well. And we think we shall call him "Jack".

'And what have you got covered there?'
He nods to the waggon and mare.
'Oh, a coffin for old John Thinn:
We are just going to put him in.'
' – So he's gone at last. He always had a good constitution.'
' – He was ninety-odd. He could call up the French Revolution.'

BAGS OF MEAT

'Here's a fine bag of meat,'
Says the master-auctioneer,
As the timid, quivering steer,
Starting a couple of feet
At the prod of a drover's stick,
And trotting lightly and quick,
A ticket stuck on his rump,
Enters with a bewildered jump.

'Where he's lived lately, friends,
I'd live till lifetime ends:
They've a whole life everyday
Down there in the Vale, have they!
He'd be worth the money to kill
And give away Christmas for good-will.'

'Now here's a heifer – worth more
Than bid, were she bone-poor;
Yet she's round as a barrel of beer';
'She's a plum,' said the second auctioneer.

'Now this young bull – for thirty pound?
Worth that to manure your ground!'
'Or to stand,' chimed the second one,
'And have his picter done!'
The beast was rapped on the horns and snout
To make him turn about.
'Well,' cried a buyer, 'another crown –
Since I've dragged here from Taunton Town!'

'That calf, she sucked three cows,
Which is not matched for bouse
In the nurseries of high life
By the first-born of a nobleman's wife!'
The stick falls, meaning, 'A true tale's told',
On the buttock of the creature sold,
       And the buyer leans over and snips
His mark on one of the animal's hips.

Each beast, when driven in,
Looks round at the ring of bidders there
With a much-amazed reproachful stare,
       As at unnatural kin,
For bringing him to a sinister scene
So strange, unhomelike, hungry, mean;
His fate the while suspended between
       A butcher, to kill out of hand,
       And a farmer, to keep on the land;
One can fancy a tear runs down his face
When the butcher wins, and he's driven from the place.

A POPULAR PERSONAGE AT HOME

'I LIVE here: "Wessex" is my name:
I am a dog known rather well:
I guard the house; but how that came
To be my whim I cannot tell.

'With a leap and a heart elate I go
At the end of an hour's expectancy
To take a walk of a mile or so
With the folk I let live here with me.

'Along the path, amid the grass
I sniff, and find out rarest smells
For rolling over as I pass
The open fields towards the dells.

'No doubt I shall always cross this sill,
And turn the corner, and stand steady,
Gazing back for my mistress till
She reaches where I have run already,

'And that this meadow with its brook,
And bulrush, even as it appears
As I plunge by with hasty look,
Will stay the same a thousand years.'

Thus 'Wessex'. But a dubious ray
At times informs his steadfast eye,
Just for a trice, as though to say,
'Yet, will this pass, and pass shall I?'

1924

NO BUYERS

A STREET SCENE

A LOAD of brushes and baskets and cradles and chairs
  Labours along the street in the rain:
With it a man, a woman, a pony with whiteybrown hairs. –
  The man foots in front of the horse with a shambling sway
   At a slower tread than a funeral train,
  While to a dirge-like tune he chants his wares,
Swinging a Turk's-head brush (in a drum-major's way
   When the bandsmen march and play).

A yard from the back of the man is the whiteybrown pony's nose:
He mirrors his master in every item of pace and pose:
   He stops when the man stops, without being told,
  And seems to be eased by a pause; too plainly he's old,
    Indeed, not strength enough shows
   To steer the disjointed waggon straight,
  Which wriggles left and right in a rambling line,
  Deflected thus by its own warp and weight,
  And pushing the pony with it in each incline.

The woman walks on the pavement verge,
Parallel to the man:
She wears an apron white and wide in span,
And carries a like Turk's-head, but more in nursing-wise:
Now and then she joins in his dirge,
But as if her thoughts were on distant things.
The rain clams her apron till it clings. –
So, step by step, they move with their merchandize,
And nobody buys.

AN EAST-END CURATE

A SMALL blind street off East Commercial Road;
Window, door; window, door;
Every house like the one before,
Is where the curate, Mr. Dowle, has found a pinched abode.
Spectacled, pale, moustache straw-coloured, and with a long thin
face,
Day or dark his lodgings' narrow doorstep does he pace.

A bleached pianoforte, with its drawn silk plaitings faded,
Stands in his room, its keys much yellowed, cyphering, and
abraded,
'Novello's Anthems' lie at hand, and also a few glees,
And 'Laws of Heaven for Earth' in a frame upon the wall one sees.

He goes through his neighbours' houses as his own, and none
regards,
And opens their back-doors off-hand, to look for them in their
yards:
A man is threatening his wife on the other side of the wall,
But the curate lets it pass as knowing the history of it all.

Freely within his hearing the children skip and laugh and say:
'There's Mister Dow-well! There's Mister Dow-well!' in
their play;
And the long, pallid, devoted face notes not,
But stoops along abstractedly, for good, or in vain, God wot!

A REFUSAL

SAID the grave Dean of Westminster:
Mine is the best minster
Seen in Great Britain,
As many have written:
So therefore I cannot
Rule here if I ban not
Such liberty-taking
As movements for making

Its grayness environ
The memory of Byron,
Which some are demanding
Who think them of standing,
But in my own viewing
Require some subduing
For tendering suggestions
On Abbey-wall questions
That must interfere here
With my proper sphere here,
And bring to disaster
This fane and its master,
Whose dict is but Christian
Though nicknamed Philistian.

A lax Christian charity –
No mental clarity
Ruling its movements
For fabric improvements –
Demands admonition
And strict supervision
When bent on enshrining
Rapscallions, and signing
Their names on God's stonework,
As if like His own work
Were their lucubrations:
And passed is my patience
That such a creed-scorner
(Not mentioning horner)
Should claim Poet's Corner.

'Tis urged that some sinners
Are here for worms' dinners
Already in person;
That he could not worsen
The walls by a name mere
With men of such fame here.
Yet nay; they but leaven
The others in heaven
In just true proportion,
While more mean distortion.

'Twill next be expected
That I get erected
To Shelley a tablet
In some niche or gablet.
Then – what makes my skin burn,
Yea, forehead to chin burn –
That I ensconce Swinburne!

August 1924

A WATERING-PLACE LADY INVENTORIED

A sweetness of temper unsurpassed and unforgettable,
A mole on the cheek whose absence would have been regrettable,
A ripple of pleasant converse full of modulation,
A bearing of inconveniences without vexation,
Till a cynic would find her amiability provoking,
Tempting him to indulge in mean and wicked joking.

Flawlessly oval of face, especially cheek and chin,
With a glance of a quality that beckoned for a glance akin,
A habit of swift assent to any intelligence broken,
Before the fact to be conveyed was fully spoken
And she could know to what her colloquist would win her, –
This from a too alive impulsion to sympathy in her, –
All with a sense of the ridiculous, keen yet charitable;
In brief, a rich, profuse attractiveness unnarratable.

I should have added her hints that her husband prized her but
    slenderly,
And that (with a sigh) 'twas a pity she'd no one to treat her
    tenderly.

A HURRIED MEETING

It is August moonlight in the tall plantation,
Whose elms, by aged squirrels' footsteps worn,
    Outscreen the noon, and eve, and morn.
On the facing slope a faint irradiation
From a mansion's marble front is borne,
    Mute in its woodland wreathing.
Up here the night-jar whirrs forlorn,
And the trees seem to withhold their softest breathing.

To the moonshade slips a woman in muslin vesture:
Her naked neck the gossamer-web besmears,
    And she sweeps it away with a hasty gesture
Again it touches her forehead, her neck, her ears,
    Her fingers, the backs of her hands.
    She sweeps it away again
    Impatiently, and then
She takes no notice; and listens, and sighs, and stands.

The night-hawk stops. A man shows in the obscure:
    They meet, and passively kiss,
And he says: 'Well, I've come quickly. About this –
    Is it really so? You are sure?'
    'I am sure. In February it will be.
    That such a thing should come to me!
We should have known. We should have left off meeting.
Love is a terrible thing: a sweet allure
    That ends in heart-outeating!'

'But what shall we do, my Love, and how?'
'You need not call me by that name now.'
Then he more coldly: 'What is your suggestion?'
'I've told my mother, and she sees a way,
Since of our marriage there can be no question.
We are crossing South – near about New Year's Day
  The event will happen there.
It is the only thing that we can dare
   To keep them unaware!'
    'Well, you can marry me.'
She shook her head. 'No: that can never be.

' 'Twill be brought home as hers. She's forty-one,
When many a woman's bearing is not done,
  And well might have a son. –
We should have left off specious self-deceiving:
   I feared that such might come,
   And knowledge struck me numb.
Love is a terrible thing: witching when first begun,
   To end in grieving, grieving!'

And with one kiss again the couple parted:
Inferior clearly he; she haughty-hearted.
He watched her down the slope to return to her place,
The marble mansion of her ancient race,
And saw her brush the gossamers from her face
As she emerged from shade to the moonlight ray.
   And when she had gone away
  The night-jar seemed to imp, and say,
   'You should have taken warning:
Love is a terrible thing: sweet for a space,
   And then all mourning, mourning!'

QUEEN CAROLINE TO HER GUESTS

  DEAR friends, stay!
 Lamplit wafts of wit keep sorrow
 In the purlieus of to-morrow:
  Dear friends, stay!

Haste not away!
Even now may Time be weaving
Tricks of ravage, wrack, bereaving:
Haste not away!

Through the pane,
Lurking along the street, there may be
Heartwrings, keeping hid till day be,
Through the pane.

Check their reign:
Since while here we are the masters,
And can barricade dim disasters:
Check their reign!

Give no ear
To those ghosts withoutside mumming,
Mouthing, threatening, 'We are coming!'
Give no ear!

Sheltered here
Care we not that next day bring us
Pains, perversions! No racks wring us
Sheltered here.

Homeward gone,
Sleep will slay this merrymaking;
No resuming it at waking,
Homeward gone.

After dawn
Something sad may be befalling;
Mood like ours there's no recalling
After dawn!

Morrow-day
Present joy that moments strengthen
May be past our power to lengthen,
Morrow-day!

> Dear friends, stay!
> Lamplit wafts of wit keep sorrow
> In the limbo of to-morrow:
> Dear friends, stay!

AN EVENING IN GALILEE

SHE looks far west towards Carmel, shading her eyes with her hand,
And she then looks east to the Jordan, and the smooth Tiberias'
    strand.
'Is my son mad?' she asks; and never an answer has she,
Save from herself, aghast at the possibility.
'He professes as his firm faiths things far too grotesque to be true,
And his vesture is odd – too careless for one of his fair young
    hue! . . .

'He lays down doctrines as if he were old – aye, fifty at least:
In the Temple he terrified me, opposing the very High-Priest!
Why did he say to me, "Woman, what have I to do with thee?"
O it cuts to the heart that a child of mine thus spoke to me!
And he said, too, "Who is my mother?" – when he knows so very
    well.
He might have said, "Who is my father?" – and I'd found it hard
    to tell!
That no one knows but Joseph and – one other, nor ever will;
One who'll not see me again. . . . How it chanced! – I dreaming no
    ill! . . .

'Would he'd not mix with the lowest folk – like those fishermen –
The while so capable, culling new knowledge, beyond our ken! . . .
That woman of no good character, ever following him,
Adores him if I mistake not: his wish of her is but a whim
Of his madness, it may be, outmarking his lack of coherency;
After his "Keep the Commandments!" to smile upon such as she!
It is just what all those do who are wandering in their wit.
I don't know – dare not say – what harm may grow from it.

'O a mad son is a terrible thing; it even may lead
To arrest, and death! . . . And how he can preach, expound, and
    read!
Here comes my husband. Shall I unveil him this tragedy-brink?
No. He has nightmares enough. I'll pray, and think, and
    think.' . . .
She remembers she's never put on any pot for his evening meal,
And pondering a plea looks vaguely to south of her – towards
    Jezreel.

CHRISTMAS IN THE ELGIN ROOM

BRITISH MUSEUM: EARLY LAST CENTURY

'WHAT is the noise that shakes the night,
   And seems to soar to the Pole-star height?'
      – 'Christmas bells,
      The watchman tells
Who walks this hall that blears us captives with its blight.'

   'And what, then, mean such clangs, so clear?'
   ' – 'Tis said to have been a day of cheer,
      And source of grace
      To the human race
Long ere their woven sails winged us to exile here.

   'We are those whom Christmas overthrew
   Some centuries after Pheidias knew
      How to shape us
      And bedrape us
And to set us in Athena's temple for men's view.

   'O it is sad now we are sold –
   We gods! for Borean people's gold,
      And brought to the gloom
      Of this gaunt room
Which sunlight shuns, and sweet Aurore but enters cold.

'For all these bells, would I were still
Radiant as on Athenai's Hill.'
    – 'And I, and I!'
    The others sigh,
'Before this Christ was known, and we had men's good will.'

Thereat old Helios could but nod,
Throbbed, too, the Ilissus River-god,
        And the torsos there
        Of deities fair,
Whose limbs were shards beneath some Acropolitan clod:

Demeter too, Poseidon hoar,
Persephone, and many more
        Of Zeus' high breed, –
        All loth to heed
What the bells sang that night which shook them to the core.

1905 and 1926

A PRACTICAL WOMAN

'O WHO'LL get me a healthy child:–
        I should prefer a son –
Seven have I had in thirteen years,
        Sickly every one!

'Three mope about as feeble shapes;
        Weak; white; they'll be no good.
One came deformed; an idiot next;
        And two are crass as wood.

'I purpose one not only sound
        In flesh, but bright in mind:
And duly for producing him
        A means I've now to find.'

She went away. She disappeared,
    Years, years. Then back she came:
In her hand was a blooming boy
    Mentally and in frame.

'I found a father at last who'd suit
    The purpose in my head,
And used him till he'd done his job,'
    Was all thereon she said.

HER SECOND HUSBAND HEARS HER STORY

'STILL, Dear, it is incredible to me
    That here, alone,
You should have sewed him up until he died,
And in this very bed. I do not see
How you could do it, seeing what might betide.'

'Well, he came home one midnight, liquored deep –
    Worse than I'd known –
And lay down heavily, and soundly slept:
Then, desperate driven, I thought of it, to keep
Him from me when he woke. Being an adept

'With needle and thimble, as he snored, click-click
    An hour I'd sewn,
Till, had he roused, he couldn't have moved from bed,
So tightly laced in sheet and quilt and tick
He lay. And in the morning he was dead.

'Ere people came I drew the stitches out,
    And thus 'twas shown
To be a stroke.' – 'It's a strange tale!' said he.
'And this same bed?' – 'Yes, here it came about.'
'Well, it sounds strange – told here and now to me.

'Did you intend his death by your tight lacing?'
'O, that I cannot own.
I could not think of else that would avail
When he should wake up, and attempt embracing.' –
'Well, it's a cool queer tale!'

SUSPENSE

A CLAMMINESS hangs over all like a clout,
The fields are a water-colour washed out,
The sky at its rim leaves a chink of light,
Like the lid of a pot that will not close tight.

She is away by the groaning sea,
Strained at the heart, and waiting for me:
Between us our foe from a hid retreat
Is watching, to wither us if we meet. . . .

But it matters little, however we fare –
Whether we meet, or I get not there;
The sky will look the same thereupon,
And the wind and the sea go groaning on.

PART V

BALLADS AND NARRATIVE POEMS

THE BRIDE-NIGHT FIRE

(A WESSEX TRADITION)

THEY had long met o' Zundays – her true love and she –
    And at junketings, maypoles, and flings;
But she bode wi' a thirtover[1] uncle, and he
Swore by noon and by night that her goodman should be
Naibour Sweatley – a wight often weak at the knee
From taking o' sommat more cheerful than tea –
    Who tranted,[2] and moved people's things.

She cried, 'O pray pity me!' Nought would he hear;
    Then with wild rainy eyes she obeyed.
She chid when her Love was for clinking off wi' her:
The pa'son was told, as the season drew near,
To throw over pu'pit the names of the pair
    As fitting one flesh to be made.

The wedding-day dawned and the morning drew on;
    The couple stood bridegroom and bride;
The evening was passed, and when midnight had gone
The feasters horned,[3] 'God save the King,' and anon
    The pair took their homealong[4] ride.

The lover Tim Tankens mourned heart-sick and leer[5]
    To be thus of his darling deprived:
He roamed in the dark ath'art field, mound, and mere,
And, a'most without knowing it, found himself near
The house of the tranter, and now of his Dear,
    Where the lantern-light showed 'em arrived.

The bride sought her chamber so calm and so pale
    That a Northern had thought her resigned;
But to eyes that had seen her in tidetimes[6] of weal,
Like the white cloud o' smoke, the red battlefield's vail,
    That look spak' of havoc behind.

---

[1] *thirtover*, cross   [2] *tranted*, traded as carrier
[3] *horned*, sang loudly   [4] *homealong*, homeward
[5] *leer*, empty-stomached   [6] *tidetimes*, holidays

The bridegroom yet laitered a beaker to drain,
  Then reeled to the linhay[1] for more,
When the candle-snoff kindled some chaff from his grain –
Flames spread, and red vlankers[2] wi' might and wi' main
  Around beams, thatch, and chimley-tun[3] roar.

Young Tim away yond, rafted[4] up by the light,
  Through brimbles and underwood tears,
Till he comes to the orchet, when crooping[5] from sight
In the lewth[6] of a codlin-tree, bivering[7] wi' fright,
Wi' on'y her night-rail to cover her plight,
  His lonesome young Barbree appears.

Her cwold little figure half-naked he views
  Played about by the frolicsome breeze,
Her light-tripping totties,[8] her ten little tooes,
All bare and besprinkled wi' Fall's[9] chilly dews,
While her great gallied[10] eyes through her hair hanging loose
  Shone as stars through a tardle[11] o' trees.

She eyed him; and, as when a weir-hatch is drawn,
  Her tears, penned by terror afore,
With a rushing of sobs in a shower were strawn,
Till her power to pour 'em seemed wasted and gone
From the heft[12] o' misfortune she bore.

'O Tim, my *own* Tim I must call 'ee – I will!
  All the world has turned round on me so!
Can you help her who loved 'ee, though acting so ill?
Can you pity her misery – feel for her still?
When worse than her body so quivering and chill
  Is her heart in its winter o' woe!

---

[1] *linhay*, lean-to building   [2] *vlankers*, fire-flakes
[3] *chimley-tun*, chimney-stack   [4] *rafted*, roused
[5] *crooping*, squatting down   [6] *lewth*, shelter
[7] *bivering*, with chattering teeth   [8] *totties*, feet
[9] *Fall*, autumn   [10] *gallied*, frightened
[11] *tardle*, entanglement   [12] *heft*, weight

'I think I mid[1] almost ha' borne it,' she said,
   'Had my griefs one by one come to hand;
But O, to be slave to thik husbird,[2] for bread,
And then, upon top o' that, driven to wed,
And then, upon top o' that, burnt out o' bed,
   Is more than my nater can stand!'

Like a lion 'ithin en Tim's spirit outsprung –
(Tim had a great soul when his feelings were wrung) –
   'Feel for 'ee, dear Barbree?' he cried;
And his warm working-jacket then straightway he flung
Round about her, and horsed her by jerks, till she clung
Like a chiel on a gipsy, her figure uphung
   By the sleeves that he tightly had tied.

Over piggeries, and mixens,[3] and apples, and hay,
   They lumpered[4] straight into the night;
And finding ere long where a halter-path[5] lay,
Sighted Tim's house by dawn, on'y seen on their way
By a naibour or two who were up wi' the day,
   But who gathered no clue to the sight.

Then tender Tim Tankens he searched here and there
   For some garment to clothe her fair skin;
But though he had breeches and waistcoats to spare,
He had nothing quite seemly for Barbree to wear,
Who, half shrammed[6] to death, stood and cried on a chair
   At the caddle[7] she found herself in.

There was one thing to do, and that one thing he did,
   He lent her some clothes of his own,
And she took 'em perforce; and while swiftly she slid
Them upon her Tim turned to the winder, as bid,
Thinking, 'O that the picter my duty keeps hid
   To the sight o' my eyes mid[1] be shown!'

[1] *mid*, might   [2] *thik husbird*, that rascal
[3] *mixens*, manure-heaps   [4] *lumpered*, stumbled
[5] *halter-path*, bridle-path   [6] *shrammed*, numbed
[7] *caddle*, quandary

In the tallet[1] he stowed her; there huddied[2] she lay
   Shortening sleeves, legs, and tails to her limbs.
But most o' the time in a mortal bad way,
Well knowing that there'd be the divel to pay
If 'twere found that, instead o' the element's prey,
   She was living in lodgings at Tim's.

'Where's the tranter?' said men and boys; 'where can
   he be?'
   'Where's the tranter?' said Barbree alone.
'Where on e'th is the tranter?' said everybod-y:
They sifted the dust of his perished roof-tree,
   And all they could find was a bone.

Then the uncle cried, 'Lord, pray have mercy on me!'
   And in terror began to repent.
But before 'twas complete, and till sure she was free,
Barbree drew up her loft-ladder, tight turned her key –
Tim bringing up breakfast and dinner and tea –
   Till the news of her hiding got vent.

Then followed the custom-kept rout, shout, and flare
Of a skimmity-ride[3] through the naibourhood, ere
   Folk had proof o' wold[4] Sweatley's decay.
Whereupon decent people all stood in a stare,
Saying Tim and his lodger should risk it, and pair:
So he took her to church. An' some laughing lads there
Cried to Tim, 'After Sweatley!' She said, 'I declare
   I stand as a maiden to-day!'

Written 1866; printed 1875

---

[1] *tallet*, loft   [2] *huddied*, hidden
[3] *skimmity-ride*, satirical procession   [4] *wold*, old
   with effigies

VALENCIENNES

(1793)

BY CORP'L TULLIDGE, in *The Trumpet-Major*

In memory of S. C. (Pensioner). Died 184–

WE trenched, we trumpeted and drummed,
And from our mortars tons of iron hummed
   Ath'art the ditch, the month we bombed
     The Town o' Valencieën.

'Twas in the June o' Ninety-dree
(The Duke o' Yark, our then Commander been)
   The German Legion, Guards, and we
     Laid siege to Valencieën.

This was the first time in the war
That French and English spilled each other's gore;
   – Few dreamt how far would roll the roar
     Begun at Valencieën!

'Twas said that we'd no business there
A-topperèn the French for disagreën;
   However, that's not my affair –
     We were at Valencieën.

Such snocks and slats, since war began
Never knew raw recruit or veteràn:
   Stone-deaf therence went many a man
     Who served at Valencieën.

Into the streets, ath'art the sky,
A hundred thousand balls and bombs were fleën;
   And harmless townsfolk fell to die
     Each hour at Valencieën!

And, sweatèn wi' the bombardiers,
A shell was slent to shards anighst my ears:
   – 'Twas nigh the end of hopes and fears
     For me at Valencieën!

They bore my wownded frame to camp,
And shut my gapèn skull, and washed en cleän,
And jined en wi' a zilver clamp
Thik night at Valencieën.

'We've fetched en back to quick from dead;
But never more on earth while rose is red
Will drum rouse Corpel!' Doctor said
O' me at Valencieën.

'Twer true. No voice o' friend or foe
Can reach me now, or any livèn beën;
And little have I power to know
Since then at Valencieën!

I never hear the zummer hums
O' bees; and don' know when the cuckoo comes;
But night and day I hear the bombs
We threw at Valencieën. . . .

As for the Duke o' Yark in war,
There may be volk whose judgment o' en is meän;
But this I say – he was not far
From great at Valencieën.

O' wild wet nights, when all seems sad,
My wownds come back, as though new wownds I'd had;
But yet – at times I'm sort o' glad
I fout at Valencieën.

Well: Heaven wi' its jasper halls
Is now the on'y Town I care to be in. . . .
Good Lord, if Nick should bomb the walls
As we did Valencieën!

1878–1897

SAN SEBASTIAN

(AUGUST 1813)

With thoughts of Sergeant M—— (Pensioner), who died 185–

'WHY, Sergeant, stray on the Ivel Way,
As though at home there were spectres rife?
From first to last 'twas a proud career!
And your sunny years with a gracious wife
    Have brought you a daughter dear.

'I watched her to-day; a more comely maid,
As she danced in her muslin bowed with blue,
Round a Hintock maypole never gayed.'
– 'Aye, aye; I watched her this day, too,
    As it happens,' the Sergeant said.

'My daughter is now,' he again began,
'Of just such an age as one I knew
When we of the Line, the Forlorn-hope van,
On an August morning – a chosen few –
    Stormed San Sebastian.

'She's a score less three; so about was *she* –
The maiden I wronged in Peninsular days. . . .
You may prate of your prowess in lusty times,
But as years gnaw inward you blink your bays,
    And see too well your crimes!

'We'd stormed it at night, by the flapping light
Of burning towers, and the mortar's boom:
We'd topped the breach; but had failed to stay,
For our files were misled by the baffling gloom;
    And we said we'd storm by day.

'So, out of the trenches, with features set,
On that hot, still morning, in measured pace,
Our column climbed; climbed higher yet,
Past the fauss'bray, scarp, up the curtain-face,
    And along the parapet.

'From the battered hornwork the cannoneers
Hove crashing balls of iron fire;
On the shaking gap mount the volunteers
In files, and as they mount expire
    Amid curses, groans, and cheers.

'Five hours did we storm, five hours re-form,
As Death cooled those hot blood pricked on;
Till our cause was helped by a woe within:
They were blown from the summit we'd leapt upon,
    And madly we entered in.

'On end for plunder, 'mid rain and thunder
That burst with the lull of our cannonade,
We vamped the streets in the stifling air –
Our hunger unsoothed, our thirst unstayed –
    And ransacked the buildings there.

'From the shady vaults of their walls of white
We rolled rich puncheons of Spanish grape,
Till at length, with the fire of the wine alight,
I saw at a doorway a fair fresh shape –
    A woman, a sylph, or sprite.

'Afeard she fled, and with heated head
I pursued to the chamber she called her own;
– When might is right no qualms deter,
And having her helpless and alone
    I wreaked my will on her.

'She raised her beseeching eyes to me,
And I heard the words of prayer she sent
In her own soft language. . . . Fatefully
I copied those eyes for my punishment
    In begetting the girl you see!

'So, to-day I stand with a God-set brand
Like Cain's, when he wandered from kindred's ken. . . .
I served through the war that made Europe free;
I wived me in peace-year. But, hid from men,
    I bear that mark on me.

'Maybe we shape our offspring's guise
From fancy, or we know not what,
And that no deep impression dies, –
    For the mother of my child is not
        The mother of her eyes.

'And I nightly stray on the Ivel Way
As though at home there were spectres rife;
I delight me not in my proud career;
    And 'tis coals of fire that a gracious wife
        Should have brought me a daughter dear!'

LEIPZIG

(1813)

SCENE – *The Master-tradesmen's Parlour at the Old Ship Inn,*
Casterbridge.   Evening.

'OLD Norbert with the flat blue cap –
    A German said to be –
Why let your pipe die on your lap,
    Your eyes blink absently?'

– 'Ah! . . . Well, I had thought till my cheek was wet
    Of my mother – her voice and mien
When she used to sing and pirouette,
    And tap the tambourine

'To the march that yon street-fiddler plies:
    She told me 'twas the same
She'd heard from the trumpets, when the Allies
    Burst on her home like flame.

'My father was one of the German Hussars,
    My mother of Leipzig; but he,
Being quartered here, fetched her at close of the wars,
    And a Wessex lad reared me.

'And as I grew up, again and again
  She'd tell, after trilling that air,
Of her youth, and the battles on Leipzig plain
  And of all that was suffered there! . . .

' – 'Twas a time of alarms. Three Chiefs-at-arms
  Combined them to crush One,
And by numbers' might, for in equal fight
  He stood the matched of none.

'Carl Schwarzenberg was of the plot,
  And Blücher, prompt and prow,
And Jean the Crown-Prince Bernadotte:
  Buonaparte was the foe.

'City and plain had felt his reign
  From the North to the Middle Sea,
And he'd now sat down in the noble town
  Of the King of Saxony.

'October's deep dew its wet gossamer threw
  Upon Leipzig's lawns, leaf-strewn,
Where lately each fair avenue
  Wrought shade for summer moon.

'To westward two dull rivers crept
  Through miles of marsh and slough,
Whereover a streak of whiteness swept –
  The Bridge of Lindenau.

'Hard by, in the City, the One, care-tossed,
  Sat pondering his shrunken power;
And without the walls the hemming host
  Waxed denser every hour.

'He had speech that night on the morrow's designs
  With his chiefs by the bivouac fire,
While the belt of flames from the enemy's lines
  Flared nigher him yet and nigher.

'Three rockets them from the girdling trine
   Told, "Ready!" As they rose
Their flashes seemed his Judgment-Sign
   For bleeding Europe's woes.

' 'Twas seen how the French watch-fires that night
   Glowed still and steadily;
And the Three rejoiced, for they read in the sight
   That the One disdained to flee. . . .

' – Five hundred guns began the affray
   On next day morn at nine;
Such mad and mangling cannon-play
   Had never torn human line.

'Around the town three battles beat,
   Contracting like a gin;
As nearer marched the million feet
   Of columns closing in.

'The first battle nighed on the low Southern side;
   The second by the Western way;
The nearing of the third on the North was heard;
   – The French held all at bay.

'Against the first band did the Emperor stand;
   Against the second stood Ney;
Marmont against the third gave the order-word:
   – Thus raged it throughout the day.

'Fifty thousand sturdy souls on those trampled plains
     and knolls,
   Who met the dawn hopefully,
And were lotted their shares in a quarrel not theirs,
   Dropt then in their agony.

' "O", the old folks said, "ye Preachers stern!
   O so-called Christian time!
When will men's swords to ploughshares turn?
   When come the promised prime?" . . .

' – The clash of horse and man which that day began
    Closed not as evening wore;
And the morrow's armies, rear and van,
    Still mustered more and more.

'From the City towers the Confederate Powers
    Were eyed in glittering lines,
And up from the vast a murmuring passed
    As from a wood of pines.

' " " 'Tis well to cover a feeble skill
    By numbers' might!" scoffed He;
"But give me a third of their strength, I'd fill
    Half Hell with their soldiery!"

'All that day raged the war they waged,
    And again dumb night held reign,
Save that ever upspread from the dank deathbed
    A miles-wide pant of pain.

'Hard had striven brave Ney, the true Bertrand,
    Victor, and Augereau,
Bold Poniatowski, and Lauriston,
    To stay their overthrow;

'But, as in the dream of one sick to death
    There comes a narrowing room
That pens him, body and limbs and breath,
    To wait a hideous doom,

'So to Napoleon, in the hush
    That held the town and towers
Through these dire nights, a creeping crush
    Seemed borne in with the hours.

'One road to the rearward, and but one,
    Did fitful Chance allow;
'Twas where the Pleiss' and Elster run –
    The Bridge of Lindenau.

'The nineteenth dawned. Down street and Platz
   The wasted French sank back,
Stretching long lines across the Flats
   And on the bridgeway track:

'When there surged on the sky an earthen wave,
   And stones, and men, as though
Some rebel churchyard crew updrave
   Their sepulchres from below.

'To Heaven is blown Bridge Lindenau;
   Wrecked regiments reel therefrom;
And rank and file in masses plough
   The sullen Elster-Strom.

'A gulf was Lindenau; and dead
   Were fifties, hundreds, tens;
And every current rippled red
   With Marshal's blood and men's.

'The smart Macdonald swam therein,
   And barely won the verge;
Bold Poniatowski plunged him in
   Never to re-emerge.

'Then stayed the strife. The remnants wound
   Their Rhineward way pell-mell;
And thus did Leipzig City sound
   An Empire's passing bell;

'While in cavalcade, with band and blade,
   Came Marshals, Princes, Kings;
And the town was theirs. . . . Ay, as simple maid,
   My mother saw these things!

'And whenever those notes in the street begin,
   I recall her, and that far scene,
And her acting of how the Allies marched in,
   And her tap of the tambourine!'

THE PEASANT'S CONFESSION

'Si le maréchal Grouchy avait été rejoint par l'officier que Napoléon lui avait expédié
la veille à dix heures du soir, toute question eût disparu. Mais cet officier n'était point
parvenu à sa destination, ainsi que le maréchal n'a cessé de l'affirmer toute sa vie, et il
faut l'en croire, car autrement il n'aurait eu aucune raison pour hésiter. Cet officier
avait-il été pris? avait-il passé à l'ennemi? C'est ce qu'on a toujours ignoré.' – THIERS,
Histoire de l'Empire, 'Waterloo'.

GOOD Father! . . . It was eve in middle June,
        And war was waged anew
By great Napoleon, who for years had strewn
        Men's bones all Europe through.

Three nights ere this, with columned corps he'd cross'd
        The Sambre at Charleroi,
To move on Brussels, where the English host
        Dallied in Parc and Bois.

The yestertide we'd heard the gloomy gun
        Growl through the long-sunned day
From Quatre-Bras and Ligny; till the dun
        Twilight suppressed the fray;

Albeit therein – as lated tongues bespoke –
        Brunswick's high heart was drained,
And Prussia's Line and Landwehr, though unbroke,
        Stood cornered and constrained.

And at next noon-time Grouchy slowly passed
        With thirty thousand men:
We hoped thenceforth no army, small or vast,
        Would trouble us again.

My hut lay deeply in a vale recessed,
        And never a soul seemed nigh
When, reassured at length, we went to rest –
        My children, wife, and I.

But what was this that broke our humble ease?
        What noise, above the rain,
Above the dripping of the poplar trees
        That smote along the pane?

K

- A call of mastery, bidding me arise,
    Compelled me to the door,
At which a horseman stood in martial guise –
    Splashed – sweating from every pore.

Had I seen Grouchy! Yes? What track took he?
    Could I lead thither on? –
Fulfilment would ensure much gold for me,
    Perhaps more gifts anon.

'I bear the Emperor's mandate,' then he said.
    'Charging the Marshal straight
To strike between the double host ahead
    Ere they co-operate,

'Engaging Blücher till the Emperor put
    Lord Wellington to flight,
And next the Prussians. This to set afoot
    Is my emprise to-night.'

I joined him in the mist; but, pausing, sought
    To estimate his say.
Grouchy had made for Wavre; and yet, on thought,
    I did not lead that way.

I mused: 'If Grouchy thus and thus be told,
    The clash comes sheer hereon;
My farm is stript. While, as for gifts of gold,
    Money the French have none.

'Grouchy unwarned, moreo'er, the English win,
    And mine is left to me –
They buy, not borrow.' – Hence did I begin
    To lead him treacherously.

And as we edged Joidoigne with cautious view
    Dawn pierced the humid air;
And still I easted with him, though I knew
    Never marched Grouchy there.

Near Ottignies we passed, across the Dyle
    (Lim'lette left far aside),
And thence direct toward Pervez and Noville
    Through green grain, till he cried:

'I doubt thy conduct, man! no track is here –
    I doubt thy gagèd word!'
Thereat he scowled on me, and prancing near,
    He pricked me with his sword.

'Nay, Captain, hold! We skirt, not trace the course
    Of Grouchy,' said I then:
'As we go, yonder went he, with his force
    Of thirty thousand men.'

– At length noon nighed; when west, from Saint-John's-
    A hoarse artillery boomed,   [Mound,
And from Saint-Lambert's upland, chapel-crowned,
    The Prussian squadrons loomed.

Then leaping to the wet wild path we had kept,
    'My mission fails!' he cried;
'Too late for Grouchy now to intercept,
    For, peasant, you have lied!'

He turned to pistol me. I sprang, and drew
    The sabre from his flank,
And 'twixt his nape and shoulder, ere he knew,
    I struck, and dead he sank.

I hid him deep in nodding rye and oat –
    His shroud green stalks and loam;
His requiem the corn-blade's husky note –
    And then I hastened home. . . .

– Two armies writhe in coils of red and blue,
    And brass and iron clang
From Goumont, past the front of Waterloo,
    To Pap'lotte and Smohain.

The Guard Imperial wavered on the height;
    The Emperor's face grew glum;
'I sent', he said, 'to Grouchy yesternight,
    And yet he does not come!'

'Twas then, Good Father, that the French espied,
    Streaking the summer land,
The men of Blücher. But the Emperor cried,
    'Grouchy is now at hand!'

And meanwhile Vand'leur, Vivian, Maitland, Kempt,
    Met d'Erlon, Friant, Ney;
But Grouchy – mis-sent, blamed, yet blame-exempt –
    Grouchy was far away.

By even, slain or struck, Michel the strong,
    Bold Travers, Dnop, Delord,
Smart Guyot, Reil-le, l'Heriter, Friant,
    Scattered that champaign o'er.

Fallen likewise wronged Duhesme, and skilled Lobar
    Did that red sunset see;
Colbert, Legros, Blancard! . . . And of the foe
    Picton and Ponsonby;

With Gordon, Canning, Blackman, Ompteda,
    L'Estrange, Delancey, Packe,
Grose, D'Oyly, Stables, Morice, Howard, Hay,
    Von Schwerin, Watzdorf, Boek,

Smith, Phelips, Fuller, Lind, and Battersby,
    And hosts of ranksmen round. . . .
Memorials linger yet to speak to thee
    Of those that bit the ground!

The Guards' last column yielded; dykes of dead
    Lay between vale and ridge,
As, thinned yet closing, faint yet fierce, they sped
    In packs to Genappe Bridge.

Safe was my stock; my capple cow unslain;
    Intact each cock and hen;
But Grouchy far at Wavre all day had lain,
    And thirty thousand men.

O Saints, had I but lost my earing corn
    And saved the cause once prized!
O Saints, why such false witness had I borne
    When late I'd sympathized! . . .

So now, being old, my children eye askance
    My slowly dwindling store,
And crave my mite; till, worn with tarriance,
    I care for life no more.

To Almighty God henceforth I stand confessed,
    And Virgin-Saint Marie;
O Michael, John, and Holy Ones in rest,
    Entreat the Lord for me!

THE BURGHERS

(17—)

THE sun had wheeled from Grey's to Dammer's Crest,
And still I mused on that Thing imminent:
At length I sought the High-street to the West.

The level flare raked pane and pediment
And my wrecked face, and shaped my nearing friend
Like one of those the Furnace held unshent.

'I've news concerning her,' he said. 'Attend.
They fly to-night at the late moon's first gleam:
Watch with thy steel: two righteous thrusts will end

Her shameless visions and his passioned dream.
I'll watch with thee, to testify thy wrong –
To aid, maybe. – Law consecrates the scheme.'

I started, and we paced the flags along
Till I replied: 'Since it has come to this
I'll do it! But alone. I can be strong.'

Three hours past Curfew, when the Froom's mild hiss
Reigned sole, undulled by whirr of merchandize,
From Pummery-Tout to where the Gibbet is,

I crossed my pleasaunce hard by Glyd'path Rise,
And stood beneath the wall. Eleven strokes went,
And to the door they came, contrariwise,

And met in clasp so close I had but bent
My lifted blade on either to have let
Their two souls loose upon the firmament.

But something held my arm. 'A moment yet
As pray-time ere you wantons die!' I said;
And then they saw me. Swift her gaze was set

With eye and cry of love illimited
Upon her Heart-king. Never upon me
Had she thrown look of love so thoroughsped! . . .

At once she flung her faint form shieldingly
On his, against the vengeance of my vows;
The which o'erruling, her shape shielded he.

Blanked by such love, I stood as in a drowse,
And the slow moon edged from the upland nigh,
My sad thoughts moving thuswise: 'I may house

And I may husband her, yet what am I
But licensed tyrant to this bonded pair?
Says Charity, Do as ye would be done by.' . . .

Hurling my iron to the bushes there,
I bade them stay. And, as if brain and breast
Were passive, they walked with me to the stair.

Inside the house none watched; and on we prest
Before a mirror, in whose gleam I read
Her beauty, his, – and mine own mien unblest;

Till at her room I turned. 'Madam,' I said,
'Have you the wherewithal for this? Pray speak.
Love fills no cupboard. You'll need daily bread.'

'We've nothing, sire,' she lipped; 'and nothing seek.
'Twere base in me to rob my lord unware;
Our hands will earn a pittance week by week.'

And next I saw she had piled her raiment rare
Within the garde-robes, and her household purse,
Her jewels, her least lace of personal wear;

And stood in homespun. Now grown wholly hers,
I handed her the gold, her jewels all,
And him the choicest of her robes diverse.

'I'll take you to the doorway in the wall,
And then adieu,' I told them. 'Friends, withdraw.'
They did so; and she went – beyond recall.

And as I paused beneath the arch I saw
Their moonlit figures – slow, as in surprise –
Descend the slope, and vanish on the haw.

' "Fool," some will say,' I thought. – 'But who is wise,
Save God alone, to weigh my reasons why?'
– 'Hast thou struck home?' came with the boughs' night-sighs.

It was my friend. 'I have struck well. They fly,
But carry wounds that none can cicatrize.'
– 'Mortal?' said he. 'Remorseful – worse,' said I.

MY CICELY

(17—)

'ALIVE?' – And I leapt in my wonder,
    Was faint of my joyance,
And grasses and grove shone in garments
    Of glory to me.

'She lives, in a plenteous well-being,
    To-day as aforehand;
The dead bore the name – though a rare one –
    The name that bore she.'

She lived . . . I, afar in the city
    Of frenzy-led factions,
Had squandered green years and maturer
    In bowing the knee.

To Baals illusive and specious,
    Till chance had there voiced me
That one I loved vainly in nonage
    Had ceased her to be.

The passion the planets had scowled on,
    And change had let dwindle,
Her death-rumour smartly relifted
    To full apogee.

I mounted a steed in the dawning
    With acheful remembrance,
And made for the ancient West Highway
    To far Exonb'ry.

Passing heaths, and the House of Long Sieging,
    I neared the thin steeple
That tops the fair fane of Poore's olden
    Episcopal see;

And, changing anew my blown bearer,
   I traversed the downland
Whereon the bleak hill-graves of Chieftains
   Bulge barren of tree;

And still sadly onward I followed
   That Highway the Icen,
Which trails its pale riband down Wessex
   By lynchet and lea.

Along through the Stour-bordered Forum
   Where Legions had wayfared,
And where the slow river-face glasses
   Its green canopy,

And by Weatherbury Castle, and thencefrom
   Through Casterbridge held I
Still on, to entomb her my mindsight
   Saw stretched pallidly.

No highwayman's trot blew the night-wind
   To me so life-weary,
But only the creak of a gibbet
   Or waggoner's jee.

Triple-ramparted Maidon gloomed grayly
   Above me from southward,
And north the hill-fortress of Eggar
   And square Pummerie.

The Nine-Pillared Cromlech, the Bride-streams,
   The Axe, and the Otter
I passed, to the gate of the city
   Where Exe scents the sea;

Till, spent, in the graveacre pausing,
   I learnt 'twas not *my* Love
To whom Mother Church had just murmured
   A last lullaby.

– 'Then, where dwells the Canon's kinswoman,
    My friend of aforetime?'
I asked, to disguise my heart-heavings
    And new ecstasy.

'She wedded.' – 'Ah!' – 'Wedded beneath her –
    She keeps the stage-hostel
Ten miles hence, beside the great Highway –
    The famed Lions-Three.

'Her spouse was her lackey – no option
    'Twixt wedlock and worse things;
A lapse over-sad for a lady
    Of her pedigree!'

I shuddered, said nothing, and wandered
    To shades of green laurel:
More ghastly than death were these tidings
    Of life's irony!

For, on my ride down I had halted
    Awhile at the Lions,
And her – her whose name had once opened
    My heart as a key –

I'd looked on, unknowing, and witnessed
    Her jests with the tapsters,
Her liquor-fired face, her thick accents
    In naming her fee.

'O God, why this seeming derision!
    I cried in my anguish:
'O once Loved, O fair Unforgotten –
    That Thing – meant it thee!

'Inurned and at peace, lost but sainted,
    Were grief I could compass;
Depraved – 'tis for Christ's poor dependent
    A cruel decree!'

I backed on the Highway; but passed not
   The hostel. Within there
Too mocking to Love's re-expression
   Was Time's repartee!

Uptracking where Legions had wayfared
   By cromlechs unstoried,
And lynchets, and sepultured Chieftains,
   In self-colloquy,

A feeling stirred in me and strengthened
   That *she* was not my Love,
But she of the garth, who lay rapt in
   Her long reverie.

And thence till to-day I persuade me
   That this was the true one;
That Death stole intact her young dearness
   And innocency.

Frail-witted, illuded they call me;
   I may be. Far better
To dream than to own the debasement
   Of sweet Cicely.

Moreover I rate it unseemly
   To hold that kind Heaven
Could work such device – to her ruin
   And my misery.

So, lest I disturb my choice vision,
   I shun the West Highway,
Even now, when the knaps ring with rhythms
   From blackbird and bee;

And feel that with slumber half-conscious
   She rests in the church-hay,
Her spirit unsoiled as in youth-time
   When lovers were we.

A TRAMPWOMAN'S TRAGEDY

(182–)

I

FROM Wynyard's Gap the livelong day,
The livelong day,
We beat afoot the northward way
We had travelled times before.
The sun-blaze burning on our backs,
Our shoulders sticking to our packs,
By fosseway, fields, and turnpike tracks
We skirted sad Sedge-Moor.

II

Full twenty miles we jaunted on,
We jaunted on, –
My fancy-man, and jeering John,
And Mother Lee, and I.
And, as the sun drew down to west,
We climbed the toilsome Poldon crest,
And saw, of landskip sights the best,
The inn that beamed thereby.

III

For months we had padded side by side,
Ay, side by side
Through the Great Forest, Blackmoor wide,
And where the Parret ran.
We'd faced the gusts on Mendip ridge,
Had crossed the Yeo unhelped by bridge,
Been stung by every Marshwood midge,
I and my fancy-man.

IV

Lone inns we loved, my man and I,
        My man and I;
'King's Stag', 'Windwhistle' high and dry,
        'The Horse' on Hintock Green,
The cosy house at Wynyard's Gap,
'The Hut' renowned on Bredy Knap,
And many another wayside tap
        Where folk might sit unseen.

V

Now as we trudged – O deadly day,
        O deadly day! –
I teased my fancy-man in play
        And wanton idleness.
I walked alongside jeering John,
I laid his hand my waist upon;
I would not bend my glances on
        My lover's dark distress.

VI

Thus Poldon top at last we won,
        At last we won,
And gained the inn at sink of sun
        Far-famed as 'Marshal's Elm'.
Beneath us figured tor and lea,
From Mendip to the western sea –
I doubt if finer sight there be
        Within this royal realm.

VII

Inside the settle all a-row –
        All four a-row
We sat, I next to John, to show
        That he had wooed and won.
And then he took me on his knee,
And swore it was his turn to be
My favoured mate, and Mother Lee
        Passed to my former one.

VIII

Then in a voice I had never heard,
    I had never heard,
My only Love to me: 'One word,
    My lady, if you please!
Whose is the child you are like to bear? –
His? After all my months o' care?'
God knows 'twas not! But, O despair!
    I nodded – still to tease.

IX

Then up he sprung, and with his knife –
    And with his knife
He let out jeering Johnny's life,
    Yes; there, at set of sun.
The slant ray through the window nigh
Gilded John's blood and glazing eye,
Ere scarcely Mother Lee and I
    Knew that the deed was done.

X

The taverns tell the gloomy tale,
    The gloomy tale,
How that at Ivel-chester jail
    My love, my sweetheart swung;
Though stained till now by no misdeed
Save one horse ta'en in time o' need;
(Blue Jimmy stole right many a steed
    Ere his last fling he flung.)

XI

Thereaft I walked the world alone,
    Alone, alone!
On his death-day I gave my groan
    And dropt his dead-born child.
'Twas nigh the jail, beneath a tree,
None tending me; for Mother Lee
Had died at Glaston, leaving me
    Unfriended on the wild.

XII

And in the night as I lay weak,
    As I lay weak,
The leaves a-falling on my cheek,
    The red moon low declined –
The ghost of him I'd die to kiss
Rose up and said: 'Ah, tell me this!
Was the child mine, or was it his?
    Speak, that I rest may find!'

XIII

O doubt not but I told him then,
    I told him then,
That I had kept me from all men
    Since we joined lips and swore.
Whereat he smiled, and thinned away
As the wind stirred to call up day . . .
– 'Tis past! And here alone I stray
    Haunting the Western Moor.

NOTES – *Windwhistle* (stanza IV). The highness and dryness of Windwhistle Inn was impressed upon the writer two or three years ago, when, after climbing on a hot afternoon to the beautiful spot near which it stands and entering the inn for tea, he was informed by the landlady that none could be had, unless he would fetch water from a valley half a mile off, the house containing not a drop, owing to its situation. However, a tantalizing row of full barrels behind her back testified to a wetness of a certain sort, which was not at that time desired.

Marshal's Elm (stanza VI), so picturesquely situated, is no longer an inn, though the house, or part of it, still remains. It used to exhibit a fine old swinging sign.

Blue Jimmy (stanza X) was a notorious horse-stealer of Wessex in those days, who appropriated more than a hundred horses before he was caught, among others one belonging to a neighbour of the writer's grandfather. He was hanged at the now demolished Ivel-chester or Ilchester jail above mentioned – that building formerly of so many sinister associations in the minds of the local peasantry, and the continual haunt of fever, which at last led to its condemnation. Its site is now an innocent-looking green meadow.

April 1902

PANTHERA

(For other forms of this legend – first met with in the second century – see
Origen contra Celsum; the Talmud; Sepher Toldoth Jeschu; quoted
fragments of lost Apocryphal gospels; Strauss, Haeckel; etc.)

YEA, as I sit here, crutched, and cricked, and bent,
I think of Panthera, who underwent
Much from insidious aches in his decline;
But his aches were not radical like mine;
They were the twinges of old wounds – the feel
Of the hand he had lost, shorn by barbarian steel,
Which came back, so he said, at a change in the air,
Fingers and all, as if it still were there.
My pains are otherwise: upclosing cramps
And stiffened tendons from this country's damps,
Where Panthera was never commandant. –
The Fates sent him by way of the Levant.

He had been blithe in his young manhood's time,
And as centurion carried well his prime.
In Ethiop, Araby, climes fair and fell,
He had seen service and had borne him well.
Nought shook him then: he was serene as brave;
Yet later knew some shocks, and would grow grave
When pondering them; shocks less of corporal kind
Than phantom-like, that disarranged his mind;
And it was in the way of warning me
(By much his junior) against levity
That he recounted them; and one in chief
Panthera loved to set in bold relief.

This was a tragedy of his Eastern days,
Personal in touch – though I have sometimes thought
That touch a possible delusion – wrought
Of half-conviction carried to a craze –
His mind at last being stressed by ails and age:–
Yet his good faith thereon I well could wage.

  I had said it long had been a wish with me
That I might leave a scion – some small tree
As channel for my sap, if not my name –
Ay, offspring even of no legitimate claim,
In whose advance I secretly could joy.
Thereat he warmed.
      'Cancel such wishes, boy!
A son may be a comfort or a curse,
A seer, a doer, a coward, a fool; yea, worse –
A criminal. . . . That I could testify!' . . .
'Panthera has no guilty son!' cried I
All unbelieving. 'Friend, you do not know,'
He darkly dropt: 'True, I've none now to show,
For *the law took him*. Ay, in sooth, Jove shaped it so!'

  'This noon is not unlike,' he again began,
'The noon these pricking memories print on me –
Yea, that day, when the sun grew copper-red,
And I served in Judæa . . . 'Twas a date
Of rest for arms. The *Pax Romana* ruled,
To the chagrin of frontier legionaries!
Palestine was annexed – though sullen yet, –
I, being in age some two-score years and ten,
And having the garrison in Jerusalem
Part in my hands as acting officer
Under the Governor. A tedious time
I found it, of routine, amid a folk
Restless, contentless, and irascible. –
Quelling some riot, sentrying court and hall,
Sending men forth on public meeting-days
To maintain order, were my duties there.

  'Then came a morn in spring, and the cheerful sun
Whitened the city and the hills around,
And every mountain-road that clambered them,
Tincturing the greyness of the olives warm,
And the rank cacti round the valley's sides.
The day was one whereon death-penalties
Were put in force, and here and there were set
The soldiery for order, as I said,

Since one of the condemned had raised some heat,
And crowds surged passionately to see him slain.
I, mounted on a Cappadocian horse,
With some half-company of auxiliaries,
Had captained the procession through the streets
When it came streaming from the judgment-hall
After the verdicts of the Governor.
It drew to the great gate of the northern way
That bears towards Damascus; and to a knoll
Upon the common, just beyond the walls –
Whence could be swept a wide horizon round
Over the housetops to the remotest heights.
Here was the public execution-ground
For city crimes, called then and doubtless now
Golgotha, Kranion, or Calvaria.

'The usual dooms were duly meted out;
Some three or four were stript, transfixed, and nailed,
And no great stir occurred. A day of wont
It was to me, so far, and would have slid
Clean from my memory at its squalid close
But for an incident that followed these.

'Among the tag-rag rabble of either sex
That hung around the wretches as they writhed,
Till thrust back by our spears, one held my eye –
A weeping woman, whose strained countenance,
Sharpened against a looming livid cloud,
Was mocked by the crude rays of afternoon –
The mother of one of those who suffered there
I had heard her called when spoken roughly to
By my ranged men for pressing forward so.
It stole upon me hers was a face I knew;
Yet when, or how, I had known it, for a while
Eluded me. And then at once it came.

'Some thirty years or more before that noon
I was sub-captain of a company
Drawn from the legion of Calabria,
That marched up from Judæa north to Tyre.
We had pierced the old flat country of Jezreel,
The great Esdraelon Plain and fighting-floor
Of Jew with Canaanite, and with the host
Of Pharaoh-Necho, king of Egypt, met
While crossing there to strike the Assyrian pride.
We left behind Gilboa; passed by Nain;
Till bulging Tabor rose, embossed to the top
With arbute, terebinth, and locust growths.

'Encumbering me were sundry sick, so fallen
Through drinking from a swamp beside the way;
But we pressed on, till, bearing over a ridge,
We dipt into a world of pleasantness –
A vale, the fairest I had gazed upon –
Which lapped a village on its furthest slopes
Called Nazareth, brimmed round by uplands nigh.
In the midst thereof a fountain bubbled, where,
Lime-dry from marching, our glad halt we made
To rest our sick ones, and refresh us all.

'Here a day onward, towards the eventide,
Our men were piping to a Pyrrhic dance
Trod by their comrades, when the young women came
To fill their pitchers, as their custom was.
I proffered help to one – a slim girl, coy
Even as a fawn, meek, and as innocent.
Her long blue gown, the string of silver coins
That hung down by her banded beautiful hair,
Symboled in full immaculate modesty.

'Well, I was young, and hot, and readily stirred
To quick desire. 'Twas tedious timing out
The convalescence of the soldiery;
And I beguiled the long and empty days
By blissful yieldance to her sweet allure,
Who had no arts, but what out-arted all,
The tremulous tender charm of trustfulness.
We met, and met, and under the winking stars
That passed which peoples earth – true union, yea,
To the pure eye of her simplicity.

'Meanwhile the sick found health; and we pricked on.
I made her no rash promise of return,
As some do use; I was sincere in that;
I said we sundered never to meet again –
And yet I spoke untruth unknowingly! –
For meet again we did. Now, guess you aught?
The weeping mother on Calvaria
Was she I had known – albeit that time and tears
Had wasted rudely her once flowerlike form,
And her soft eyes, now swollen with sorrowing.

'Though I betrayed some qualms, she marked me not;
And I was scarce of mood to comrade her
And close the silence of so wide a time
To claim a malefactor as my son –
(For so I guessed him). And inquiry made
Brought rumour how at Nazareth long before
An old man wedded her for pity's sake
On finding she had grown pregnant, none knew how,
Cared for her child, and loved her till he died.

'Well; there it ended; save that then I learnt
That he – the man whose ardent blood was mine –
Had waked sedition long among the Jews,
And hurled insulting parlance at their god,
Whose temple bulked upon the adjoining hill,
Vowing that he would raze it, that himself
Was god as great as he whom they adored,
And by descent, moreover, was their king;
With sundry other incitements to misrule.

'The impalements done, and done the soldiers' game
Of raffling for the clothes, a legionary,
Longinus, pierced the young man with his lance
At signs from me, moved by his agonies
Through naysaying the drug they had offered him.
It brought the end. And when he had breathed his last
The woman went. I saw her never again. . . .
Now glares my moody meaning on you, friend? –
That when you talk of offspring as sheer joy
So trustingly, you blink contingencies.
Fors Fortuna! He who goes fathering
Gives frightful hostages to hazardry!'

Thus Panthera's tale. 'Twas one he seldom told,
But yet it got abroad. He would unfold,
At other times, a story of less gloom,
Though his was not a heart where jests had room.
He would regret discovery of the truth
Was made too late to influence to ruth
The Procurator who had condemned his son –
Or rather him so deemed. For there was none
To prove that Panthera erred not: and indeed,
When vagueness of identity I would plead,
Panther himself would sometimes own as much –
Yet lothly. But, assuming fact was such,
That the said woman did not recognize
Her lover's face, is matter for surprise.
However, there's his tale, fantasy or otherwise.

Thereafter shone not men of Panthera's kind:
The indolent heads at home were ill-inclined
To press campaigning that would hoist the star
Of their lieutenants valorous afar.
Jealousies kept him irked abroad, controlled
And stinted by an Empire no more bold.

Yet in some actions southward he had share –
In Mauretania and Numidia; there
With eagle eye, and sword and steed and spur,
Quelling uprisings promptly. Some small stir
In Parthia next engaged him, until maimed,
As I have said; and cynic Time proclaimed
His noble spirit broken. What a waste
Of such a Roman! – one in youth-time graced
With indescribable charm, so I have heard,
Yea, magnetism impossible to word
When faltering as I saw him. What a fame,
O Son of Saturn, had adorned his name,
Might the Three so have urged Thee! – Hour by hour
His own disorders hampered Panthera's power
To brood upon the fate of those he had known,
Even of that one he always called his own –
Either in morbid dream or memory. . . .
He died at no great age, untroublously,
An exit rare for ardent soldiers such as he.

THE CHAPEL-ORGANIST

(A.D. 185–)

I'VE been thinking it through, as I play here to-night, to play never
    again,
By the light of that lowering sun peering in at the window-pane,
And over the back-street roofs, throwing shades from the boys of
    the chore
In the gallery, right upon me, sitting up to these keys once
    more. . . .
How I used to hear tongues ask, as I sat here when I was new:
'Who is she playing the organ? She touches it mightily true!'
'She travels from Havenpool Town,' the deacon would softly
    speak,
'The stipend can hardly cover her fare hither twice in the week.'
(It fell far short of doing, indeed; but I never told,
For I have craved minstrelsy more than lovers, or beauty, or gold.)

'Twas so he answered at first, but the story grew different later:
'It cannot go on much longer, from what we hear of her now!'
At the meaning wheeze in the words the inquirer would shift his
place
Till he could see round the curtain that screened me from people
below.
'A handsome girl,' he would murmur, upstaring (and so I am).
'But – too much sex in her build; fine eyes, but eyelids too heavy;
A bosom too full for her age; in her lips too voluptuous a dye.'
(It may be. But who put it there? Assuredly it was not I.)

I went on playing and singing when this I had heard, and more,
Though tears half-blinded me; yes, I remained going on and on,
Just as I used me to chord and to sing at the selfsame time! . . .
For it's a contralto – my voice is; they'll hear it again here to-night
In the psalmody notes that I love far beyond every lower delight.

Well, the deacon, in fact, that day had learnt new tidings about me;
They troubled his mind not a little, for he was a worthy man.
(He trades as a chemist in High Street, and during the week he had
sought
His fellow-deacon, who throve as a bookbinder over the way.)
'These are strange rumours,' he said. 'We must guard the good
name of the chapel.
If, sooth, she's of evil report, what else can we do but dismiss her?'
'– But get such another to play here we cannot for double the
price!'
It settled the point for the time, and I triumphed awhile in their
strait,
And my much-beloved grand semibreves went living on, pending
my fate.

At length in the congregation more headshakes and murmurs were
rife,
And my dismissal was ruled, though I was not warned of it then.
But a day came when they declared it. The news entered me as a
sword;
I was broken; so pallid of face that they thought I should faint,
they said.
I rallied. 'O, rather than go, I will play you for nothing!' said I.

'Twas in much desperation I spoke it, for bring me to forfeit I
    could not
Those melodies chorded so richly for which I had laboured and
    lived.
They paused. And for nothing I played at the chapel through
    Sundays again,
Upheld by that art which I loved more than blandishments lavished
    of men.

But it fell that murmurs anew from the flock broke the pastor's
    peace.
Some member had seen me at Havenpool, comrading close a sea-
    captain.
(O yes; I was thereto constrained, lacking means for the fare to and
    fro.)
Yet God knows, if aught He knows ever, I loved the Old-Hundredth,
    Saint Stephen's,
Mount Zion, New Sabbath, Miles-Lane, Holy Rest, and Arabia, and
    Eaton,
Above all embraces of body by wooers who sought me and
    won! . . .
Next week 'twas declared I was seen coming home with a swain ere
    the sun.

The deacons insisted then, strong; and forgiveness I did not
    implore.
I saw all was lost for me, quite, but I made a last bid in my throbs.
My bent, finding victual in lust, men's senses had libelled my soul,
But the soul should die game, if I knew it! I turned to my masters
    and said:
'I yield, Gentlemen, without parlance. But – let me just hymn you
    once more!
It's a little thing, Sirs, that I ask; and a passion is music with me!'
They saw that consent would cost nothing, and show as good grace,
    as knew I,
Though tremble I did, and feel sick, as I paused thereat, dumb for
    their words.
They gloomily nodded assent, saying, 'Yes, if you care to. Once
    more,
And only once more, understand.' To that with a bend I agreed.

– 'You've a fixed and a far-reaching look,' spoke one who had eyed
me awhile.
'I've a fixed and a far-reaching plan, and my look only showed it,' I
smile.

This evening of Sunday is come – the last of my functioning here.
'She plays as if she were possessed!' they exclaim, glancing upward
and round.
'Such harmonies I never dreamt the old instrument capable of!'
Meantime the sun lowers and goes; shades deepen; the lights are
turned up,
And the people voice out the last singing: tune Tallis: the Evening
Hymn.
(I wonder Dissenters sing Ken: it shows them more liberal in spirit
At this little chapel down here than at certain new others I know.)
I sing as I play. Murmurs some one: 'No woman's throat richer
than hers!'
'True: in these parts,' think I. 'But, my man, never more will its
richness outspread.'
And I sing with them onward: 'The grave dread as little do I as my
bed.'

I lift up my feet from the pedals; and then, while my eyes are still
wet
From the symphonies born of my fingers, I do that whereon I am
set,
And draw from my 'full round bosom' (their words; how can *I*
help its heave?)
A bottle blue-coloured and fluted – a vinaigrette, they may conceive –
And before the choir measures my meaning, reads aught in my
moves to and fro,
I drink from the phial at a draught, and they think it a pick-me-up;
so.
Then I gather my books as to leave, bend over the keys as to pray.
When they come to me motionless, stooping, quick death will have
whisked me away.

'Sure, nobody meant her to poison herself in her haste, after all!'
The deacons will say as they carry me down and the night shadows
fall,

'Though the charges were true,' they will add. 'It's a case red as
　　scarlet withal!'
I have never once minced it. Lived chaste I have not. Heaven
　　knows it above! . . .
But past all the heavings of passion – it's music has been my life-
　　love! . . .
That tune did go well – this last playing! . . . I reckon they'll bury
　　me here. . . .
Not a soul from the seaport my birthplace – will come, or bestow
　　me . . . a tear.

THE TURNIP-HOER

　　　Of tides that toss the souls of men
　　Some are foreseen, and weathered warefully;
　　More burst at flood, none witting why or when,
　　　　And are called Destiny.

　　　– Years past there was a turnip-hoer,
　　Who loved his wife and child, and worked amain
　　In the turnip-time from dawn till day out-wore
　　　　And night bedimmed the plain.

　　　The thronging plants of blueish green
　　Would fall in lanes before his skilful blade,
　　Which, as by sleight, would deftly slip between
　　　　Those spared and those low-laid.

　　　'Twas afternoon: he hoed his best,
　　Unlifting head or eye, when, through the fence,
　　He heard a gallop dropping from the crest
　　　　Of the hill above him, whence.

　　　Descending at a crashing pace,
　　An open carriage came, horsed by a pair:
　　A lady sat therein, with lilywhite face
　　　　And wildly windblown hair.

The man sprang over, and horse and horse
Faced in the highway as the pair ondrew;
Like Terminus stood he there, and barred their course,
        And almost ere he knew

The lady was limp within his arms,
And, half-unconscious, clutched his hair and beard;
And so he held her, till from neighbouring farms
        Came hinds, and soon appeared

Footman and coachman on the way:–
The steeds were guided back, now breath-bespent,
And the hoer was rewarded with good pay:–
        So passed the accident.

'She was the Duchess of Southernshire,
They tell me,' said the second hoe, next day:
'She's come a-visiting not far from here;
        This week will end her stay.'

The hoer's wife that evening set
Her hand to a crusted stew in the three-legged pot,
And he sat looking on in silence; yet
        The cooking saw he not,

But a woman, with her arms around him,
Glove-handed, clasping his neck and clutching his blouse,
And ere he went to bed that night he found him
        Outside a manor-house.

A page there smoking answered him:
'Her Grace's room is where you see that light;
By now she's up there slipping off her trim:
        The Dook's is on the right.'

She was, indeed, just saying through the door,
'That dauntless fellow saved me from collapse:
I'd not much with me, or 'd have given him more:
        'Twas not enough, perhaps!'

Up till she left, before he slept,
He walked, though tired, to where her window shined,
And mused till it went dark; but close he kept
    All that was in his mind.

'What is it, Ike?' inquired his wife;
'You are not so nice now as you used to be.
What have I done? You seem quite tired of life!'
    'Nothing at all,' said he.

In the next shire this lady of rank,
So 'twas made known, would open a bazaar:
He took his money from the savings-bank
    To go there, for 'twas far.

And reached her stall, and sighted, clad
In her ripe beauty and the goodliest guise,
His Vision of late. He straight spent all he had,
    But not once caught her eyes.

Next week he heard, with heart of clay,
That London held her for three months or so:
Fearing to tell his wife he went for a day,
    Pawning his watch to go;

And scanned the Square of her abode,
And timed her moves, as well as he could guess,
That he might glimpse her; till afoot by road
    He came home penniless. . . .

– The Duke in Wessex once again,
Glanced at the Wessex paper, where he read
Of a man, late taken to drink, killed by a train
    At a crossing, so it said.

'Why – he who saved your life, I think?'
– 'O no,' said she. 'It cannot be the same:
He was sweet-breath'd, without a taint of drink;
    Yet it is like his name.'

AT SHAG'S HEATH

1685

(TRADITIONAL)

I GRIEVE and grieve for what I have done,
And nothing now is left to me
But straight to drown; yea, I have slain
The rarest soul the world shall see!
– My husband said: 'Now thou art wed
Thou must beware! And should a man
Cajole, mind, he means ill to thee,
Depend on't: fool him if ye can!'
    But 'twas King Monmouth, he!

As truth I took what was not true:
Till darked my door just such a one.
He asked me but the way to go,
Though looking all so down and done.
And as he stood he said, unsued,
'The prettiest wife I've eyed to-day!'
And then he kissed me tenderly
Before he footed fast away
    Did dear King Monmouth, he!

Builded was he so beautiful! –
Why did I pout a pettish word
For what he'd done? – Then whisking off –
For his pursuers' feet were heard –
'Dear one, keep faith!' he turns and saith.
And next he vanished in the copse
Before I knew what such might be,
And how great fears and how great hopes
    Had rare King Monmouth – he!

Up rode the soldiers. 'Where's this man? –
He is the rebel Duke,' say they.
'And calls himself King Monmouth, sure!'
Then I believed my husband; aye,
Though he'd spoke lies in jealous-wise!
– To Shag's nigh copse beyond the road
I moved my finger mercilessly;
And there lay hidden where I showed:
    My dear King Monmouth, he!

The soldiers brought him by my door,
His elbows bounded behind him, fast;
Passing, he me-ward cast his eyes –
What eyes of beauty did he cast!
Grieved was his glance at me askance:
'I wished all weal might thee attend,
But this is what th'st done to me,
O heartless woman, held my friend!'
    Said sweet King Monmouth, he!

O then I saw he was no hind,
But a great lord of loftihood,
Come here to claim his rule and rights,
Who'd wished me, as he'd said, but good. –
With tug and jolt, then, out to Holt,
To Justice Ettricke, he was led,
And thence to London speedily,
Where under yester's headsman bled
    The rare King Monmouth, he!

Last night, the while my husband slept,
He rose up at the window there,
All blood and blear, and hacked about,
With heavy eyes, and rumpled hair;
And said: 'My Love, 'twas cruel of
A Fair like thee to use me so!
But now it's nought; from foes I'm free!
Sooner or later all must go,'
    Said dear King Monmouth, he!

'Yes, lovely cruel one!' he said
In through the mullioned pane, shroud-pale,
'I love you still, would kiss you now,
But blood would stain your nighty-rail!'
– That's all. And so to drown I go:
O wear no weeds, my friends, for me . . .
When comes the waterman, he'll say,
'Who's done her thuswise?' – 'Twill be, yea,
    Sweet, slain King Monmouth – he!

THE PAPHIAN BALL

ANOTHER CHRISTMAS EXPERIENCE OF THE MELLSTOCK QUIRE

WE went our Christmas rounds once more,
With quire and viols as theretofore.

Our path was near by Rushy-Pond,
Where Egdon-Heath outstretched beyond.

There stood a figure against the moon,
Tall, spare, and humming a weirdsome tune.

'You tire of Christian carols,' he said:
'Come and lute at a ball instead.

' 'Tis to your gain, for it ensures
That many guineas will be yours.

'A slight condition hangs on't, true,
But you will scarce say nay thereto:

'That you go blindfold; that anon
The place may not be gossiped on.'

They stood and argued with each other:
'Why sing from one house to another

'These ancient hymns in the freezing night,
And all for nought? 'Tis foolish, quite!'

' – 'Tis serving God, and shunning evil:
Might not elsedoing serve the devil?'

'But grand pay!' . . . They were lured by his call,
Agreeing to go blindfold all.

They walked, he guiding, some new track,
Doubting to find the pathway back.

In a strange hall they found them when
They were unblinded all again.

Gilded alcoves, great chandeliers,
Voluptuous paintings ranged in tiers,

In brief, a mansion large and rare,
With rows of dancers waiting there.

They tuned and played; the couples danced;
Half-naked women tripped, advanced,

With handsome partners footing fast,
Who swore strange oaths, and whirled them past.

And thus and thus the slow hours wore them:
While shone their guineas heaped before them.

Drowsy at length, in lieu of the dance
'*While Shepherds watched* . . .' they bowed by chance;

And in a moment, at a blink,
There flashed a change; ere they could think

The ball-room vanished and all its crew:
Only the well-known heath they view –

The spot of their crossing overnight,
When wheedled by the stranger's sleight.

There, east, the Christmas dawn hung red,
And dark Rainbarrow with its dead

Bulged like a supine negress' breast
Against Clyffe-Clump's faint far-off crest.

Yea; the rare mansion, gorgeous, bright,
The ladies, gallants, gone were quite.

The heaped-up guineas, too, were gone
With the gold table they were on.

'Why did not grasp we what was owed!'
Cried some, as homeward, shamed, they strode.

Now comes the marvel and the warning:
When they had dragged to church next morning,

With downcast heads and scarce a word,
They were astound at what they heard.

Praises from all came forth in showers
For how they'd cheered the midnight hours.

'We've heard you many times,' friends said,
'But like *that* never have you played!

'*Rejoice, ye tenants of the earth,
And celebrate your Saviour's birth.*

'Never so thrilled the darkness through,
Or more inspired us so to do!' . . .

— The man who used to tell this tale
Was the tenor-viol, Michael Mail;

Yes; Mail the tenor, now but earth! —
I give it for what it may be worth.

L

APPENDIX I

HARDY'S PREFACES

Wessex Poems (1898)

PREFACE

OF the miscellaneous collection of verse that follows, only four pieces have been published, though many were written long ago, and others partly written. In some few cases the verses were turned into prose and printed as such, it having been unanticipated at that time that they might see the light.

Whenever an ancient and legitimate word of the district, for which there was no equivalent in received English, suggested itself as the most natural, nearest, and often only expression of a thought, it has been made use of, on what seemed good grounds.

The pieces are in a large degree dramatic or personative in conception; and this even where they are not obviously so.

The dates attached to some of the poems do not apply to the rough sketches given in illustration,[1] which have been recently made, and, as may be surmised, are inserted for personal and local reasons rather than for their intrinsic qualities.

T. H.

September 1898

Poems of the Past and the Present (1902)

PREFACE

HEREWITH I tender my thanks to the editors and proprietors of the *Times*, the *Morning Post*, the *Daily Chronicle*, the *Westminster Gazette*, *Literature*, the *Graphic*, *Cornhill*, *Sphere*, and other papers, for permission to reprint from their pages such of the following pieces of verse as have already been published.

Of the subject-matter of this volume – even that which is in other than narrative form – much is dramatic or impersonative even where not explicitly so. Moreover, that portion which may be regarded as individual comprises a series of feelings and

---

[1] The early editions were illustrated by the writer.

fancies written down in widely differing moods and circumstances, and at various dates. It will probably be found, therefore, to possess little cohesion of thought or harmony of colouring. I do not greatly regret this. Unadjusted impressions have their value, and the road to a true philosophy of life seems to lie in humbly recording diverse readings of its phenomena as they are forced upon us by chance and change.

T. H.

August 1901

Time's Laughingstocks and Other Verses (1909)

PREFACE

IN collecting the following poems I have to thank the editors and proprietors of the periodicals in which certain of them have appeared for permission to reclaim them.

Now that the miscellany is brought together, some lack of concord in pieces written at widely severed dates, and in contrasting moods and circumstances, will be obvious enough. This I cannot help, but the sense of disconnection, particularly in respect of those lyrics penned in the first person, will be immaterial when it is borne in mind that they are to be regarded, in the main, as dramatic monologues by different characters.

As a whole they will, I hope, take the reader forward, even if not far, rather than backward. I should add that some lines in the early-dated poems have been rewritten, though they have been left substantially unchanged.

T. H.

September 1909

[*Satires of Circumstance* (1914) and *Moments of Vision* (1917) have no prefaces.]

Late Lyrics and Earlier (1922)

APOLOGY

ABOUT half the verses that follow were written quite lately. The rest are older, having been held over in MS. when past volumes were published, on considering that these would contain a sufficient number of pages to offer readers at one time, more especially during the distractions of the war. The unusually far back poems to be found here are, however, but some that were overlooked in gathering previous collections. A freshness in them, now unattainable, seemed to make up for their inexperience and to justify their inclusion. A few are dated; the dates of others are not discoverable.

The launching of a volume of this kind in neo-Georgian days by one who began writing in mid-Victorian, and has published nothing to speak of for some years, may seem to call for a few words of excuse or explanation. Whether or no, readers may feel assured that a new book is submitted to them with great hesitation at so belated a date. Insistent practical reasons, however, among which were requests from some illustrious men of letters who are in sympathy with my productions, the accident that several of the poems have already seen the light, and that dozens of them have been lying about for years, compelled the course adopted, in spite of the natural disinclination of a writer whose works have been so frequently regarded askance by a pragmatic section here and there, to draw attention to them once more.

I do not know that it is necessary to say much on the contents of the book, even in deference to suggestions that will be mentioned presently. I believe that those readers who care for my poems at all – readers to whom no passport is required – will care for this new instalment of them, perhaps the last, as much as for any that have preceded them. Moreover, in the eyes of a less friendly class the pieces, though a very mixed collection indeed, contain, so far as I am able to see, little or nothing in technic or teaching that can be considered a Star-Chamber matter, or so much as agitating to a ladies' school; even though, to use Wordsworth's observation in his Preface to *Lyrical Ballads*, such readers may suppose 'that by the act of writing in verse an author makes a formal engagement that he will gratify certain known habits of association: that he not only thus apprises the reader that certain classes of ideas and expressions will be found in his book, but that others will be carefully excluded'.

It is true, nevertheless, that some grave, positive, stark, delineations are interspersed among those of the passive, lighter, and traditional sort presumably nearer to stereo-typed tastes. For – while I am quite aware that a thinker is not expected, and, indeed, is scarcely allowed, now more than heretofore, to state all that crosses his mind concerning existence in this universe, in his attempts to explain or excuse the presence of evil and the incongruity of penalizing the irresponsible – it must be obvious to open intelligences that, without denying the beauty and faithful service of certain venerable cults, such disallowance of 'obstinate questionings' and 'blank misgivings' tends to a paralysed intellectual stalemate. Heine observed nearly a hundred years ago that the soul has her eternal rights; that she will not be darkened by statutes, nor lullabied by the music of bells. And what is to-day, in allusions to the present author's pages, alleged to be 'pessimism' is, in truth, only such 'questionings' in the exploration of reality, and is the first step towards the soul's betterment, and the body's also.

If I may be forgiven for quoting my own old words, let me repeat what I printed in this relation more than twenty years ago, and wrote much earlier, in a poem entitled 'In Tenebris':

If way to the Better there be, it exacts a full look at the Worst:

that is to say, by the exploration of reality and its frank recognition stage by stage along the survey, with an eye to the best consummation possible: briefly, evolutionary meliorism. But it is called pessimism nevertheless; under which word, expressed with condemnatory emphasis, it is regarded by many as some pernicious new thing (though so old as to underlie the Gospel scheme, and even to permeate the Greek drama);

and the subject is charitably left to decent silence, as if further comment were needless.

Happily there are some who feel such Levitical passing-by to be, alas, by no means a permanent dismissal of the matter; that comment on where the world stands is very much the reverse of needless in these disordered years of our prematurely afflicted century: that amendment and not madness lies that way. And looking down the future these few hold fast to the same: that whether the human and kindred animal races survive till the exhaustion or destruction of the globe, or whether these races perish and are succeeded by others before that conclusion comes, pain to all upon it, tongued or dumb, shall be kept down to a minimum by loving-kindness, operating through scientific knowledge, and actuated by the modicum of free will conjecturally possessed by organic life when the mighty necessitating forces – unconscious or other – that have 'the balancings of the clouds', happen to be in equilibrium, which may or may not be often.

To conclude this question I may add that the argument of the so-called optimists is neatly summarized in a stern pronouncement against me by my friend Mr. Frederic Harrison in a late essay of his, in the words: 'This view of life is not mine.' The solemn declaration does not seem to me to be so annihilating to the said 'view' (really a series of fugitive impressions which I have never tried to co-ordinate) as is complacently assumed. Surely it embodies a too human fallacy quite familiar in logic. Next, a knowing reviewer, apparently a Roman Catholic young man, speaks, with some rather gross instances of the *suggestio falsi* in his whole article, of 'Mr. Hardy refusing consolation', the 'dark gravity of his ideas', and so on. When a Positivist and a Romanist agree there must be something wonderful in it, which should make a poet sit up. But . . . O that 'twere possible!

I would not have alluded in this place or anywhere else to such casual personal criticisms – for casual and unreflecting they must be – but for the satisfaction of two or three friends in whose opinion a short answer was deemed desirable, on account of the continual repetition of these criticisms, or more precisely, quizzings. After all, the serious and truly literary inquiry in this connection is: Should a shaper of such stuff as dreams are made on disregard considerations of what is customary and expected, and apply himself to the real function of poetry, the application of ideas to life (in Matthew Arnold's familiar phrase)? This bears more particularly on what has been called the 'philosophy' of these poems – usually reproved as 'queer'. Whoever the author may be that undertakes such application of ideas in this 'philosophic' direction – where it is specially required – glacial judgments must inevitably fall upon him amid opinion whose arbiters largely decry individuality, to whom *ideas* are oddities to smile at, who are moved by a yearning the reverse of that of the Athenian inquirers on Mars Hill; and stiffen their features not only at sound of a new thing, but at a restatement of old things in new terms. Hence should anything of this sort in the following adumbrations seem 'queer' – should any of them seem to good Panglossians to embody strange and disrespectful conceptions of this best of all possible worlds, I apologize; but cannot help it.

Such divergences, which, though piquant for the nonce, it would be affectation to say are not saddening and discouraging likewise, may, to be sure, arise sometimes from superficial aspect only, writer and reader seeing the same thing at different angles. But in palpable cases of divergence they arise, as already said, whenever a serious effort is made towards that which the authority I have cited – who would now be called old-fashioned, possibly even parochial – affirmed to be what no good critic could deny as the poet's province, the application of ideas to life. One might shrewdly guess, by the by, that in such recommendation the famous writer may have overlooked the cold-shouldering results upon an enthusiastic disciple that would be pretty certain to follow his putting the high aim in practice, and have forgotten the disconcerting experience of Gil Blas with the Archbishop.

To add a few more words to what has already taken up too many, there is a contingency liable to miscellanies of verse that I have never seen mentioned, so far as I can remember; I mean the chance little shocks that may be caused over a book of various character like the present and its predecessors by the juxtaposition of unrelated, even discordant, effusions; poems perhaps years apart in the making, yet facing each other. An odd result of this has been that dramatic anecdotes of a satirical and humorous intention following verse in graver voice, have been read as misfires because they raise the smile that they were intended to raise, the journalist, deaf to the sudden change of key, being unconscious that he is laughing with the author and not at him. I admit that I did not foresee such contingencies as I ought to have done, and that people might not perceive when the tone altered. But the difficulties of arranging the themes in a graduated kinship of moods would have been so great that irrelation was almost unavoidable with efforts so diverse. I must trust for right note-catching to those finely-touched spirits who can divine without half a whisper, whose intuitiveness is proof against all the accidents of inconsequence. In respect of the less alert, however, should any one's train of thought be thrown out of gear by a consecutive piping of vocal reeds in jarring tonics, without a semiquaver's rest between, and be led thereby to miss the writer's aim and meaning in one out of two contiguous compositions, I shall deeply regret it.

Having at last, I think, finished with the personal points that I was recommended to notice, I will forsake the immediate object of this Preface; and, leaving *Late Lyrics* to whatever fate it deserves, digress for a few moments to more general considerations. The thoughts of any man of letters concerned to keep poetry alive cannot but run uncomfortably on the precarious prospects of English verse at the present day. Verily the hazards and casualties surrounding the birth and setting forth of almost every modern creation in numbers are ominously like those of one of Shelley's paper-boats on a windy lake. And a forward conjecture scarcely permits the hope of a better time, unless men's tendencies should change. So indeed of all art, literature, and 'high thinking' nowadays. Whether owing to the barbarizing of taste in the younger minds by the dark madness of the late war, the unabashed cultivation of selfishness in all classes, the plethoric growth of knowledge simultaneously with the stunting of wisdom, 'a degrading thirst after outrageous stimulation' (to quote Wordsworth again), or from any other cause, we seem threatened with a new Dark Age.

I formerly thought, like other much exercised writers, that so far as literature was concerned a partial cause might be impotent or mischievous criticism; the satirizing of individuality, the lack of whole-seeing in contemporary estimates of poetry and kindred work, the knowingness affected by junior reviewers, the overgrowth of meticulousness in their peerings for an opinion, as if it were a cultivated habit in them to scrutinize the tool-marks and be blind to the building, to hearken for the key-creaks and be deaf to the diapason, to judge the landscape by a nocturnal exploration with a flash-lantern. In other words, to carry on the old game of sampling the poem or drama by quoting the worst line or worst passage only, in ignorance or not of Coleridge's proof that a versification of any length neither can be nor ought to be all poetry; of reading meanings into a book that its author never dreamt of writing there. I might go on interminably.

But I do not now think any such temporary obstructions to be the cause of the hazard, for these negligences and ignorances, though they may have stifled a few true poets in the run of generations, disperse like stricken leaves before the wind of next week, and are no more heard of again in the region of letters than their writers themselves. No: we may be convinced that something of the deeper sort mentioned must be the cause.

In any event poetry, pure literature in general, religion – I include religion, in its essential and undogmatic sense, because poetry and religion touch each other, or rather modulate into each other; are, indeed, often but different names for the same thing – these, I say, the visible signs of mental and emotional life, must like all other things keep moving, becoming; even though at present, when belief in witches of Endor is displacing the Darwinian theory and 'the truth that shall make you free', men's minds appear, as above noted, to be moving backwards rather than on. I speak somewhat sweepingly, and should except many thoughtful writers in verse and prose; also men in certain worthy but small bodies of various denominations, and perhaps in the homely quarter where advance might have been the very least expected a few years back – the English Church – if one reads it rightly as showing evidence of 'removing those things that are shaken', in accordance with the wise Epistolary recommendation to the Hebrews. For since the historic and once august hierarchy of Rome some generation ago lost its chance of being the religion of the future by doing otherwise, and throwing over the little band of New Catholics who were making a struggle for continuity by applying the principle of evolution to their own faith, joining hands with modern science, and outflanking the hesitating English instinct towards liturgical restatement (a flank march which I at the time quite expected to witness, with the gathering of many millions of waiting agnostics into its fold); since then, one may ask, what other purely English establishment than the Church, of sufficient dignity and footing, with such strength of old association, such scope for transmutability, such architectural spell, is left in this country to keep the shreds of morality together?[1]

It may indeed be a forlorn hope, a mere dream, that of an alliance between religion, which must be retained unless the world is to perish, and complete rationality, which must come, unless also the world is to perish, by means of the interfusing effect of poetry – 'the breath and finer spirit of all knowledge; the impassioned expression of science', as it was defined by an English poet who was quite orthodox in his ideas. But if it be true, as Comte argued, that advance is never in a straight line, but in a looped orbit, we may, in the aforesaid ominous moving backward, be doing it *pour mieux sauter*, drawing back for a spring. I repeat that I forlornly hope so, notwithstanding the supercilious regard of hope by Schopenhauer, von Hartmann, and other philosophers down to Einstein who have my respect. But one dares not prophesy. Physical, chronological, and other contingencies keep me in these days from critical studies and literary circles

> Where once we held debate, a band
> Of youthful friends, on mind and art

(if one may quote Tennyson in this century). Hence I cannot know how things are going so well as I used to know them. and the aforesaid limitations must quite prevent my knowing henceforward.

I have to thank the editors and owners of *The Times, Fortnightly, Mercury*, and other

---

[1] However, one must not be too sanguine in reading signs, and since the above was written evidence that the Church will go far in the removal of 'things that are shaken' has not been encouraging.

periodicals in which a few of the poems have appeared for kindly assenting to their being reclaimed for collected publication.

T. H.

February 1922

[*Human Shows* (1925) has no preface.]

Winter Words (1928)

[Winter Words, *though prepared for the press, would have undergone further revision, had the author lived to issue it on the birthday of which he left the number uninserted below.*]

INTRODUCTORY NOTE

So far as I am aware, I happen to be the only English poet who has brought out a new volume of his verse on his . . . birthday, whatever may have been the case with the ancient Greeks, for it must be remembered that poets did not die young in those days.

This, however, is not the point of the present few preliminary words. My last volume of poems was pronounced wholly gloomy and pessimistic by reviewers – even by some of the more able class. My sense of the oddity of this verdict may be imagined when, in selecting them, I had been, as I thought, rather too liberal in admitting flippant, not to say farcical, pieces into the collection. However, I did not suppose that the licensed tasters had wilfully misrepresented the book, and said nothing, knowing well that they could not have read it.

As labels stick, I foresee readily enough that the same perennial inscription will be set on the following pages, and therefore take no trouble to argue on the proceeding, notwithstanding the surprises to which I could treat my critics by uncovering a place here and there to them in the volume.

This being probably my last appearance on the literary stage, I would say, more seriously, that though, alas, it would be idle to pretend that the publication of these poems can have much interest for me, the track having been adventured so many times before to-day, the pieces themselves have been prepared with reasonable care, if not quite with the zest of a young man new to print.

I also repeat what I have often stated on such occasions, that no harmonious philosophy is attempted in these pages – or in any bygone pages of mine, for that matter.

T. H.

APPENDIX II

SOME THOUGHTS OF HARDY'S
ON POETRY AND THE ARTS*

'READ again Addison, Macaulay, Newman, Sterne, Defoe, Lamb, Gibbon, Burke, *Times* leaders, etc., in a study of style. Am more and more confirmed in an idea I have long held, as a matter of common sense, long before I thought of any old aphorism bearing on the subject: "Ars est celare artem". The whole secret of a living style and the difference between it and a dead style, lies in not having too much style – being, in fact, a little careless, or rather seeming to be, here and there. It brings wonderful life into the writing:

> A sweet disorder in the dress . . .
> A careless shoe-string, in whose tie
> I see a wild civility,
> Do more bewitch me than when art
> Is too precise in every part.

'Otherwise your style is like worn half-pence – all the fresh images rounded off by rubbing, and no crispness or movement at all.

'It is, of course, simply a carrying into prose the knowledge I have acquired in poetry – that inexact rhymes and rhythms now and then are far more pleasing than correct ones.'

Life, p. 105 (1875).

★

'THERE is enough poetry in what is left [in life], after all the false romance has been abstracted, to make a sweet pattern: *e.g.* the poem by H. Coleridge:

She is not fair to outward view.

'So, then, if Nature's defects must be looked in the face and transcribed, whence arises the *art* in poetry and novel-writing? which must certainly show art, or it becomes

---

* Excerpts from the *Life* introduced by quotation marks are diary or note-book entries quoted there by H and are contemporary with the date at the end of the excerpt. All others are from the text H wrote in his later years, in the third person, attributing authorship to his second wife, and final dates are of the period of his life he is describing. See 331 (II).

merely mechanical reporting. I think the art lies in making these defects the basis of a hitherto unperceived beauty, by irradiating them with "the light that never was" on their surface, but is seen to be latent in them by the spiritual eye.'

Life, p. 114 (1877).

[*Cf. this very late note:*]
On this day also he copied a quotation from an essay by L. Pearsall Smith:

'In every representation of Nature which is a work of art there is to be found, as Professor Courthope said, something which is not to be found in the aspect of Nature which it represents; and what that something is has been a matter of dispute from the earliest days of criticism.'

'The same writer adds', notes Hardy, ' "Better use the word 'inspiration' than 'genius' for inborn daemonic genius as distinct from conscious artistry."

'(It seems to me it might be called "temperamental impulse", which, of course, must be inborn.)'

Life, p. 427 (1924).

★

'SINCE coming into contact with Leslie Stephen about 1873, as has been shown, Hardy had been much influenced by his philosophy, and also by his criticism. He quotes the following sentence from Stephen in his note-book under the date of July 1, 1879:

'The ultimate aim of the poet should be to touch our hearts by showing his own, and not to exhibit his learning, or his fine taste, or his skill in mimicking the notes of his predecessors.' That Hardy adhered pretty closely to this principle when he resumed the writing of poetry can hardly be denied.

Life, p. 128 (1879).

★

' . . . As, in looking at a carpet, by following one colour a certain pattern is suggested, by following another colour, another; so in life the seer should watch that pattern among general things which his idiosyncrasy moves him to observe, and describe that alone. This is, quite accurately, a going to Nature; yet the result is no mere photograph, but purely the product of the writer's own mind.'

Life, p. 153 (1882).

★

'THE business of the poet and novelist is to show the sorriness underlying the grandest things, and the grandeur underlying the sorriest things.'

Life, p. 171 (1885).

★

'WHAT Ruskin says as to the cause of the want of imagination in works of the present age is probably true – that it is the flippant sarcasm of the time. "Men dare not open their hearts to us if we are to broil them on a thorn fire." '

Life, p. 172 (1886).

★

'AFTER looking at the landscape ascribed to Bonington in our drawing-room I feel that Nature is played out as a Beauty, but not as a Mystery. I don't want to see landscapes, *i.e.*, scenic paintings of them, because I don't want to see the original realities – as optical effects, that is. I want to see the deeper reality underlying the scenic, the expression of what are sometimes called abstract imaginings.

'The "simply natural" is interesting no longer. The much decried, mad, late-Turner rendering is now necessary to create my interest. The exact truth as to material fact ceases to be of importance in art – it is a student's style – the style of a period when the mind is serene and unawakened to the tragical mysteries of life; when it does not bring anything to the object that coalesces with and translates the qualities that are already there, – half hidden, it may be – and the two united are depicted as the All.'

Life, p. 185 (1886).

*

' . . . FOR my part, if there is any way of getting a melancholy satisfaction out of life, it lies in dying, so to speak, before one is out of the flesh; by which I mean putting on the manners of ghosts, wandering in their haunts, and taking their views of surrounding things. To think of life as passing away is a sadness; to think of it as past is at least tolerable. Hence even when I enter into a room to pay a simple morning call I have unconsciously the habit of regarding the scene as if I were a spectre not solid enough to influence my environment; only fit to behold and say, as another spectre said: "Peace be unto you!"'

Life, pp. 209–10 (1888).

*

'To find beauty in ugliness is the province of the poet.'

Life, p. 213 (1888).

*

'THE besetting sin of modern literature is its insincerity. Half its utterances are qualified, even contradicted, by an aside, and this particularly in morals and religion. When dogma has to be balanced on its feet by such hair-splitting as the late Mr. M. Arnold's it must be in a very bad way.'

Life, p. 215 (1888).

*

'AT the Old Masters, Royal Academy. Turner's water-colours: each is a landscape *plus* a man's soul. . . . What he paints chiefly is *light as modified by objects*. He first recognizes the impossibility of really reproducing on canvas all that is in a landscape; then gives for that which cannot be reproduced a something else which shall have upon the spectator an approximative effect to that of the real. He said, in his maddest and greatest days: "What pictorial drug can I dose man with, which shall affect his eyes somewhat in the manner of this reality which I cannot carry to him?" – and set to make such strange mixtures as he was tending towards in "Rain, Steam and Speed", "The Burial of Wilkie", "Agrippina landing with the ashes of Germanicus", "Approach to Venice", "Snowstorm and a Steamboat", etc. Hence, one may say, Art is the secret of how to produce by a false thing the effect of a true. . . .

'I am struck by the red glow of Romney's backgrounds, and his red flesh shades. . . . Watteau paints claws for hands. They are unnatural – hideous sometimes. . . . Then the pictures of Sir Joshua, in which middle-aged people sit out of doors without hats, on damp stone seats under porticoes, and expose themselves imprudently to draughts and chills, as if they had lost their senses. . . .

Life, pp. 216–17 (1889).

*

'REFLECTIONS on Art. Art is a changing of the actual proportions and order of things, so as to bring out more forcibly than might otherwise be done that feature in them which appeals most strongly to the idiosyncrasy of the artist. The changing, or distortion, may be of two kinds: (1) The kind which increases the sense of vraisemblance: (2) That which diminishes it. (1) is high art: (2) is low art.

'High art may choose to depict evil as well as good, without losing its quality. Its choice of evil, however, must be limited by the sense of worthiness.' A continuation of the same note was made a little later, and can be given here:

'Art is a disproportioning – (*i.e.* distorting, throwing out of proportion) – of realities, to show more clearly the features that matter in those realities, which, if merely copied or reported inventorially, might possibly be observed, but would more probably be overlooked. Hence "realism" is not Art.'

Life, pp. 228–9 (1890).

*

'POETRY. Perhaps I can express more fully in verse ideas and emotions which run counter to the inert crystallized opinion – hard as a rock – which the vast body of men have vested interests in supporting. To cry out in a passionate poem that (for instance) the Supreme Mover or Movers, the Prime Force or Forces, must be either limited in power, unknowing, or cruel – which is obvious enough, and has been for centuries – will cause them merely a shake of the head; but to put it in argumentative prose will make them sneer, or foam, and set all the literary contortionists jumping upon me, a harmless agnostic, as if I were a clamorous atheist, which in their crass illiteracy they seem to think is the same thing. . . . If Galileo had said in verse that the world moved, the Inquisition might have let him alone.'

Life, pp. 284–5 (1896).

*

[*Hardy was incensed by some criticisms of* Wessex Poems *(1898) which treated his first volume of verse as the mere caprice of an ageing novelist who would do better to stick to prose. He always regarded himself as a poet who had to write novels for a living. The following passage resulted from this:*]

'ALMOST all the fault-finding was, in fact, based on the one great antecedent conclusion that an author who has published prose first, and that largely, must necessarily express himself badly in verse, no reservation being added to except cases in which he may have published prose for temporary or compulsory reasons, or prose of a poetical kind, or have written verse first of all, or for a long time intermediately.

'In criticism generally, the fact that the date of publication is but an accident in the life of a literary creation, that the printing of a book is the least individual occurrence in the history of its contents, is often overlooked. In its visible history the publication is what counts, and that alone. It is then that the contents start into being for the outside public. In the present case, although it was shown that many of the verses had been written before their author dreamt of novels, the critics' view was little affected that he had "at the eleventh hour", as they untruly put it, taken up a hitherto uncared-for art.

'It may be observed that in the art-history of the century there was an example staring them in the face of a similar modulation from one style into another by a great artist. Verdi was the instance, "that amazing old man" as he was called. Someone of insight wrote concerning him: "From the ashes of his early popularity, from *Il Trovatore* and its kind, there arose on a sudden a sort of phoenix Verdi. Had he died at Mozart's death-age he would now be practically unknown." And another: "With long life enough Verdi might have done almost anything; but the trouble with him was that he had only just arrived at maturity at the age of threescore and ten or thereabouts, so that to complete his life he ought to have lived a hundred and fifty years."

But probably few literary critics discern the solidarity of all the arts. Curiously enough Hardy himself dwelt upon it in a poem that seems to have been little understood, though the subject is of such interest. It is called 'Rome: The Vatican: Sala delle Muse'; in which a sort of composite Muse addresses him:

> 'Be not perturbed', said she. 'Though apart in fame,
> I and my sisters are one.'*
>
> > *Life*, pp. 299–300 (1898)

★

[*The reception of* Wessex Poems]

In short, this was a particular instance of the general and rather appalling conclusion to which he came – had indeed known before – that a volume of poetry, by clever manipulation, can be made to support any *a priori* theory about its quality. Presuppose its outstanding feature to be the defects aforesaid; instances can be found. Presuppose, as here was done, that it is overloaded with derivations from the Latin or Greek when really below the average in such words; they can be found. Presuppose that Wordsworth is unorthodox; instances can be found; that Byron is devout; instances can also be found. (The foregoing paragraphs are abridged from memoranda which Hardy set down, apparently for publication; though he never published them.)

He wrote somewhere: 'There is no new poetry; but the new poet – if he carry the flame on further (and if not he is no new poet) – comes with a new note. And that new note it is that troubles the critical waters.

'Poetry is emotion put into measure. The emotion must come by nature, but the measure can be acquired by art.'

In the reception of this and later volumes of Hardy's poems there was, he said, as regards form, the inevitable ascription to ignorance of what was really choice after full knowledge. That the author loved the art of concealing art was undiscerned. For instance, as to rhythm. Years earlier he had decided that too regular a beat was bad art. He had fortified himself in his opinion by thinking of the analogy of architecture, between which art and that of poetry he had discovered, to use his own words, that there existed a close and curious parallel, both arts, unlike some others, having to carry a rational content inside their artistic form. He knew that in architecture cunning irregularity is of enormous worth, and it is obvious that he carried on into his verse. perhaps in part unconsciously, the Gothic art-principle in which he had been trained –

---

* See *Life*, p. 176, 'Be not perturbed'. H here misquotes himself. See 104.

the principle of spontaneity found in mouldings, tracery, and such like – resulting in the 'unforeseen' (as it has been called) character of his metres and stanzas, that of stress rather than of syllable, poetic texture rather than poetic veneer; the latter kind of thing, under the name of 'constructed ornament', being what he, in common with every Gothic student, had been taught to avoid as the plague. He shaped his poetry accordingly, introducing metrical pauses, and reversed beats; and found for his trouble that some particular line of a poem exemplifying this principle was greeted with a would-be jocular remark that such a line 'did not make for immortality'. The same critic might have gone to one of our cathedrals (to follow up the analogy of architecture), and on discovering that the carved leafage of some capital or spandrel in the best period of Gothic art strayed freakishly out of its bounds over the moulding, where by rule it had no business to be, or that the enrichments of a string-course were not accurately spaced; or that there was a sudden blank in a wall where a window was to be expected from formal measurement, have declared with equally merry conviction, 'This does not make for immortality'.

One case of the kind, in which the poem 'On Sturminster Foot-Bridge'* was quoted with the remark that one could make as good music as that out of a milk-cart, betrayed the reviewer's ignorance of any perception that the metre was intended to be onomatopoeic, plainly as it was shown; and another in the same tone disclosed that the reviewer had tried to scan the author's sapphics as heroics.

If any proof were wanted that Hardy was not at this time and later the apprentice at verse that he was supposed to be, it could be found in an examination of his studies over many years. Among his papers were quantities of notes on rhythm and metre: with outlines and experiments in innumerable original measures, some of which he adopted from time to time. These verse skeletons were mostly blank, and only designated by the usual marks for long and short syllables, accentuations, etc., but they were occasionally made up of 'nonsense verses' – such as, he said, were written when he was a boy by students of Latin prosody with the aid of a 'Gradus'.

Lastly, Hardy had a born sense of humour, even a too keen sense occasionally: but his poetry was sometimes placed by editors in the hands of reviewers deficient in that quality. Even if they were accustomed to Dickensian humour they were not to Swiftian. Hence it unfortunately happened that verses of a satirical, dry, caustic, or farcical cast were regarded by them with the deepest seriousness. In one case the tragic nature of his verse was instanced by the ballad called 'The Bride-night Fire', or 'The Fire at Tranter Sweatley's', the criticism being by an accomplished old friend of his own, Frederic Harrison, who deplored the painful nature of the bridegroom's end in leaving only a bone behind him. This piece of work Hardy had written and published when quite a young man, and had hesitated to reprint because of its too pronounced obviousness as a jest.

But he had looked the before-mentioned obstacles in the face, and their consideration did not move him much. He had written his poems entirely because he liked doing them, without any ulterior thought; because he wanted to say the things they contained and would contain. He offered his publishers to take on his own shoulders the risk of producing the volume, so that if nobody bought it they should not be out of pocket. They were kind enough to refuse this offer, and took the risk on themselves; and fortunately they did not suffer.

* Not in this volume.

A more serious meditation of Hardy's at this time than that on critics was the following:

'*January* (1899). No man's poetry can be truly judged till its last line is written. What is the last line? The death of the poet. And hence there is this quaint consolation to any writer of verse – that it may be imperishable for all that anybody can tell him to the contrary; and that if worthless he can never know it, unless he be a greater adept at self-criticism than poets usually are.'

Life, pp. 300–2 (1899).

*

IN a pocket-book of this date [1899] appears a diagram illustrating 'the language of verse':

Verse

| Fanciful | Meditative | Sentimental | Passionate |

Language of Common Speech

Poetic Diction

and the following note thereon:

'The confusion of thought to be observed in Wordsworth's teaching in his essay in the Appendix to *Lyrical Ballads* seems to arise chiefly out of his use of the word "imagination". He should have put the matter somewhat like this: In works of *passion and sentiment* (not "imagination and sentiment") the language of verse is the language of prose. In works of *fancy* (or *imagination*), "poetic diction" (of the real kind) is proper, and even necessary. The diagram illustrates my meaning.'

Life, p. 306 (1899).

*

'THE longer I live, the more does Browning's character seem *the* literary puzzle of the 19th Century. How could Christian optimism worthy of a dissenting grocer find a place inside a man who was so vast a seer and feeler when on neutral ground?'

Letter to Edmund Gosse, 1899 (in the British Museum).

*

'PICTURES. My weakness has always been to prefer the large intention of an unskilful artist to the trivial intention of an accomplished one: in other words, I am more interested in the high ideas of a feeble executant than in the high execution of a feeble thinker.'

Life, p. 310 (1901).

*

'POETRY. There is a latent music in the sincere utterance of deep emotion, however expressed, which fills the place of the actual word-music in rhythmic phraseology on thinner emotive subjects, or on subjects with next to none at all. And supposing a total poetic effect to be represented by a unit, its component fractions may be either, say:

'Emotion three-quarters, plus Expression one quarter, or

'Emotion one quarter, plus Expression three-quarters.

'This suggested conception seems to me to be the only one which explains all cases, including those instances of verse that apparently infringe all rules, and yet bring unreasoned convictions that they are poetry.'

Life, p. 311 (1901).

★

'THE artistic spirit is at bottom a spirit of caprice, and in some of its finest productions in the past it could have given no clear reason why they were run in this or that particular mould, and not in some more obvious one.'

(Letter to *The Times Literary Supplement*, 5 February 1904 (reprinted in Orel, p. 141).

★

'I PREFER late Wagner, as I prefer late Turner, to early (which I suppose is all wrong in taste), the idiosyncrasies of each master being more strongly shown in these strains. When a man not contented with the grounds of his success goes on and on, and tries to achieve the impossible, then he gets profoundly interesting to me. To-day it was early Wagner for the most part: fine music, but not so particularly his – no spectacle of the inside of a brain at work like the inside of a hive.'

Life, p. 329 (1906).

★

[*The following letter was the answer to an invitation to join a committee to establish a Shakespeare Memorial Theatre:*]

'IF I felt at all strongly, or indeed weakly, on the desirability of a memorial to Shakespeare in the shape of a theatre, I would join the Committee. But I do not think that Shakespeare appertains particularly to the theatrical world nowadays, if ever he did. His distinction as a minister to the theatre is infinitesimal beside his distinction as a poet, man of letters, and seer of life, and that his expression of himself was cast in the form of words for actors and not in the form of books to be read was an accident of his social circumstances that he himself despised. I would, besides, hazard the guess that he, of all poets of high rank whose works have taken a stage direction, will some day cease altogether to be acted, and be simply studied.

'I therefore do not see the good of a memorial theatre, or for that matter any other material monument to him and prefer not to join the Committee. . . .'

Hardy afterwards modified the latter part of the above opinion in favour of a colossal statue in some public place.

Life, pp. 341–2 (1908).

★

'FOR several reasons I could not bring myself to write on Swinburne immediately I heard that, to use his own words, "Fate had undone the bondage of the gods" for him. . . .

'No doubt the press will say some good words about him now he is dead and does not care whether it says them or no. Well, I remember what it said in 1866, when he did care, though you do not remember it, and how it made the blood of some of us young men boil.

'Was there ever such a country – looking back at the life, work, and death of Swinburne – is there any other country in Europe whose attitude towards a deceased poet of his rank would have been so ignoring and almost contemptuous? I except *The Times*, which has the fairest estimate I have yet seen. But read the *Academy* and the *Nation*.

'The kindly cowardice of many papers is overwhelming him with such toleration, such theological judgements, hypocritical sympathy, and misdirected eulogy that, to use his own words again, "it makes one sick in a corner" – or as we say down here in Wessex, "it is enough to make every little dog run to mixen".

'However, we are getting on in our appreciativeness of poets. One thinks of those other two lyricists, Burns and Shelley, at this time, for obvious reasons, and of how much harder it was with them. We know how Burns was treated at Dumfries, but by the time that Swinburne was a young man Burns had advanced so far as to be regarded as no worse than "the glory and the shame of literature" (in the words of a critic of that date). As for Shelley, he was not tolerated at all in his lifetime. But Swinburne has been tolerated – at any rate since he has not written anything to speak of. And a few months ago, when old and enfeebled, he was honoured by a rumour that he had been offered a complimentary degree at Oxford. And Shelley too, in these latter days of our memory, has been favoured so far as to be considered no lower than an ineffectual angel beating his luminous wings in vain. . . .

'I was so late in getting my poetical barge under way, and he was so early with his flotilla – besides my being between three and four years younger, and being nominally an architect (an awful impostor at that, really) – that though I read him as he came out I did not personally know him till many years after the *Poems and Ballads* year. . . .'

Life, pp. 344–5 (1909).

[Letter to an unidentified recipient.]

*

'HERE is a sentence from the *Edinburgh Review* of a short time back which I might have written myself: "The division [of poems] into separate groups [ballad, lyrical, narrative, &c.] is frequently a question of the preponderance, not of the exclusive possession, of certain aesthetic elements." '

Life, p. 359 (1912).

*

'IN these days when the literature of narrative and verse seems to be losing its qualities as an art, and to be assuming a structureless and conglomerate character, it is a privilege that we should have come into our midst a writer [Anatole France] who is faithful to the principles that make for permanence, who never forgets the value of organic form and symmetry, the force of reserve, and the emphasis of understatement, even in his lighter works.'

Life, p. 363 (1913).

*

'GEORGIAN POETS'. It is a pity that these promising young writers adopted such a title. The use of it lacks the modesty of true genius, as it confuses the poetic chronology, and implies that the hitherto recognized original Georgians – Shelley, Keats, Words-worth, Byron, etc., are negligible; or at any rate says that they do not care whether it implies such or no.'

Life, p. 370 (1915).

*

'I HOLD that the mission of poetry is to record impressions, not convictions. Wordsworth in his later writings fell into the error of recording the latter. So also did Tennyson, and so do many poets when they grow old. *Absit omen!*

'I fear I have always been considered the Dark Horse of contemporary English literature.

'I was quick to bloom; late to ripen. . . .'

Life, pp. 377–8 (1917).

*

'As to reviewing. Apart from a few brilliant exceptions, poetry is not at bottom criticized as such, that is, as a particular man's artistic interpretation of life, but with a secret eye on its theological and political propriety. Swinburne used to say to me that so it would be two thousand years hence; but I doubt it.

'As to pessimism. My motto is, first correctly diagnose the complaint – in this case human ills – and ascertain the cause: then set about finding a remedy if one exists. The motto or practice of the optimists is: Blind the eyes to the real malady, and use empirical panaceas to suppress the symptoms.

'Browning said (in a line cited against me so often):

Never dreamed though right were worsted wrong would triumph.

'Well, that was a lucky dreamlessness for Browning. It kept him comfortably unaware of those millions who cry with the Chorus in *Hellas*: "Victorious Wrong, with vulture scream, Salutes the rising sun!"[1] – or with Hyllus in the *Trachiniae*: "Mark the vast injustice of the gods!" "[2]

'It is *the unwilling mind* that stultifies the contemporary criticism of poetry.'

Life, p. 383 (1918).

*

IN a United States periodical for March it was stated that 'Thomas Hardy is a realistic novelist who . . . has a grim determination to go down to posterity wearing the laurels of a poet'. This writer was a glaring illustration of the danger of reading motives into actions. Of course there was no 'grim determination', no thought of 'laurels'. Thomas Hardy was always a person with an unconscious, or rather unreasoning, *tendency*, and the poetic tendency had been his from the earliest. He would tell that it used to be said to him at Sir Arthur Blomfield's: 'Hardy, there can hardly have been anybody in the world with less ambition than you.' At this time the real state of his mind was, in his own words, that 'A sense of the truth of poetry, of its supreme place in literature, had awakened itself in me. At the risk of ruining all my worldly prospects I dabbled in it . . . was forced out of it. . . . It came back upon me. . . . All was of the nature of being led by a mood, without foresight, or regard to whither it led.'

Life, pp. 384–5 (1918).

*

'BY the will of God some men are born poetical. Of these some make themselves practical poets, others are made poets by lapse of time who were hardly recognized as such. Particularly has this been the case with the translators of the Bible. They translated into the language of their age; then the years began to corrupt that language as

---

[1] Shelley's *Hellas*, line 940.   [2] Sophocles' *Trachiniae*, 1266.

spoken, and to add grey lichen to the translation; until the moderns who use the cor-
rupted tongue marvel at the poetry of the old words. When new they were not more
than half so poetical. So that Coverdale, Tyndale, and the rest of them are as ghosts
what they never were in the flesh.'

Life, p. 385 (1918).

★

SOME sense of the neglect of poetry by the modern English may have led him to write
at this time:

'The poet is like one who enters and mounts a platform to give an address as announ-
ced. He opens his page, looks around, and finds the hall – *empty*.'

A little later he says:

'It bridges over the years to think that Gray might have seen Wordsworth in his
cradle, and Wordsworth might have seen me in mine.'

Some days later:

'The people in Shakespeare act as if they were not quite closely thinking of what
they are doing, but were great philosophers giving the main of their mind to the general
human situation.

'I agree with Tennyson, who said he could form no idea how Shakespeare came to
write his plays.

'My opinion is that a poet should express the emotion of all the ages and the thought
of his own.'

Life, p. 386 (1918).

★

'*November 18*. To my father's grave (he was born Nov. 18, 1811) with F. [Mrs. Hardy].
The funeral psalm formerly sung at the graveside to the tune of "St. Stephen" was the
xc. in Tate and Brady's version. Whether Dr. Watts's version, beginning "O God, our
help in ages past" – said to be a favourite with Gladstone – was written before or
after T. and B.'s (from Coverdale's prose of the same psalm) I don't know, but I think
it inferior to the other, which contains some good and concise verse, *e.g.*,

'T. and B.:

<blockquote>
For in Thy sight a thousand years
    Are like a day that's past,
Or like a watch at dead of night
    Whose hours unnumbered waste.
Thou sweep'st us off as with a flood,
    We vanish hence like dreams. . . .
</blockquote>

'Watts (more diffusely):

<blockquote>
A thousand ages in Thy sight
    Are like an evening gone;
Short as the watch that ends the night
    Before the rising sun.
Time, like an ever-rolling stream,
    Bears all its sons away;
They fly forgotten, as a dream
    Dies at the opening day.'
</blockquote>

Life, p. 393 (1919).

★

ON June 2nd of this year [1920] came Hardy's eightieth birthday, and he received a deputation from the Society of Authors, consisting of Mr. Augustine Birrell, Sir Anthony Hope Hawkins, and Mr. John Galsworthy. The occasion was a pleasant one, and the lunch lively. Many messages were received during the day, including one from the King, the Lord Mayor of London, the Cambridge Vice-Chancellor, and the Prime Minister.

Hardy pencilled down the following as 'Birthday notes':

'When, like the Psalmist, "I call mine own ways to remembrance", I find nothing in them that quite justifies this celebration.

'The value of old age depends upon the person who reaches it. To some men of early performance it is useless. To others, who are late to develop, it just enables them to complete their job.

'We have visited two cathedrals during the last month, and I could not help feeling that if men could get a little more of the reposefulness and peace of those buildings into their lives how much better it would be for them.

'Nature's indifference to the advance of her species along what we are accustomed to call civilized lines makes the late war of no importance to her, except as a sort of geological fault in her continuity.

'Though my life, like the lives of my contemporaries, covers a period of more material advance in the world than any of the same length can have done in other centuries, I do not find that real civilization has advanced equally. People are not more humane, so far as I can see, than they were in the year of my birth. Disinterested kindness is less. The spontaneous goodwill that used to characterize manual workers seems to have departed. One day of late a railway porter said to a feeble old lady, a friend of ours, "See to your luggage yourself". Human nature had not sunk so low as that in 1840.

'If, as has been lately asserted, only the young and feeble League of Nations stands between us and the *utter destruction of Civilization*, it makes one feel he would rather be old than young. For a person whose chief interest in life has been the literary art – poetry in particular – the thought is depressing that, should such an overturn arrive, poetry will be the first thing to go, probably not to revive again for many centuries. Anyhow, it behoves young poets and other writers to endeavour to stave off such a catastrophe.'

Life, pp. 405–6 (1920).

*

ON November 15th the poetic drama *The Famous Tragedy of the Queen of Cornwall* was published. Hardy's plan in writing this is clearly given in a letter to Mr. Harold Child:

'The unities are strictly preserved, whatever virtue there may be in that. (I, myself, am old-fashioned enough to think there *is* a virtue in it, if it can be done without artificiality. The only other case I remember attempting it in was *The Return of the Native*.) The original events could have been enacted in the time taken up by the performance, and they continue unbroken throughout. The change of persons on the stage is called a change of scene, there being no change of background.

'My temerity in pulling together into the space of an hour events that in the traditional stories covered a long time will doubtless be criticized, if it is noticed. But there are so many versions of the famous romance that I felt free to adapt it to my purpose in any way – as, in fact, the Greek dramatists did in their plays – notably Euripides.

'Wishing it to be thoroughly English I have dropped the name of Chorus for the conventional onlookers, and called them Chanters, though they play the part of a Greek Chorus to some extent. I have also called them Ghosts (I don't for the moment recall an instance of this in a Greek play). . . . Whether the lady ghosts in our performance will submit to have their faces whitened I don't know! . . .

'I have tried to avoid turning the rude personages of, say, the fifth century into respectable Victorians, as was done by Tennyson, Swinburne, Arnold, etc. On the other hand it would have been impossible to present them as they really were, with their barbaric manners and surroundings.'

Life, pp. 422–3 (1923).

★

'Note – It appears that the theory exhibited in *The Well-Beloved* in 1892 has been since developed by Proust still further:

'Peu de personnes comprennent le caractère purement subjectif du phénomène qu'est l'amour, et la sorte de création que c'est d'une personne supplémentaire, distincte de celle qui porte le même nom dans le monde, et dont la plupart des éléments sont tirés de nous-mêmes.' . . .

'Le désir s'élève, se satisfait, disparaît - et c'est tout. Ainsi, la jeune fille qu'on épouse n'est pas celle dont on est tombé amoureux.' (*Ombre*, I 40; II 158, 159.)

Life, p. 432 (1926).

★

[From Mrs Hardy's last chapter of the *Life*.]

'Speaking about ambition T. said to-day that he had done all that he meant to do, but he did not know whether it had been worth doing.

'His only ambition, so far as he could remember, was to have some poem or poems in a good anthology like the Golden Treasury.

'The model he had set before him was "Drink to me only", by Ben Jonson.'

Life, p. 444 (1927).

★

In the evening he asked that Robert Browning's poem 'Rabbi Ben Ezra' should be read aloud to him. While reading it his wife glanced at his face to see whether he were tired, the poem being a long one of thirty-two stanzas, and she was struck by the look of wistful intentness with which Hardy was listening. He indicated that he wished to hear the poem to the end.

. . . As it grew dusk, after a long musing silence, he asked his wife to repeat to him a verse from the *Rubáiyát of Omar Khayyám*, beginning

Oh, Thou, who Man of baser Earth –

She took his copy of this work from his bedside and read to him:

Oh, Thou, who Man of baser Earth didst make,
And ev'n with Paradise devise the Snake:
For all the Sin wherewith the Face of Man
Is blacken'd – Man's forgiveness give – and take!

He indicated that he wished no more to be read.

In the evening he had a sharp heart attack of a kind he had never had before. The doctor was summoned and came quickly, joining Mrs. Hardy at the bedside. Hardy remained conscious until a few minutes before the end. Shortly after nine he died.

An hour later one, going to his bedside yet again, saw on the death-face an expression such as she had never seen before on any being, or indeed on any presentment of the human countenance. It was a look of radiant triumph such as imagination could never have conceived. Later the first radiance passed away, but dignity and peace remained as long as eyes could see the mortal features of Thomas Hardy.

The dawn of the following day rose in almost unparalleled splendour. Flaming and magnificent, the sky stretched its banners over the dark pines that stood sentinel around.

Life, pp. 445–6 (1928).

THOMAS HARDY:
BIOGRAPHICAL SUMMARY

1840   Born 2 June at Higher Bockhampton, Stinsford ('Mellstock' in the novels and poems), near Dorchester.

1848–56   At local schools. Learnt Latin.

1856–62   Training and working as architect in Dorchester. Taught himself Greek.

        1860   Read *Essays and Reviews*.

1862–73   Architect in London or Dorset.

        1862–7   Read much poetry, philosophy and contemporary religious and scientific work. Wrote poetry; none published. Religious faith declined. Working as architect in London.

        1867   Began relationship with Tryphena Sparks. Wrote 'The Poor Man and the Lady' (never published).

        1869   Met George Meredith in London to discuss this novel.

        1870   Met Emma Gifford. Ended relationship with Tryphena Sparks.

        1870–3   *Desperate Remedies, Under the Greenwood Tree, A Pair of Blue Eyes* and *Far From the Madding Crowd*.

        1873   Abandoned architecture. Began literary correspondence with Leslie Stephen. Considered 'pursuit of poetry now for ever hindered' by the necessity of writing novels for a living (*L* 99–100). Met Leslie Stephen in London, 'the man whose philosophy was to influence his own for many years, indeed more than that of any other contemporary' (*L* 100) and who introduced him to literary and social life there.

1873–85   Living in lodgings or rented houses in Dorset or London, writing novels professionally.

        1874   17 September. Married Emma Gifford. (Nearly all subsequent activities shared with her.)

        1876   Journey to Low Countries and Germany.

        1876–8   Living at Sturminster Newton, Dorset. (The 'Sturminster Idyll', the best time of their marriage.)

        1880   Journey to France. Severe illness in London.

        1880–1   *The Hand of Ethelberta, The Return of the Native, The Trumpet-Major, A Laodicean, Two on a Tower* and *The Mayor of Casterbridge* belong to this period. Literary and financial success of novels steadily increasing; entered into London literary and social life, meeting Browning, Matthew Arnold, Henry James, Tennyson and other important people.

1885–1912   At Max Gate, near Dorchester (designed by H, built 1885).

        1886   Began research for *The Dynasts*.

        1887   Journey to Italy.

1885–1912 – *contd*

1888	Journey to Paris.
1893	The Hardys spent 'summer season' in London in this and many subsequent years; received as people of importance in the highest circles. Visit to Dublin in May. First meeting with Mrs Henniker. *The Woodlanders, Tess of the d'Urbervilles, The Well-Beloved* and *Jude the Obscure* written between 1886 and 1894.
1894	End of novel-writing.
1896	Journey to Brussels and Waterloo to gather material for *The Dynasts*.
1897	Journey to Switzerland.
1898	*Wessex Poems*.
1902	*Poems of the Past and the Present*.
1904	*The Dynasts, Part First*.
1906	*The Dynasts, Part Second*.
1908	*The Dynasts, Part Third*.
1909	*Time's Laughingstocks*.
1910	Awarded O.M. by Edward VII, and Freedom of Dorchester by the Borough.
1912	Gold Medal of R.S.L. presented to H at his home by W. B. Yeats and Henry Newbolt. 27 November, Mrs Hardy died unexpectedly.

1912–28 Continued living at Max Gate, writing poetry and walking in the country; received many honours.

1913	March. Solitary journey to Cornwall, revisiting scenes of courtship of Emma Gifford in 1870.
1914	Marriage to Florence Dugdale. *Satires of Circumstance*.
1917	*Moments of Vision*.
1922	*Late Lyrics and Earlier*.
1923	*The Famous Tragedy of the Queen of Cornwall*.
1925	*Human Shows, Far Phantasies, Songs and Trifles*.
1928	11 January, died. Ashes buried in Westminster Abbey and heart in Stinsford Churchyard. October, *Winter Words*. November, *Life*, volume I.
1930	*Life*, volume II. *Collected Poems*.

Wessex Poems and Other Verses (1898) and *Poems of the Past and the Present* (1902) were originally published by Harper & Brothers, and subsequently reissued by Macmillan & Company. All later volumes were published by Macmillan.

NOTES

EXPLANATORY NOTE

(I) ABBREVIATIONS

      CP = *Collected Poems of Thomas Hardy* (London, Macmillan, 1968) (first complete edn 1930)

      H = Hardy

      L = F. E. Hardy, *The Life of Thomas Hardy* (London, Macmillan, 1962), one vol. (orig. publ. in two vols, 1928 & 1930)

All page references are given in arabic numerals, chapter references in roman, without 'p.' or 'ch.' before them. Where a page reference is not preceded by a title it refers to the pagination of this selection. Other abbreviations are self-explanatory.

    References to books listed in the Bibliography at the end of this volume give only the author's name and the page number.

(II) *The Life of Thomas Hardy.* I accept Purdy's argument (265–6 & 272–3) that all except its last four chapters were written by H and only attributed to his second wife & regard him as the author of all quotations not from these chapters. Wherever a reference is given to L without further explanation, the reader will find some illuminating comment there on the poem under discussion.

III) DEFINITIONS. All words needing explanation which occur in *The Oxford English Dictionary* (Oxford, 1933) have been explained in terms of the definition given there, though not necessarily by a complete transcription of the text. Categories applied to words by the *O.E.D.* (e.g. 'poetic', 'archaic') have been repeated where they seemed relevant, but not otherwise. Where information about the history of a word seemed to throw light on Hardy's attitude to his poetic vocabulary it has been given (always from the *O.E.D.*). Words which do not occur in *O.E.D.* are coinages unless otherwise stated, whether defined or not. In every case therefore, where there is no statement to the contrary, a word defined in the notes is one which is accepted by the *O.E.D.* & defined in similar terms, not an innovation of Hardy's. Uncommon words used more than once have been cross-referenced in the notes when appropriate.

    The object of this lexical annotation has been to establish the true nature & quality of Hardy's poetic vocabulary. He has often been accused of wayward & uncouth word-coinages but the number of coined words in these poems is surprisingly small. With a very few exceptions the supposed neologisms prove to be revivals. What emerges is that Hardy had an unusually wide & recondite knowledge of the lexical resources of English, & an unusually exact sense of the meanings & historical resonances of words, which he took for granted in his readers. Given this knowledge, there is no affectation in the use of words such as 'patroon' (Notes, p. 332), 'irised' (Notes, p. 337), 'becall' (Notes, p. 339), 'stillicide' (Notes, p. 347), or the precise & moving image in 'beneaped' (Notes, p. 337). Hardy's practice is rather to explore unfamiliar byways of English vocabulary than, like Hopkins, to invest it with dramatic new words.

Part I: NATURE AND MAN

Order. These poems are arranged for the sake of the subject with no regard to chronology of composition or appearance. (Introduction ix–x.)

P. 3 'A Backward Spring' *Barberry: berberis,* flowering shrub
P. 4 'An Unkindly May' L 444
P. 7 'A Sheep Fair' *Postscript*: 'a bad or irrelevant verse may mar the good remainder' (H, Intro. to *Select Poems of Wm. Barnes,* London, 1908)
P. 8 'The Later Autumn' *Toadsmeat*: toad's cheese, poisonous fungus *couch-fires*: bonfires of couch grass, a weed (cf. 85)
P. 9 'Last Look round St. Martin's Fair' St Martin's Day, 11 November, traditional time of hot weather *patroon*: patron (arch.)
P. 11 'At Day-Close in November' L 173
P. 11 'Snow in the Suburbs' L ix
P. 11 'Winter Night in Woodland' *Swingels*: poachers' weapons L 443 *quire*: L 9–13
P. 14 'The Darkling Thrush' Commemorates the end of 19th century *Darkling*: see Shakespeare. *King Lear* I. iv. 218; Milton, *Paradise Lost* III. 37–40; Keats, 'Ode to a Nightingale' VI; Arnold, 'Dover Beach' *bine-stems*: climbing plants
P. 18 'Afterwards' *Dewfall-hawk*: a moth *quittance*: being freed of a debt
P. 19 'Compassion' L 425 *Ailinon*: Greek, 'cry woe'; Aeschylus, *Agamemnon* 121
P. 20 'Throwing a Tree' A very late poem

Part II: LOVE

Introductory Note. Hardy gives a characteristic account of his first feelings of love in L 25–6. He remained throughout his life what used to be called a susceptible man but combined with susceptibility a sense of the ambiguous & contradictory properties of sexual feeling, a recognition equally of its delightfulness, its transience & its destructiveness. His own intensest experiences of love began ecstatically & led on to bitterness and tragedy. If there is a dark cloud over much of his treatment of the subject, if the prevalence of disaster & 'crossed fidelities' seems sometimes perverse, we must look to the contrast between the part love played in his life & his unusually ardent expectations of it for an explanation. He sees love as a force of infinite value, capable of the utmost benignity which having been inexplicably tossed into an indifferent world of 'crass casualty' is turned by events into a curse. He may sometimes falsify events (though there are instances of happily fulfilled love in both the poems & the novels) but he never falsifies emotional and psychological processes. Very few writers have recorded with such truthfulness the delight of the feeling of love, the illusions on which it rests and its moments of blank sceptical detachment. His love poetry offers a remarkable combination of the warm romantic feeling that never left him & the coolest psychological observation. (See his quotation from Proust in *L* 432; see above, 327.)

Much of it is closely autobiographical but there can be no greater mistake than to approach it as a kind of versified diary or, as several commentators have, as a set of clues to episodes in Hardy's life that he preferred to conceal. What the poetry tells us about the facts of Hardy's experience is supremely unimportant; it is the interpretation of them by his profound & sensitive mind that matters. It is a precisely articulated presentation of a diversity of states of feeling & a wide-ranging inquiry into the nature of love. How much of it is derived from what actually happened, how much from what is imaginary or fictitious has nothing to do with the greatness & authenticity of the poetic achievement. We need no more facts & details than Hardy has given us – perhaps, even, not so many – to respond fully to what he has written & often knowledge of what may lie behind a factual allusion which he has not explained serves only to limit what should be unlimited, to drive back into personal experience what has transcended it. The borderlines between the autobiographical & the 'dramatic and personative' in Hardy's love poetry – or anywhere else in his work – cannot & should not be drawn where he has not drawn them. Many poems that could not possibly be autobiographical, 'Her Dilemma' (193), 'The Contretemps' (32) or 'A Hurried Meeting' (250) for instance, are just as much investigations or dramatisations of aspects of love as the apparently confessional *Poems of 1912–13* (49 f.). Many that read like precise records of events – 'Neutral Tones' (26) or 'The Place on the Map' (27) are good examples – are just as likely to be imaginary projections, the musings of a psychologically aware young man in love on what might happen or what in certain circumstances he might feel. Hardy shows great skill in using detailed description, factual allusion & in particular the names of places to give his poems a sense of concrete reality but their function is to convey feeling, not autobiography.

Why, then, have I grouped this selection of Hardy's more personal love poetry, as distinct from poems about love that occur all through his work & in various parts of this volume, around four different periods of or episodes in his life? There are two reasons, & neither is to produce a biographical sequence, to make each section tell a story. First, a close study of all the love poetry revealed to me a unity of tone, feeling & attitude in certain poems, which corresponded roughly to the times of his life they seemed to arise from so that the poems grouped themselves into these four sections for artistic not biographical reasons. Second, *Poems of 1912–13* unavoidably attracted to themselves many other works scattered over the *Collected Poems* which arose out of Hardy's marriage to Emma Gifford & produced a fairly large body of verse which was both artistically & biographically central. The poems in Part II, Section 2 seem to me to illuminate each other in a way that cannot be resisted, & to relate to those in other sections – & to his whole work – in a way which is illuminating. But except where Hardy has made it explicit, the reference of any poem to actual experience is both conjectural & unimportant.

Hardy's meditations on love extend over much of his poetry & most of his novels. He said himself (*L* 392) 'speaking generally there is more autobiography in a hundred lines of Mr. Hardy's poetry than in all the novels', & it is true that he put all of himself into his verse. What the reader should extract is the essence, the distillation of experience, now its record. Consequently I have restricted my biographical & topographical notes to the barest minimum.

Order. In all four sections poems which Hardy dated appear in the order suggested by his dates but I have not distinguished between the date of conception or inspiration of a poem (given at the beginning) & of composition (at the end). Undated poems have been interspersed as coherence of tone, feeling or subject required with no regard to chronology of composition or appearance. (Introduction ix–x.)

Part II: Section 1

The poems in this section probably all originate in the period of Hardy's life before he met his first wife, Emma Gifford, in 1870, though some were written long afterwards. He had an intense & passionate relation with his cousin Tryphena Sparks at this time, & was temporarily engaged to her. The relation ended in tension & bitterness & some kind of situation of 'crossed fidelities'. These facts have long been known to students of Hardy & their only critical importance is to show that his dark & tragic view of life & love had deep roots in experience as well as in temperament, as the strength of the poetry suggests, & is not, as has sometimes been thought, the perverse gloom of a neurotic young man. The conjectural & often unreliable 'revelations' & speculations of Deacon & Coleman add little to this & have hardly any critical value. The impression they create that his relation with Tryphena was immeasurably the strongest influence on Hardy at this time – & indeed on the whole of his life & work – & that all the poems of this period are 'about' it is belied by internal evidence & external fact. 'In Vision I Roamed' (24), for example, is 'about' the vast spaces of the 'universe taciturn and drear' opened up by astronomical discovery that so appalled the Tennyson of *In Memoriam* quite as much as it is about any human relationship. 'At a Bridal' (25) relates Hardy's awareness of the cold indifference of evolutionary process to a certainly imaginary connection with a woman & again recalls *In Memoriam* (section lvi for instance), though the differences in tone between the two poets is more interesting than a correspondence of thought not surprising in two sceptical minds at this time. '1967' (25) contrasts the evanescence of life & the obsessiveness of love with the 19th-century belief in 'progress'. The conjecture that Hardy & Tryphena may have had an illegitimate son receives more support from the great power of the central figure of 'At the Railway Station, Upway' (239) & 'Midnight on the Great Western' (228) than from the inability of Deacon & Coleman to find his birth certificate & it is just as likely that Hardy imagined him as that he ever existed. Readers principally concerned with poetry need not pursue this question, nor the allied one of his blood relationship to Tryphena, any further.

There are many other poems connected with this period of Hardy's life which have been placed elsewhere in this volume because they seemed to belong more congruously there.

P. 24 'In Vision I Roamed' & the two following sonnets seem to me more interesting examples of H's work at this time than the more celebrated 'She to Him' sequence (*CP* 11–13) – 'part of a much larger number which perished' (*L* 54) – which I have omitted

P. 27 'The Place on the Map' First printed with subtitle 'A Poor Schoolmaster's Story'

P. 31 'The Dawn' to 'On the Esplanade' appeared at widely different dates between
1909 & 1925. They refer to summer 1869 (*L* 63–4) when H was engaged to Try-
phena & just about to meet Emma. Put together, they show H blending the bio-
graphical & the fictitious, foresight & hindsight into a contemplation of a state
of mind & returning to feelings & drafts 50 or more years old. Though not always
of his highest quality, they are included for this interest

P. 35 'Thoughts of Phena' *L* 224 *nimb*: a nimbus or halo (cf. 121)

PART II: Section 2

This is a selection from the poems more intimately connected with Hardy's relation
with his first wife, Emma Gifford, from 1870 to 1912. Many of them were written after
her death. The subject recurs in other poems so different in attitude or treatment that
they belong in other parts of this volume.

    L continually mentions Hardy's marriage but never its increasing unhappiness &
failure. He met Emma at St Juliot on the north coast of Cornwall (see *A Pair of Blue Eyes*)
when he went as architect to restore her brother-in-law's church there in 1870. Their
meeting is described in *L* v in her 'Recollections' which give a vivid picture of her.
Hardy fell in love with her & admired her physical appearance, her daring horsemanship
('She cantered down as if she must fall / (Though she never did')) & her piano-playing,
all of which occur in the poems. Their romantic courtship took place on the Cornish
cliffs & they were married in 1874 against her father's will. His feeling that she was
marrying beneath her gave them a bad start, & as time went on they found they had
little in common. Emma later developed symptoms of madness, supposed to be heredi-
tary, which led her into hostility to Hardy & into an emotional & idiosyncratic form of
religion. This, contrasting with his progressive alienation from any conventional faith,
caused her to feel shocked disapproval of his work & thought. They had no children.

    They shared every activity of domestic & social life in the closest outward partnership
for 38 years, living after 1876 at Max Gate, designed by Hardy, just outside Dorchester.
By the early 1890s their emotional situation had become painful & estranged. It seems
to have grown a little less so later on, if only through habituation. But 'they faced but
chancewise'. The hopes of St Juliot declined into a life of reciprocal isolation. In 1912
Mrs Hardy died unexpectedly & suddenly at 72. She was buried in Stinsford churchyard,
a mile or so from Max Gate. Her photograph in Southerington 30 (without statement
of its origin), is a grim comment on time & change.

    The poems declare themselves quite explicitly without any of this biographical
information. Its interest lies in what it tells us about the relation between the threads of
remembered feeling & detail from which Hardy wove these poems & the finished works
of art. He wrote (*L* 378): 'I have a faculty (possibly not uncommon) for burying an
emotion in my heart or brain for forty years and exhuming it at the end of that time as
fresh as when interred. . . . Query: where was that sentiment hiding itself during more
than forty years?' But it is possible that what he resurrected had been so shaped &
coloured by his imagination during its long dormancy as to be very different from the
original 'sentiment'. Florence Hardy is reported as saying, with an irony unusual in her,
'all the poems about [Emma] are a fiction but fiction in which their author has now
come to believe' (W. Blunt, *Cockerell*, London, 1964, 223 n). She may not have been the
most reliable judge, since her marriage certainly had to accept some competition from

Emma's memory, but it is no derogation of Hardy's love or his art to say that these poems are mainly an interpretation of his feelings after Emma's death, not a record of their marriage.

The place-names in this Section are all of places in Emma's Cornwall or Hardy's Dorset & are used with habitual geographical accuracy, but map references would not increase their evocative power & I give no notes on them.

P. 36 'The Wind's Prophecy' *L* 65–6   *Skrymer*: Norse giant who snored like thunder (*Prose Edda*)

P. 37 'A Man was Drawing Near to Me' *L* 70

P. 38 'When I set out' *L* 65–79, 411   *Lyonnesse*: mythical Cornwall

P. 39 'At the Word "Farewell"' *L* 75

P. 40 'Under the Waterfall' *L* 71

P. 42 'We Sat at the Window' *L* 107   *Swithin's*: traditionally rain on St Swithun's Day, 15 July, means 40 wet days to follow   *wasted*: see *The Return*, bk IV, ii, 319 for same thought

P. 45 'The Interloper'   Epigraph added to later edn to make the poem 'clearer' (H). Source untraced   *Fourth Figure*: Daniel 3; a divene presence (cf. 'The Burghers' 277)

P. 47 'A Duettist' *L* 75   *E.L.H.*: Emma Lavinia Hardy   *H.C.H.*: her sister, Mrs Holder

P. 48 'Alike and Unlike' *L* 254   MS. has '*She speaks*'

P. 49 *Poems of 1912–13*

These poems were all written in the year after Mrs Hardy's death on 27 November 1912 & published in *Satires of Circumstance* in 1914. Hardy wrote: 'Many poems were written by Hardy at the end of the previous year [1912] and the early part of this [1913] – more than he had ever written before in the same space of time – as can be seen by referring to their subjects as well as to the dates attached to them. To adopt Walpole's words concerning Gray, Hardy was "in flower" in these days &, like Gray's, his flower was sad-coloured' (*L* 361). Hardy was 72 in 1912.

The poems move between 'those red-veined rocks far West' where Hardy met Emma in 1870 & the Dorset countryside where most of their marriage was spent. Past & present are linked by Hardy's feelings when he revisited Cornwall alone in 1913 (he wrote that the visit 'has been a very painful one to me' & wished he had not gone) & he fills both landscapes with Emma's remembered presence. This series is unique in Hardy's work as his only cohesive body of poems written on a single subject in a short space of time. It is central to his whole poetry & to Part II of this selection. Hardy described it as 'an expiation'. His exclusion of other poems, for instance the four that follow the group in this volume, makes it clear that he assembled it as an elegiac whole. The order of the poems is his own.

P. 49 *Epigraph*: 'Traces of an ancient flame': Virgil, *Aeneid* IV. 23

P. 53 'I found her'   *Dundagel*: Tintagel, King Arthur's Cornish castle   *Lyonnesse*: cf. 38

P. 57 'The Voice'   *wistlessness*: unknowingness, coined from 'wist', past of arch. wit = know; MS. has 'consigned to existlessness'

P. 57 'His Visitor'   *Mellstock*: H's name for Stinsford, the Hardys' parish where Emma was buried

P. 61 'Beeny Cliff' *irised*: made iridescent (cf. 167, stanza viii)

P. 63 'Places' *Three Towns* composed Plymouth, Emma's birthplace *beneaped*: 17th- & 18th-century nautical term for a ship washed up & left at the highest point of a spring tide after it has gone out or 'neaped'

P. 66 'The Spell of the Rose' *newel*: central beam of a staircase *misconceits*: misconceptions (arch.) *couched*: to couch, surgical term for removing a cataract

[End of *Poems of 1912–13*]

P. 72 'Quid Hic Agis?' *L* 32 & 157 Title: 1 Kings 13 & 19 *Kalendar*: pious archaism (Mowbray's *Churchman's Kalendar* used it till 1967) ironically contrasted with 'devouring time'

Part II: Section 3

These poems probably have their origin in the early 1890s when Hardy was working on *Jude* & first met the Hon. Mrs Arthur Henniker. (See *L* 254–7, 389, 406, 416; Purdy 342–8; Bailey 28–31; & Pinion (London, 1972).) The 'misconceits' & 'misvisions' of the Hardys' marriage were at their worst at this time as can be inferred from the tone of *Jude* & of such poems as 'Wessex Heights'. Hardy met Florence Henniker in 1893, found her 'a charming *intuitive* woman' (*L* 254) and they began to correspond & meet. She was, apparently happily, married to an army officer. A warm friendship which Mrs Henniker seems to have handled with 'intuitive' tact developed & lasted till her death in 1923. Sue Bridehead in *Jude* 'was in part drawn from Mrs. Henniker' (Purdy 345) but she must have been much more evenly balanced. Whether Hardy 'fell in love' with her, to what extent these poems are 'about' her, is irrelevant. They present an imaginative fusion of the feelings aroused in him at 53 by a friendship with an 'intuitive' woman of 38, of the contemplation of the irreversible facts of his own marriage that it aroused & of the thoughts about the emotional consequences of 19th-century attitudes to marriage expressed in *Jude*. J. M. Barrie wrote that Florence Henniker 'took [Hardy] on a holiday from himself'.

P. 75 'At an Inn' *hold*: stronghold *port*: demeanour (both arch.)

P. 78 'He Wonders' *fantocine*: puppet, 18th-century Italian loan-word (see Orel 144)

P. 78 'The Recalcitrants' First title of *Jude*

Part II: Section 4

Hardy, like Eliot, attained in a second marriage late in life to a younger woman a happiness that had been denied him earlier. Mrs Henniker brought Florence Dugdale to visit the Hardys at Max Gate in 1904 when she was 26. She helped him with research in the British Museum for *The Dynasts*. Ten years later he married her at the age of 74 (*L* 363). *L* xxxv–viii were written by her. See V. Woolf, *A Writer's Diary* (London, 1953, 89–94), for a description of their life together.

P. 82 'After the Visit' *F. E. D.*: F. E. Dugdale, later Hardy's second wife

M

P. 83 'On the Departure Platform' *young man*: an MS. dates this in Hardy's late
1960s. He often said, only partly ironically, that he grew up late (e.g. *L* 378).
Florence wrote in 1914: 'he is just like a boy'. The attribution of this poem to her
is substantiated by Purdy 142

P. 83 'A Jog-trot Pair' *joyance*: delight (arch.) (cf. 'My Cicely' 280)

Part III: THE PAST AND THE PRESENT

Section 1: Childhood and Family

Hardy was born at Higher Bockhampton in the parish of Stinsford near Dorchester
on 2 June 1840. The strongest influences on his youth were the old-fashioned Christianity
of the village church, the Dorset countryside & its traditional way of life & the close
affection of the family which he shared with a brother & two sisters. His greatest delight
was playing the violin with his father & his deepest security his mother's firm, composed
character (*L* 1–11). In these poems he contemplates these things from a great distance
in time. Though outward change destroyed the culture that supported them & inward
change his religious faith, they remained his basic pieties, the foundation of a mind that
reached out to grasp & accept new, discrepant & disturbing realities.

The Hardy family was an old one, having produced 'the Elizabethan Thomas Hardy
who endowed Dorchester Grammar School' & 'Thomas Hardy, captain of the *Victory*
at Trafalgar', but was, Hardy thought, 'of spent social energies' & 'declined from
whatever importance it might once have been able to claim' (*L* 5). His father was a
master-mason who sometimes employed as many as 15 men; his mother, Jemima Hand,
'read omnivorously' & 'knew the writings of Addison, Steele and others of the *Spectator*
group almost by heart, was familiar with Richardson and Fielding, and of course with
other such standard works as *Paradise Lost* and *The Pilgrim's Progress*' (*L* 14). They had
not much money because the father preferred making music to carrying on his business
(he was an accomplished string player & a good, if limited, all-round musician) but
they certainly never endured poverty. When Hardy thought of going to Cambridge he
'knew that what money he could not muster himself . . . his father would lend him for
a few years' (*L* 50). The often-repeated belief that Hardy came of peasant stock & was
himself a hard-worked peasant (as Burns or Clare were) is an illusion. He had a good
secondary education, became proficient in Latin & Greek, grew up in an atmosphere of
considerable if provincial culture & was self-taught only in that he did not go to a
university. There was a dignity & ceremoniousness about the Hardys' lives quite
different from those of peasant life because it rested on a certain ease & freedom from
toil, though they might have struck us today as very simple people.

Indeed simplicity, an acceptance of both good & bad in a simply conceived reality
(the calm certainties of the village church were neither more nor less real than the
scandals or brutalities of country life found in 'The Bride-Night Fire' (260) or 'Her
Second Husband' (256) & did not seem contradictory), was the keynote of their lives.
An intense reliance on custom & tradition, a sense of the presence of the generations
ranked behind one in the same way of life – see 'Sine Prole' (98) – a self-enclosed,

self-supporting culture & a recognition of man's dependence on nature characterised them. Though never a peasant, Hardy was always a countryman. He knew nature & peasant life with both a deep familiarity & a certain detachment. Unlike Wordsworth, whose birth removed him a little further from them, he found more in both to love than to idealise.

Order. The poems are arranged for the sake of the subject with no regard to date of composition or appearance (Introduction ix–x)

P. 88 'One We Knew' *L* 420 *M. H.*: Mary Head, H's maternal grandmother *manses*: mansions *cots*: cottages *dip*: wick dipped in grease *cart-tail* . . . *lash*: young offenders were tied to a moving cart & whipped through the streets in the 18th century

P. 89 'A Church Romance' Sonnet on first meeting of H's parents. 18th- to mid-19th-century English churches had singers & string band in west gallery & no organ. *L* 9–13 *Mellstock*: Stinsford *'New Sabbath' or 'Mount Ephraim'*: tunes to metrical psalms (cf. 'The Choirmaster's Burial' 225)

P. 90 'After the Last Breath' *J. H.*: H's mother

P. 90 'The Self-Unseeing' *former door*: the front door of the family house was moved after H's boyhood

P. 91 'The Oxen' The tradition that cattle kneel to honour Christ's birth occurs comically in *Tess* xvii *barton*: farmyard

P. 93 'Afternoon Service' *L* 15, 18, 393 *Tate & Brady's* metrical psalms (1696) are still sung in English churches *'Cambridge New'*: name of tune

P. 95 'Old Furniture' *nut*: projection on neck of violin over which strings pass *linen*: made of cotton-wool; not in *O.E.D.*, app. a coinage

P. 96, 97 'Logs on the Hearth' & 'Sacred to the Memory' refer to the death in 1915 of Hardy's sister Mary. He had 'Sacred to the memory of Mary, elder daughter of Thomas and Jemima Hardy' inscribed on her grave in Stinsford churchyard

P. 97 'To my Father's Violin' *L* 8–15 & 410 *eff-holes*: apertures in stringed instruments *purflings*: inlaid borders on their edges

P. 98 'Sine Prole' *L* 116 & 316 explaining headnote *Title*: without offspring

Part III: Section 2: Travel

L xv & 292–5. All these poems are from 'Poems of Pilgrimage' in *Poems of the Past and the Present* (1902). The order is Hardy's. Bailey 126–40 shows their debt to Baedeker's guide-book.

P. 103 'Rome: The Vatican' *L* 300 The Sala delle Muse contains Roman statues of all the muses *perturbed*: *L* 176 *becall*: call bad names

P. 105 'Lausanne' Gibbon, *Autobiography* (edition John Murray, London, 1897, 333), on the completion of *The Decline and Fall*: 'It was on the day, or rather night, of the 27th of June, 1787, between the hours of eleven & twelve, that I wrote the last lines of the last page in a summer house in my garden. After laying down my pen, I took several turns in a *berceau* or covered walk of acacia, which commands a prospect of the country, the lake & the mountains' *Truth*: Milton, 'Doctrine and Discipline of Divorce', *Prose Writing*, London, Everyman, 249: 'Truth is as impossible to be soiled by any outward touch as the sunbeam; though this ill hap wait on her nativity, that she never comes into the world but like a bastard, to the ignominy of him that brought her forth; till Time, the midwife rather than the mother of truth, have washed & salted the infant, & delivered her legitimate.'

P. 106 'Zermatt' *Matterhorn*, first climbed by Whymper's party, 1865. Three were killed

P. 107 'The Schreckhorn' First climbed by Leslie Stephen, critic, mountaineer, sceptic, friend of Hardy & father of Virginia Woolf

Part III: Section 3: Memory and Reflection

Order (see Introduction ix–x). The poems printed so far have been arranged for the sake of their subjects without, as has been frequently said, consistent regard to date of composition or appearance. In this section, & in each of the following sections, the poems have been arranged in the closest approximation to the order of their composition that can be attained so as to give the reader what evidence is available from the text about change & development in Hardy's style & thought. This order cannot be other than approximate & unreliable owing to Hardy's habits of composition & publication.

In each section all poems whose dates of composition are given by Hardy, or can be inferred with reasonable probability from other evidence, come in the order of those dates. Other poems assigned to the same section are interspersed among them in the order of their first appearance, occasionally in a periodical, generally in volume form. The order of printing within a given volume has not been preserved when a different order seemed to make better sense poetically. That is to say, all poems known to have been written before 1898, whichever volume they appeared in, & all poems from *Wessex Poems* (1898) come before any poems known to have been written before 1902, the date of publication of *Poems of the Past and the Present*, & before all poems from that volume, & so on up to *Winter Words* (1928). This establishes a mixed chronology of date of composition & appearance, which is the nearest approach to an accurate chronology of Hardy's poetry that can ever be made.

P. 107 'The Temporary The All' MS. has '(To be thrown out)' but H began his first volume of verse, *Wessex Poems* (1898), with this poem. The strangeness of his choice of form & subject requires its inclusion. See *L* 155 for the same idea

P. 115 'The Last Signal' *William Barnes* (1801–86), parson, scholar, schoolmaster, Dorset dialect poet, friend of Hardy's & one of the few direct influences on his poetry. See Hynes 23–32 for Welsh poetic devices learnt from Barnes & used here

Pp. 116–18 'In Tenebris' In Darkness *Epigraphs*: H uses St Jerome's Vulgate translation with different numeration from Authorised Version I: *A.V.* Ps. 102, 4: 'My heart is smitten, & withered as grass' II: Ps. 142, 4: 'I looked on my right hand & beheld, but there was no man that would know me . . . no man cared for my soul' *due time*: 1 Corinthians 15, 8 *If way . . . Worst*: see *Apology* to *Late Lyrics* (308 ff.) III: Ps. 120, 5: 'Woe is me that I sojourn in Mesech, that I dwell in the tents of Kedar. My soul dwelleth with him that hateth peace' Stanzas 2–4 refer to H's childhood & his mother *That sweets . . . untoward*: Revelation 10, 9–10

P. 119 'Wessex Heights' *Ingpen Beacon, Wyll's-Neck, Bulbarrow, Pilsdon Crest*: hills at the four corners of Wessex *her who suffereth*: charity, 1 Corinthians 13, 4

P. 120 'In Front of The Landscape' *nimb*: halo (cf. 35) *broad brow*: 59, stanza 2

P. 125 'George Meredith' Meredith read H's first (unpublished) novel in 1869 & advised him about writing. *L* 56–62 *green hills*: G.M. lived on Box Hill

P. 125 'A Singer Asleep' Swinburne's pagan iconoclasm impressed the young H in London 1862–70. They became friends. Many refs in *L* *Lesbian* . . . *Leucadian*: Sappho of Lesbos, type of early Greek artistic & moral freedom, jumped to death in the sea from the island of Leucadia for unrequited love of a man. Swinburne's grave in the Isle of Wight overlooks the sea *hydrosphere*: earth's waters collectively *orts*: remnants; only a few fragments survive of Sappho's poems *deft as wind*: Swinburne was a keen strong swimmer, as was H *L* 64, 138

P. 127 'Exeunt Omnes' *kennels*: gutters

P. 131 'The Something that Saved Him' *cit and clown*: citizen & rustic

P. 132 'The Opportunity' *H. P.*: Helen Paterson, illustrator (1873) for the *Cornhill* of *Far from the Madding Crowd* *L* 97–101

P. 134 'Waiting Both' *L* 390–1

P. 134 'In St. Paul's' MS. has '1869', dating scene, not poem *mart*: St Paul's Churchyard, a commercial centre for centuries

P. 136 'A Nightmare' *Union House*: poor-house

P. 136 'So Various' Dryden, *Absalom & Achitophel* 545–6:

> 'A man so various that he seemed to be
> Not one, but all mankind's epitome.'

P. 138 'Not Known' MS. has '1914: after reading criticism' *phasm*: anything visionary; a phantom. Cf. 'A Plaint' (159) & 'The Absolute' (166)

P. 139 'He Never Expected Much' Title left unrevised at H's death

P. 141 'He Resolves' Final poem in *Winter Words*, which H was still arranging when he died, but missing from MS. He probably meant it to stand as his last pronouncement, so it is important to see that it is not a statement of utter pessimism & despair. The last stanza allows the possibility of a visionary experience of liberating truth 'beyond / The blinkered sight of souls in bond' described in the first two. I suggest that stanza 3 refers to Einstein and relativity & links the alternatives. *L* 419, 'The Absolute' & 'So, Time' (169) & 'Drinking Song' (176) & note (345). In *Apology* to *Late Lyrics*, H suggests an equation between 'the Darwinian theory' & 'the truth that shall make you free' but does not seem satisfied by it. Relativity offered a better chance. This last poem states the tension H never resolved between the bleak & tragic picture of man & the universe he saw & the need for a visionary experience of cosmic meaning he never found *pale horse*: 'And I looked, & behold a pale horse: & the name of him that sat on him was Death' Revelation 6, 8 *magians*: members of occult priestly caste

Part III: Section 4: Belief and Unbelief

The religion of Hardy's childhood offered a simple & reassuring picture of existence. It was founded on a literal interpretation of the Old & New Testaments, an anthropomorphic view of God & a firm belief in divine providence. It sanctified the affections of family life & looked confidently beyond death to personal immortality in a heaven where those who had loved each other in this life would be reunited. It was deeply permeated by the pagan & magical superstitions of country life which did not seem to conflict with it, it placed man in a benign & harmonious relation to nature which was God's handiwork &, though it exacted certain duties & pieties from man, was more aware of the forgiveness extended to sin than of its possible punishment. The consoling beauty of such a faith, of the medieval Church where it was celebrated & of the poetry of the Anglican liturgy & the Authorised Version, the music over which his father presided as leader of the church band, all took firm possession of Hardy's imagination & emotions. But the easy-going Christianity of Stinsford church lacked spiritual or metaphysical profundity & it was defenceless against intellectual or speculative examination.

Hardy began to subject his inherited beliefs to such examination in 1860 when he read *Essays and Reviews* &, as he moved on in the next few years to evolution, astronomy, geology & the higher criticism of the Bible his intellect forced him into a complete rejection of them quite repugnant to his emotional needs & nature. He was unable to find either a spiritual & sophisticated religious belief compatible with his new knowledge or, in agnostic rationalism, the kind of liberation & enhancement of life that many of his contemporaries did. The drawing of a broken key in a lock with which he illustrated 'Nature's Questioning' (147) is a precise metaphor of his experience. It was not that he had lost an intuitive or mystical vision – in so far as he possessed one it was rather a product of his feeling for nature than for Christianity, as such poems as 'An August Midnight' (6) or 'The Darkling Thrush' (14) testify, & one that he held very sternly in check – but that an explanation of life & the universe completely satisfying to his emotions, inextricably woven into his memory & representative of the traditional life he most deeply loved was irreplaceably lost. The loss made him 'seem to be false to myself, the simple self that was / And is not now' & produced an irreconcilable tension between the claims of emotion & reason. To the end of his life his religious feelings rebelled against the scepticism of his intellect & he was forced to live as a soul divided against itself. His religious poetry is an expression of the conflict between a sensibility not so much deeply spiritual as dominated by the beauty & simplicity of a lost faith, & an intellect more capable of inflexible reasoning from contemporary premises than of philosophical subtlety or originality. But to criticise Hardy as Blackmur does as 'a sensibility violated by ideas' (51–79) is to miss the point, unless at least we see violation as involving a poetic fertilisation. The tension between sensibility & ideas is the essential foundation of the poetry, without which it could not have existed. It is great poetry because of the precision with which it articulates a state of loss, disorientation & deracination unflinchingly confronted but never resolved.

Much has been written about Hardy's 'philosophy', his doctrine of the Will as it appears in the poems & *The Dynasts* & his supposed indebtedness to Schopenhauer & von Hartmann. But it seems likely that he found in these philosophers rather a resonance of thoughts already present in part of his mind than a source of new beliefs. The Will of

The Dynasts is incompatible with Schopenhauer's *Wille*, less pessimistic & less philosophically respectable, for when the cosmic process has been completed, 'consciousness the Will informing / Till it fashion all things fair', it will be both sentient & beneficent. It will be very like the God of Stinsford church – a poetic dream, not a philosopher's concept. Hardy must be believed when he refuses to be labelled a rationalist but rather an irrationalist 'on account of his inconsistencies' (*L* 403) & when, again & again in the *Life*, he repudiates having any philosophy whether pessimistic or otherwise. 'I have no philosophy – merely . . . a confused heap of impressions like those of a bewildered child at a conjuring show' (*L* 410). 'People *will* take my mood-dictated writings as a single scientific theory' (*L* 411). 'The views [in my works of art] are *seemings*, provisional impressions only, used for artistic purposes' (*L* 375). Even when agreeing, in the 'Apology' to *Late Lyrics*, that the poet's province is 'the application of ideas to life', he describes his own outlook as 'really a series of fugitive impressions which I have never tried to co-ordinate'. Ideas for Hardy are always a scaffolding from which to construct a work of art, one which can be dismantled, reassembled or jettisoned when it has served its purpose, never a philosopher's establishment of a committed position, & he says as much in his remarks about the philosophy of *The Dynasts* in *L* 335 & in his indignant letter to Noyes (*L* 408–10). His fundamental attitudes are neither rationalistic nor philosophic, though his tough persistent intellect builds a large number of shifting rationalisations upon them; they are deep & simple emotions – a profound grief at the inexplicable & annihilating power of time & death over mortals in their 'progress through a world not worthy of them' (*L* 332), an amazed inability to discern any purpose or meaning behind a world & a universe which *ought* to have purpose & meaning, a horror at the misery, mischance & cruelty of human life & the ruthlessness of the evolutionary process, a blank incredulity that the personal God who alone could make satisfactory sense of it all so obstinately refuses to exist.

Hardy never ceased trying to bring him to life & his quest for a first cause, a power whether sentient or not behind the universe is as far as it is possible to be from scientific rationalism. 'I have been looking for God for 50 years, and I think that if he had existed I should have discovered him' (*L* 224). 'I have called this Power all sorts of names – never supposing they would be taken for more than fancies' (*L* 409). Invidious critics who called him 'Agnostic, Atheist, Infidel, Immoralist, Heretic, Pessimist . . . had never thought of calling him what they might have called him more plausibly – churchy; not in an intellectual sense but in so far as instincts and emotions ruled' (*L* 376). At the age of 80, after attending a cathedral service, he wrote: 'Felt I would prefer to be a cathedral organist to anything in the world' (*L* 404), & in the same year: 'The Scheme of Things is indeed incomprehensible . . . perhaps for the best. Knowledge might be terrible' (*L* 410). The Bible was the book he knew best & read most all his life. His poems & novels abound in Biblical allusions, as much to the Old as the New Testament. He never ceased going to church service without professing the slightest intellectual belief in what was an emotional & cultural necessity.

The poems in this section then should not be read as philosophic or didactic. They record subjectively the lifelong dialogue between Hardy's simple but inalienable Christian sentiments, his rational rejection of them & his wholly individual sense of the numinous in nature. A superficial reading may find them monotonous, indigestible, stultified & stultifying – Hardy at his most gristly as it has been, I think misguidedly, put to me. Closer inspection will reveal their startling variety & inconsistency, their wide range of poetic tone & register, & their extraordinary imaginative power.

The conclusions, for instance of ᾽ΑΓΝΩΣΤΩι ΘΕΩι (155) or 'The Graveyard of Dead Creeds' (165) are diametrically opposite to those of 'A Sign-Seeker' (142) or 'Nature's Questioning' (147). The Miltonic majesty of God in 'God-Forgotten' (149), his lyrical quality in 'New Year's Eve' (157) – ('I have strewn the leaf on the sod, / Sealed up the worm within the clod, / And let the last sun down') – have nothing in common with his existless passivity in 'A Plaint to Man' (159) or 'God's Funeral' (160): a poem whose last line, 'Mechanically I followed with the rest', epitomises Hardy's feeling about his agnosticism. In 'The Subalterns' (148) he finds comfort in what appals him in 'An Inquiry' (170). In 'The Absolute Explains' (166) & 'So, Time' (169) he finds in relativity a provisionally optimistic solution to the problem of time & death that so oppressed him earlier. ('Relativity – That things and events always were, are, and will be (e.g. Emma, Mother and Father are living still in the past)' (*L* 419)). The conscious doggerel of 'A Philosophical Fantasy' (172) & 'Drinking Song' (176) treat almost hilariously matters which have earlier seemed so grim, as if to suggest that in the ripeness of extreme old age the cosmic question no longer looked quite so important.

Throughout these poems Hardy returns to the broken key in the lock & repeatedly attempts to turn it. He never succeeds but he never fumbles. Each different movement is brisk and deft. They are the record of a sensibility always divided but never paralysed by its division, of a mind strong & capacious enough to accommodate fundamental contradictions of thought & feeling without either resolving them by sleight of hand or collapsing under their weight. They do not set out to propound a doctrine or present a picture of the universe but to explore a particular personal predicament at a particular time in history – the predicament of man whose heart remained in life as well as in death at Stinsford church while his brain took very different courses. What matters about them is the poetic power & intensity with which they describe that predicament, the compression & concentration of language they bring to bear upon its inescapable discrepancies & not any message they may seem to, but do not, contain. If they strike the reader as at times almost unbearably painful he may like to be reminded of another view of Hardy by the lady who played the part of Tess in a dramatisation of this novel late in his life: 'A great deal has been said and written . . . of the sad philosophy and pessimistic attitudes to life of Thomas Hardy but to us he was not the grim cynical man often pictured and if he sometimes emphasised the darker side of life, he never forgot the sunshine of laughter. I can still hear him laugh . . .' (G. Bugler, *Personal Recollections of T. H.*, Dorchester, 1964.)

P. 141 'Hap'   *Crass Casualty*: 'insensible' chance; H's gloss

P. 142   'A Young Man's Epigram'   *L* 409   *W.P.V.*: Westbourne Park Villas, London, where H lived in 1866

P. 142   'A Sign-Seeker'   *subtrude*: not in *O.E.D.* Webster has 'to place under, insert'; intrans. usage app. a coinage   *eccentric orbs*: comets   *moils*: toils   *general*: the general public   *word*: talk about (vb); 'Those signs most people talk about as granted to their heedlessness, which are denied to my long waiting'

P. 144   'The Impercipient'   *Hark . . . the sea*: cf. Wordsworth, 'Ode: Intimations of Immortality' ix

P. 147   'Nature's Questioning'   *L* 409

P. 150   'The Bedridden Peasant'   *L* 409

P. 151   'By the Earth's Corpse'   *repenteth*: Genesis 6, 6

P. 153   'The To-be-Forgotten'   MS. has epigraph, Ecclesiastes 9, 5: 'neither have they any more a reward, for the memory of them is forgotten' *second death*: Revelation 20, 14 *Things . . . report*: Philippians 4, 8

P. 154 'Yell'ham-Wood's Story' All the woods are near H's birthplace

P. 155 ʼΑΓΝΩΣΤΩι ΘΕΩι 'To the Unknown God': Acts 17, 23

P. 156 'Before Life' *earth's testimonies*: geological evidence

P. 157 'New Year's Eve' *L* 409 In a letter (1907) to E. Clodd, now in B.M., H described this poem as a 'fantasy or dream', deplored the fact that people would 'mistake it for a belief', quoted Feuerbach that God is a product of man & ended that it was 'paralyzing to think what if, of all that is so incomprehensible to us (the Universe) there exists no comprehension anywhere' *tabernacle*: 2 Corinthians 5, 4

P. 159 'A Plaint' *phasm*: anything visionary, a phantom, but here in Greek sense of 'appearance'; cf. 'Not Known' (139) & 'The Absolute' (166) *decide . . . seers*: modern churchmen, rationalists & scientists who have killed the anthropomorphic God

P. 160 'God's Funeral' *L* 354 No evidence that H read Nietzsche on 'the death of God' but comparison is interesting with *The Joyful Wisdom* (trans. T. Common) Edinburgh & London 1910) esp. 'The Madman' 125: 'Do we not hear the voice of the grave-diggers who are burying God? Do we not smell the divine putre-faction? – for even Gods putrefy.' *L* 315 & 364 shows H's antipathy to Nietzsche

P. 164 'According to The Mighty Working' Words of Anglican burial-service as earth is cast into the grave, derived from Ephesians 1, 19 *moiling*: toiling

P. 165 'The Graveyard of Dead Creeds' *Catholicons*: panaceas, comprehensive formulae

P. 165 'A Cathedral Façade' *L* 296

P. 166 'Our Old Friend Dualism' *L* 369 *Dualism*: doctrine that mind & matter, good & evil, in religion God & Devil, exist as separate entities *Protean*: able to assume many different shapes *Spinoza . . . monists*: Spinoza, 17th-century philoso-pher & monist, denied distinction between mind & matter, equated God with 'the fixed & unalterable order of nature & the interconnection of natural beings', denied personal immortality *Bergson* (*L* 369–70, 449–51) & *James*: 19th-century philosophers, taught various forms of dualism *pragmatic*: James's 'pragmatism' taught that ideas are true if they 'work' & harmonise with our experience and accepted ideas *flamens*: priests

P. 166 'The Absolute' *L* 419 on relativity *toothless*: *Measure for Measure* v. i. 12 *phasmal*: not real (coined from *phasm*); cf. 'Not Known' (138) & 'A Plaint' (159) *irised*: made iridescent; cf. 'Beeny Cliff' (61)

P. 169 'So, Time' Placed by H as PS. to 'The Absolute' in *Human Shows*

P. 170 'An Inquiry' *Epigraph*: 'The sorrows of death encompassed me around' Ps. 18, 4

P. 171 'The Aërolite' The Meteorite

P. 172 'A Philosophical Fantasy' *L* 436 *Epigraph* from Bagehot's review of Masson's *Life of Milton* 1859 *life-shotten*: drained of life (of a spawned fish, see *1 Henry IV* II. v. 126) *unfulfilled intention*: see *Woodlanders* VII 'but dream-projected', 'blind force persisting', 'purposeless propension': concepts from Schopenhauer, *Die Welt als Wille und Idee*

P. 176 'Drinking Song' traces eclectically the waning of some human illusions about the universe over 2500 years. Thales (*c*. 600 B.C.) thought earth the centre of the universe. Copernicus (16th century) disproved this. Hume (18th century) attacked miracles. Darwin's *Origin* (1849) undermined conventional anthropomorphism. Einstein's theory of relativity (1915–17) questioned all accepted thought about time & space. Dr Cheyne (1841–1915), uneasy in august company, denied Christ's virgin birth & stands for Higher Criticism (cf. 199)

P. 179   'We are Getting to the End'   *warely*: advisedly.

Part III: Section 5: War

P. 180   'Drummer Hodge' refers to Boer War 1899–1902
P. 180   'The Souls Of The Slain'   Orig. pub. *Cornhill* during Boer War with a note by H that a bird on a 'great circle' from South Africa might land at Portland Bill. This is the most southerly point of England, locally called the Isle, & has a lighthouse on its tip   *bent-bearded*: overgrown with bent grass, a reedy grass   *mighty-vanned*: mighty-winged
P. 184   'The Man He Killed'   *nipperkin*: half-pint measure (dial.)
P. 184   'In Time Of "The Breaking Of Nations" '   *L* 79, 378   *couch-grass*: weed which farmers burn in piles; cf. 'The Later Autumn' (8)
P. 185   'A New Year's Eve'   *gable-cock*: weathercock   *hand-hid*: minute hand hides hour hand at midnight   *Death*: Revelation 6, 8   *Tears . . . Shock*: Revelation 6, 2–5
P. 186   'I Met A Man'   *shining face*: Exodus 34, 29   *antiphonic*: in liturgical response   *Cockers*: promoters of cock fights   *pit liege men*: set subjects to fight; *pit* is vb   *death-mains*: fights to death between two cocks; technicalities of cockfight are used precisely   *Malign compeer*: Jehovah & H disagree about 'Our Old Friend Dualism' (166)   *Saul*: type of military leader; made king by Jehovah & defied Him   *repenteth*: 1 Samuel 15, 11   *chartered*: licensed (by Jehovah's mistake)   *armipotents*: warriors, orig. Mars
P. 188   'I Looked Up' is placed in ironic contrast immediately after the two preceding poems in *Moments of Vision*
P. 189   'And There Was A Great Calm'   *L* 407   *Title*: Matthew 8, 26; Mark 4, 39   *Spirits of Pity, Irony, & Sinister* occur in celestial chorus in *Dynasts* (1903–8)   *Sirius*: brightest star, seemed to stop twinkling. Guns in France were often heard at night in southern England

Part IV: POEMS DRAMATIC AND PERSONATIVE

P. 192   'Dream of the City Shopwoman'   *garreteer*: one living in a garret
P. 193   'Her Dilemma'   *poppy-head*: carved end of pew
P. 193   'The Ruined Maid'   *barton*: farmyard   *megrims*: migraines
P. 194   'The Levelled Churchyard'   *L* 44–5   As architect, H was responsible for moving skeletons, often mixed up, from London graveyards demolished to let railways through

P. 196 'Friends Beyond' *tranter*: carrier (dial.) *stillicide*: dripping of water *hold the manse in fee*: inherit the mansion *charlock*: weeds *grinterns*: corn-bins (dial.) *stage*: stage-coach *Trine*: the Trinity

P. 199 'The Respectable Burgher' *Higher Criticism*: scholarly study of Biblical texts begun Germany late 18th century; cast doubt on truth of many (esp. miraculous) stories in O. & N.T. Critics were mainly liberal Christians trying to find rational-not superstitious bases for religion, but shocked conventional Victorians. The Burgher's dependence on miracles and literal truth is satirised. The blanks for 'Jesus Christ' are *his*, not H's, false reticence. The crude vocabulary and rhyme scheme are his *Piombo*: Renaissance painter whose *Lazarus* is in National Gallery, London

P. 200 'The Curate's Kindness' *Workhouse*: poor-house; paupers able to had to work for their keep; maintained by the *Union of Boards of Guardians of the Poor* for several districts. *Union* was 19th-century paupers' slang

P. 201 'Reminiscences of A Dancing Man' *L* 34, 42-3, 123 *Almack's, Cremorne Gardens, the Argyle*: popular London dance halls in 19th century. H was a keen dancing man *Jullien*: composer of popular quadrille music, square dance in which large numbers of people participated; also a serious musician; whenever he conducted Beethoven he used a jewelled baton & had a clean pair of kid gloves brought him *moue*: to make faces at

P. 203 'Liddell & Scott' compiled definitive Greek-English lexicon *college living*: appointment by one's Oxford or Cambridge college to incumbency of (prob. rural) parish with fine house & good pay; honourable retirement *Donnegan* compiled lexicon 1826, which *L. & S.* was meant to replace & *Passow* Greek-German one, 1819, on which it is based Greek words cited are first and last in Lexicon, pron. 'äägos', 'öödees' in 19th century

P. 205 'At Casterbridge Fair' Title of a series of 7 poems in 'A Set of Country Songs' in *Time's Laughingstocks* from which these 3 are taken 'The Market-Girl' *causey*: causeway (arch. or dial.) 'After The Fair' *drongs*: lanes (dial.) *burghees*: not in *O.E.D.*, Webster or Dial. Dictionary; app. a coinage for rhyme's sake; if so, the only one in H's work

P. 207 'Julie-Jane' *L* 258

P. 212 'Beyond the Last Lamp' *Tooting Common*: open ground in south London where H lived 1878-81 *L* IX-XI; cf. Tess & Angel's walk in *Tess* xxxv

P. 213 'A King's Soliloquy' *L* 350 Edward VII buried, 20 May 1910

P. 214 'The Coronation' George V crowned 22 June 1911. H took historical liberty for his fantasy. Henry VIII was not buried in the Abbey *Edward the Pious . . . he who loved confession*: Edward the Confessor, traditionally reputed holy

P. 216 'The Convergence' The British *Titanic*, first transatlantic luxury liner, considered unsinkable, struck an iceberg in the night on her maiden voyage to New York on 15 April 1912 & sank in a few hours with loss of 1500 lives. The poem was printed in aid of Titanic Disaster Fund *august* may seem a strange adjective for such a catastrophe, but reflects both the air of heroism with which public opinion invested this blow to its technological & economic confidence, & H's sense of the overwhelming force of 'crass casualty'

P. 218 'Channel Firing' *L* 365 British ships are practising gunnery off the south coast of England shortly before the 1914-18 war *glebe*: parson's fields *Christë's*:

God, timeless whether or not existent, mixes archaisms with colloquialisms *Parson Thirdly*: the name occurs in Dorset; see *Far from the Madding Crowd* XXXIII & XLII   *Stourton Tower . . . Stonehenge*: scenes of earlier battles, now evocative place-names

Pp. 219–21   'In Church' to 'Over the Coffin'. 4 poems from 15 'Satires Of Circumstance', in the longer volume of that name.   *L* 367

P. 220   'In the Cemetery'   *L* 44–5

P. 222   'In the Servants' Quarters'   Matthew 26, 55–75; Mark 14, 48–72; Luke 22, 52–62; John 18, 12–27

P. 224   'Aquae Sulis' (the Waters of Sul), Roman name for Bath which has medicinal springs. Sul was pre-Roman native goddess of waters; Romans syncretistically dedicated a temple to Sul-Minerva   *interlune*: dark period between old & new moon (arch.)   *parle*: discussion (arch.)   *baldachined*: from baldachin, ornamental awning over altar   *Jumping-jack . . . jill*: puppets

P. 225   'The Choirmaster's Burial'   *L* 12–13   *lutes*: puzzling term from musically expert H for the violin family actually played by Dorset musicians   *Mount Ephraim*: metrical psalm tune; cf. 'A Church Romance' (89)   *tenor*: tenor violin, cello

P. 226   'During Wind and Rain' describes incidents from Emma Hardy's early life

P. 234   'Barthélémon at Vauxhall'   *L* 414   *Barthélémon*: chief violinist at Vauxhall pleasure gardens, London 1770; wrote famous tune to Bishop Ken's 'Awake my soul & with the sun'

P. 234   'Haunting Fingers'   *phosphor*: Morning Star   *Amphion*: Gk musician, patron of players   *clavier*: keyboard   *nebulous . . . mould*: phosphorescent light emitted by decomposing bodies   *mufflings*: drums were covered with black crape at ceremonial funerals in 19th century   *shawm*: medieval ancestor of oboe   *sock*: symbol of comedy

P. 236   'Voices from Things Growing'   *L* 92, 413–14   *Voss*: see *Under the Greenwood Tree* I, IV   *withwind*: clematis known as 'the virgin's bower' (cf. H's note)

P. 239   'At the Railway Station'   '*This Life . . . for me*': prob. refrain of Victorian popular song

P. 240   'An Ancient'   Prob. written 1920. The *persona* evokes the 1860s in London when H 'was strong and vigorous and enjoyed his life immensely' (*L* 442). Allusions to the old-fashioned dance instruments (stanza 1), attitudes to women (stanza 2), dances & operas (stanza 4), painters & writers, (stanza 5) culminate in allusion to the opening of Tennyson's 'Mariana' (stanza 6). It is hard to realise how 'roof-wrecked' all these, except possibly George Sand, looked in the era of 'The Waste Land', the later Yeats, Lawrence, Huxley & Joyce   '*Girl*': *The Bohemian Girl* (1843), popular opera by Balfe   *Aïdes*: Greek god of world of the dead   *Sophocles . . . Origen* all did their best work in old age

P. 244   'Bags of Meat'   *L* 434   *stand*: bucolic pun; bulls or stallions 'stand' to mate   *bouse*: drink (arch.)   *tear*: rural belief that cattle could weep was common (see Blunden 153, quoting Kilvert)

P. 245   'A Popular Personage'   *L* 427–8 & 434–5   Written for a children's annual. H's terrier used to walk on the table taking food from guests' forks, bit many visitors incl. Galsworthy but spared Barrie, Sassoon, V. Woolf & Cynthia Asquith, who commissioned the poem

P. 246   'No Buyers'   *Turk's head*: long-handled broom

P. 247   'An East-End Curate'   *cyphering*: sticking down

P. 248 'A Refusal' Byron's remains were refused burial in the Abbey. In 1924 H with other eminent men asked that a memorial to him be placed there. The Dean declined, blaming B's 'dissolute life . . . the influence of the licentious verse' & his 'world-wide reputation for immorality'. The Dean's verse reflects his philistinism, not a fading of H's powers *horner*: cuckolder

P. 249 'A Watering-Place Lady' *Watering-place*: seaside resort

P. 250 'A Hurried Meeting' *night-jar*: bird which makes a whirring sound *to imp*: to enlarge the meaning

P. 251 'Queen Caroline' See *Dynasts* II, VI. vi, & III, IV. iii. Caroline, spurned wife of George IV, led a life of hectic social activity apart from him & became queen against his wish a month before her death – a neurotic & pathetic person

P. 254 'Christmas in the Elgin Room' Elgin Room in British Museum houses sculptures from the Parthenon frieze brought to England by Lord Elgin in 19th century *Borean people's gold*: northerners' money

Part V: BALLADS AND NARRATIVE POEMS

P. 260 'The Bride-Night Fire' L 302 H's first published poem (*Gentleman's Magazine* 1875). H suggests dialect by mixing Dorset diction & phonetics with normal English. He never attempted full dialect reproduction as did Barnes & Tennyson *Northern*: a northerner, not a Dorset man who knew her *vail*: veil (dial.); her pale face was the veil covering inner conflict like smoke covering a battle *orchet*: orchard (dial.) *codlin*: kind of apple *night-rail*: night dress (dial.) *horsed*: put her on his back *skimmity-ride*: skimmington-ride; grotesque procession organised to deride adulterers; see *The Mayor of Casterbridge* XXXIX

P. 264 'Valenciennes' H's interest in the Napoleonic wars began when, aged 10, he read a *History of the Wars* found in a closet & attended a supper where old soldiers were present, & culminated in *The Dynasts*. He sought out & talked to many veterans. S.C. (Pensioner) must be one. Tullidge (see *Trumpet-Major* IV where song does not occur) & much of the detail in this & the 3 succeeding poems grew out of such interviews as well as H's wide reading in the period. Valenciennes was besieged by allied armies 1793, & bombarded continuously for several weeks. Each side undermined the other's positions but British commander exploded his mines first & captured town. Name is stressed *Valenciéen* to rhyme with disagreën, etc. *topperen*: toppering, knocking on head (dial.) *shent to shards*: blown to bits (arch.)

P. 266 'San Sebastian' Battle won by Wellington in Spain with great loss of life *Sergeant M*: another veteran H knew *faussbray*: faussebraie, mound or wall built in front of main fortification *horn*: projection from main fortification *woe within*: during attack a pile of explosives inside Fr. position blew up & killed many

P. 268 'Leipzig' L 417-18. *Dynasts* III, iii. Napoleon's defeat at Leipzig, 1813, began his downfall. Norbert's details are historically accurate inc. Polish & Scottish names of some of Napoleon's commanders. German troops were quartered near Dorchester in the wars (see 'The Melancholy Hussar' in *Life's Little Ironies*).

Norbert is son of one who settled. The consistent ballad metre must be scanned acc. to stress, not feet (e.g. stanza 19).

P. 273   'The Peasant's Confession' *L* 298, *Dynasts* III, VII, 2–3. For Waterloo generally, III, VI & VII. Headnote: 'If Marshal Grouchy had been joined by the officer whom Napoleon had sent to him at ten o'clock on the previous evening, all doubt [of the outcome of Waterloo] would have disappeared. But this officer never did arrive at his destination, as the Marshal never ceased to state all his life, and he must be believed for otherwise he would have had no reason at all to hesitate. Had this officer been captured? Had he defected to the enemy? That is what no one will ever know.' No historical source for this story is known. Prob. H's invention. But many historians believe that if Grouchy had got a message from Napoleon (which he plainly had not) the Fr. might have won. Strategic & (with few minor exceptions) geographical details are accurate. Names are all of real people   *Landwehr*: (Prussian) Army   *Goumont*: contraction of Hougoumont   *capple*: white-faced with red or dun specks (dial., not in *O.E.D.*)

P. 277   'The Burghers'   Set in Dorchester; geography precise   *Grey's to Dammer's Crest*: hills to east & west of Dorchester; from sunrise to sunset   *Furnace*: Daniel 7, 3–25; cf. 'The Interloper' (45)   *unshent*: unharmed (arch.)   *Froom*: river encircling Dorchester

P. 280   'My Cicely'   H was proud of this poem. It has been much attacked, esp. by P. N. Furbank (*Selected Poems of H*, London, 1967, xvii) for 'incompetence'. But to maintain the anapaestic rhythm of galloping hooves over 31 stanzas & to rhyme the last lines of 31 internally unrhymed ones is near virtuosity. Stylised diction & contorted syntax are to give height & dignity to a potentially ludicrous subject. Whether successful or not, H knows what he is doing & is never simply incompetent. Metre & rhyme are those of Barnes's 'Old Woak', used for a different purpose. Geographical features between London & Exeter (Exonbury) are precisely chosen to evoke the past   *joyance*: delight (arch.); cf. 'A Jog-Trot Pair' (83)   *nonage*: youth   *Long Sieging*: Basing House, besieged by Cromwell's forces 1634–5   *Poore*: Bishop Poore founded Salisbury Cathedral 1220   *Icen, Forum, Weatherbury, Maidon, Eggar, Pummerie, Cromlech*: relics of ancient British or Roman England   *lynchet*: prehistoric strip-field   *jee*: gee-up   *Bride-streams . . . Otter*: rivers   *knaps*: hillocks (dial.)   *church-hay*: churchyard (dial.)

P. 284   'A Trampwoman's Tragedy' *L* 311–12 (where H describes this as 'on the whole his most successful poem') & 317–18. Geographical references to places in western England trace the journey precisely   *Fosseway*: a Roman road   *landskip*: landscape (arch.)   *tor*: hill (dial.)

P. 288   'Panthera'   H's rather random headnote indicates that he found legend of Christ's human parentage in Strauss & Haeckel, who quote ancient if unreliable authorities between 2nd & 13th centuries to try to reconcile magical claims of primitive Christianity with rationalistic findings of 19th century. Panthera or Pandira is mentioned as Christ's father. Geography & history are as accurate as in H's Wessex.   *Governor, Procurator*: Pilate   *Kranion*: the place of a skull (Gk)   *arbute . . . locust growths*: shrubs   *Fors Fortuna*: goddess of chance, deification of 'crass casualty'   *Son of Saturn*: Jupiter   *Three*: the Fates

P. 294   'The Chapel-Organist' *L* 29–30 (Baptists) & 404 (organ-playing). The organist is relating to herself what is about to happen.   *Chore*: choir (arch.)   *Old Hundredth . . . Eaton*: names of tunes   *Tallis*: Tallis's canon sung to Bishop Ken's Evening

Hymn containing lines 'Teach me to live that I may dread / The grave as little as my bed'

P. 298 'The Turnip Hoer' *Terminus*: God of Boundaries, immovable

P. 301 'At Shag's Heath' Duke of Monmouth, illeg. son of Charles II, raised rebellion in western England on his father's death to assert his claim to succeed as Protestant instead of Catholic James II. Captured at Shag's Heath, he was executed in London a week later. Amy Farrant, his betrayer, was paid £50 from the King's secret service fund. *nighty-rail*: nightdress (dial.)

P. 303 'The Paphian Ball' See 'Absent-Mindedness in a Parish Choir' in *Life's Little Ironies*. *Paphian*: sacred to Venus *Michael Mail*, the tenor man occurs in *Under the Greenwood Tree*

BIBLIOGRAPHY

I. SELECT BIBLIOGRAPHY OF WRITING ON HARDY'S POETRY

Auden W. H., 'A Literary Transference', Hardy Centennial Number, *The Southern Review*, no. VI, 1940, reprinted in *Hardy*, 20th Century Views Series (New Jersey, Prentice-Hall (ed. Guérard)), 1963.

Bailey, J. O., *The Poetry of Thomas Hardy: A Handbook and Commentary* (Chapel Hill, University of North Carolina Press, 1970).

Blackmur, R. P., 'The Shorter Poems of Thomas Hardy' in *Language as Gesture* (London, Allen & Unwin, 1954; New York, Arrow Editions, 1940).

Brown, Douglas, 'The Harvest of The Novels' in *Thomas Hardy* (London, Longmans, Green & Co., 1954).

Davie, Donald, *Thomas Hardy and British Poetry* (London, Routledge, 1973).

Hickson, E., *The Versification of Thomas Hardy* (Philadelphia, University of Pennsylvania Press, 1931).

Hynes, S., *The Pattern of Hardy's Poetry* (Chapel Hill, University of North Carolina Press, 1961).

MacDowall, A. S., chapters XI to XIV in *Thomas Hardy: A Critical Study* (London, Faber & Faber, 1931).

Miller, J. Hillis, *Thomas Hardy. Distance and Desire* (Cambridge, Mass., Belknap Press, Harvard, 1970). (This book places poems and novels in a single perspective.)

Ransome, J. C., 'Honey and Gall', Hardy Centennial Number (*The Southern Review*, no. VI, 1940).

—, 'Hardy – Old Poet', *New Republic*, CXXVI (12 May 1952).

—, 'Thomas Hardy's Poems and the Religious Difficulties of a Naturalist', *Kenyon Review*, XXII (Spring 1960).

Schwartz, D., 'Poetry and Belief in Thomas Hardy', Hardy Centennial Number, *The Southern Review*, no. VI, 1940, reprinted in *Hardy*, 20th Century Views Series (New Jersey, Prentice-Hall (ed. Guérard)), 1963.

Southworth, J. G., *The Poetry of Thomas Hardy* (New York, Columbia University Press, 1947).

Stevenson, L., 'Thomas Hardy' in *Darwin Among The Poets* (Chicago, University of Chicago Press, 1933).

II. SELECT BIBLIOGRAPHY OF OTHER WORKS ON HARDY

Blunden, E., *Thomas Hardy* (London, Macmillan, 1942).

Deacon, L., and Coleman, T., *Providence and Mr Hardy* (London, Hutchinson, 1966).

Eliot, T. S., 'Thomas Hardy' from *After Strange Gods*, London, Faber & Faber, 1934, reprinted in *Selected Prose* (London, Peregrine, 1953).

Hardy, E. (ed.), *Thomas Hardy's Notebooks and Some Letters from Julia Augusta Martin* (London, Hogarth Press, 1958).

— and Gittings, R. (eds), *Some Recollections by Emma Hardy with Some Relevant Poems by Thomas Hardy* (London, Oxford University Press, 1961).

Hardy, Evelyn, and Pinion, F. B. (eds), *One Rare Fair Woman: Thomas Hardy's Letters to Florence Henniker 1893–1922* (London, Macmillan, 1972).

Hardy, F. E., *The Life of Thomas Hardy 1840–1928* (London, Macmillan, 1962). Originally published in two volumes, *The Early Life of Thomas Hardy 1840–1891* (London, Macmillan, 1928) and *The Later Years of Thomas Hardy 1892–1928* (London, Macmillan, 1930).

Lawrence, D. H., 'A Study of Thomas Hardy' in *Phœnix* (London, Heinemann, 1936 (1961)).

Morrell, R., *Thomas Hardy: The Will and The Way* (Kuala Lumpur, University of Malaya Press, 1965).

Orel, H. (ed.), *Thomas Hardy's Personal Writings* (London, Macmillan, 1967).

Purdy, R. L., *Thomas Hardy: A Bibliographical Study* (Oxford, Clarendon Press, 1954).

Southerington, F. R., *Hardy's Vision of Man* (London, Chatto & Windus, 1971).

Stewart, J. I. M., *Thomas Hardy. A Critical Biography* (London, Longman, 1971).

Weber, C., *Hardy of Wessex* (London, Routledge & Kegan Paul, 1965; New York, Columbia University Press, 1965).

Webster, H. C., *On a Darkling Plain: The Art and Thought of Thomas Hardy* (Chicago, University of Chicago Press, 1947).

INDEX TO POEM-TITLES

The original volume-sources are indicated by the following abbreviations

HS: *Human Shows, Far Phantasies* . . . (1925)
LLE: *Late Lyrics and Earlier* (1922)
MV: *Movements of Vision* (1917)
PPP: *Poems of the Past and the Present* (1902)
SC: *Satires of Circumstance, Lyrics and Reveries* (1914)
TL: *Time's Laughingstocks and Other Verses* (1909)
WP: *Wessex Poems and Other Verses* (1898)
WW: *Winter Words* (1928)

INDEX TO FIRST LINES

Sue Cowley Books Ltd
PO Box 1172
Bristol BS39 4ZJ

www.suecowley.co.uk

© Sue Cowley Books Ltd 2013

First published 2013

Part of the 'Alphabet Sevens' Series

ISBN: 978-1489537836

The Seven T's of Practical Differentiation

SUE COWLEY

Sue Cowley Books Ltd
2013

The Seven T's of Practical Differentiation

Contents

Introduction

This book offers you a concise, practical and easy to read guide to the subject of differentiation. My aim is to give you realistic advice that you can use straight away with your students in your classroom – today! The ideas that I give in this short guide will help you differentiate your lessons, without needing to spend huge amounts of extra time and energy on planning and preparation. The strategies described in this book are suitable for students of all different ages. Remember: if a child doesn't learn in the way that you currently teach him, then both he and you are wasting valuable learning time. By making some simple adaptations to the teaching and learning strategies you use, you can reach and teach all of your students.

In my first few years as a teacher, I can remember being totally confused by the term 'differentiation'. What on earth did it mean? How on earth was I supposed to do it? And where exactly was I going to find the time? I had a vague idea that differentiation meant creating different activities for different students. So, in the early days I would spend hours creating and adapting worksheets to suit individual children. In those days I thought that differentiation always meant adapting the task to suit each learner, but of course there are many more ways to differentiate than just that.

All teachers differentiate, all the time. You do it every single day, even if you are not conscious of actually doing it. Perhaps you pick a particular child to answer a question, because you want to build her confidence about speaking in front of the class? That's differentiation. Maybe you move a child to sit nearer the front of the room, because you know he struggles to write down what's on the board? That's differentiation as well. Perhaps you use slightly different vocabulary with one child than you do with another? That's differentiation too. Put simply, differentiation means the teacher acknowledges that students are individuals, who learn in different ways. It stands to reason, therefore, that the teacher must do different things to help them learn.

Children really do come in all shapes and sizes. When we talk about 'difference', we mean so much more than just different ability levels. The children in your class will have different cultural or social backgrounds, different levels of listening skills, different interests, different stages of written and spoken English, different kinds of motivation, different speeds of work, different maturity levels, different physical or psychological needs, and so on. A key technique for effective differentiation is to get to know your students: what makes them tick, where do their strengths lie, what kind of people are they, what do they really enjoy? In this book you will discover how to find out this and much, much more.

Differentiation should be part of your daily teaching routine. In this short book you will find out how to embed it into your practice, so that every single child you ever teach gets the best possible learning experience. My 'Seven T's' will help you achieve a properly differentiated classroom, full of happy, confident learners. Your students will be able to access the learning you give them at the appropriate level. And you will be able to enjoy your work, sure and certain that you're reaching and teaching every single child in your class.

Sue Cowley
www.suecowley.co.uk

The First T:

Top and Tail

The First T: Top and Tail

The simplest way in which you can differentiate is to use the 'top and tail' technique. You can use this approach right away, and it will not take up a huge amount of your time. By using this technique you get into the habit of thinking about differentiation every single time you plan a lesson activity. Even if you don't manage to use a differentiated activity every time, or you don't manage to write down all the strategies you use in your lesson plans, you will still be thinking about creative ways to achieve differentiated learning.

Clearly, your students have a huge range of different levels of ability: they are all unique individuals. However, it is just not possible to prepare a personalised and individualised activity for every single child that you teach in every single lesson. There are too many other demands on a teacher's time. So, the top and tail technique achieves the next best thing: it touches all the bases.

It is probably fair to say that you could divide your students into three categories – the able ones, the middling ones, and the ones struggling at the bottom. What teachers often do is to aim for the middle when they are planning. So a lesson activity might be difficult for the strugglers, just right for the middle group, and easy for the top end. (Or, to put it another way, the teacher only gets it exactly right for one third of the class.) By topping and tailing each activity, you create an extension for the most able, and a support mechanism for the least able.

Techniques for the Able Students

Always have a plan in place for those very able students who find most activities fairly easy. Think about how you can extend these students within the task itself; think also about what these students can do next, after they finish the activity. When a student finishes a task quickly and you have not planned ahead, you may find yourself suggesting that the student 'checks over their work' or 'colours in the pictures'. Far better to have something more interesting, challenging and valuable up your sleeve.

To stretch your most able students:

✓ Ask them to do more of the activity than the rest of the class, for example, to complete eight questions rather than five, in the same amount of time.

✓ Get them to do a more difficult version of the activity, for instance completing five sums using three digit numbers, rather than five sums using two digit numbers.

✓ Ask them to do the same activity, but with an added twist that makes the task more challenging or complex. For example, you could ask them to write for a really specific audience, or from the perspective of a particular character. Imagine the students are writing a description of a scientific experiment they have done in class. The most able students could imagine they are government scientists, who have to present their report to a high-level government committee, and write it using the appropriate tone, language and format.

✓ Get them to do a tightly focused, pared down version of a whole class writing activity. For instance, while the rest of the class write a news report which is roughly half a page long, the very able students could be asked to write the report in exactly fifty words.

✓ Put the activity into a different context, preferably a 'real life' one, which makes it slightly more difficult to complete. For instance, with a series of multiplication sums you could use the context of buying something in a shop. So, while the rest of the class are trying to figure out 5 x 20, the most able students are asked to figure out how much it costs to buy five apples each costing 20p.

✓ Present some activities as a competition – either group against group, or for the individual student against him or herself. Your most academically able students will typically respond very well to a competitive challenge. For instance, you could have a 'tricky words' word bank, and challenge the most able students to use at least three tricky words in each lesson.

✓ Encourage your students to learn how to edit their writing early on, by giving them access to the full range of editing marks. It is useful to have a set of these editing marks stuck in the front of the student's exercise book.

To stretch your most able students when they finish a task early:

✓ Get them to teach what they have learned during the activity to someone else within the class.

✓ If several students have finished simultaneously, ask them to swap books and to write comments on each other's writing.

✓ Ask them to 'be teacher' and to support another less able or less well-motivated student in completing the task. Don't feel awkward about using this technique, or worry that you are somehow unfairly imposing a job on the child. Teaching something to someone else is one of the very best ways to consolidate learning.

✓ Get them to devise a new and different version of the skill you have been learning about in the lesson. For instance, the student could create his or her own series of three digit sums.

✓ Where you have been doing a class activity that requires remembering a technical term, a name or a date, ask the student to come up with a mnemonic or other memory strategy to teach to the rest of the class, to help them remember it in the future. The student can share this with the class in the plenary part of your lesson.

✓ Ask the student to underline or highlight five key words within the piece of writing they have done, and to write a definition for each one.

✓ Get them to highlight three words, phrases or sentences within their piece of writing that they feel are really effective. Ask them to talk with a partner about why they feel these parts work so well.

✓ For some kinds of activity, particularly those involving writing, it works very well to do a 'paring down' exercise. This forces the student to work out which words really matter, and which can be cut. Ask the student to re-write or cut down the piece, this time using exactly half (or a quarter, or an eighth) of the number of words used previously.

✓ Have a 'bank' of interesting and challenging puzzles or questions that your students can visit and choose from, whenever they finish a task. You could use generic puzzles and challenges or find something related to the subject you are teaching.

✓ Set up a class blog online, or get your students to set one up. I recommend weebly.com as a great free website building and blogging tool. When your able students finish a task, ask them to blog about it online, for their parents and others to read. They could describe what they did, why they did it, how they did it and what they learned from it. This will also give you a sense of how well you have achieved your learning objectives for the lesson.

✓ Give the students a digital camera, and ask them to go around the classroom taking close-up photos of very good examples of work done by other students. They could put these into a display, with an explanation of why they felt they were good examples. They could also upload these to your class blog or your school's virtual learning environment (VLE).

Techniques for the Weakest Students

For your less able students, and for those students who face a barrier to learning, such as having English as an additional language (EAL), you should offer a variety of methods of support. Those students who struggle with learning may have low self-esteem, and they may also be loath to get going on an activity for fear of getting it wrong. Aim to encourage an ethos of risk taking, where 'giving it a go' is far preferable to 'getting it completely right'.

To support your tail students, and help them access the learning:

✓ When preparing a worksheet, create a second version for those students who need extra support. Add a text box with definitions of key words, to support those with poor literacy skills or with EAL. Make the text box large and use a clear font, to make it as easy as possible to read.

✓ Have a high frequency word bank on your wall, with high frequency words on Velcro strips, so that the students can borrow these to help with spelling whenever they need. For secondary age students, your word bank could include a list of subject specific terminology. You could involve your students in creating the words for the word bank.

✓ Allow your weakest students to use a mini whiteboard during whole class teaching sessions, making notes as you explain a topic or activity to the class. They can then read and use their mini whiteboard notes during subsequent activities, rather than having to remember everything you said to them.

✓ When you have finished setting a whole class activity, go directly to your least able students to ensure that they understand what you want them to do and how they are meant to do it.

✓ If you have a teaching assistant or learning support assistant working with you in your classroom, ask him or her to go to the tail students first, to check for understanding.

✓ Partner the students up with 'study buddies', so that they always have someone to turn to when they are unsure about an activity. Use mixed ability groups for your study buddy pairings. Secondary aged students could swap email addresses, so that they can support each other with homework activities as well.

✓ Film yourself delivering an explanation of a topic or activity, or find suitable clips online. Allow your less able students to watch the clips several times, as required. To save time, film yourself during the lesson itself, and allow the students to replay this.

✓ Use physical resources to make an activity feel more concrete for the less able, and to help students feel more confident about participating. For instance, when working on sorting or division, give your weaker students some blocks or some Lego bricks, so that they can do some hands on practice.

✓ Adapt the format in which you present the learning, so that it works better for your weaker students. For example, when you read a passage of text to the whole class, make a recording as you speak. Allow your less able students to listen to the recording several times, before answering questions on the passage.

✓ Adapt the format in which you ask your students to record their learning. For instance, your weaker students could write directly onto a laptop, they could film or record their ideas, or they could work with a scribe who supports them with their writing.

✓ For students with very poor literacy skills, and for those who currently speak very little English, it is important to find something to create a sense of success. When working with text, cloze procedure activities work well. Take the main text that you will be working with in class, then blank out some of the words. Ask the weakest students to 'fill in the blanks' or (even simpler), provide them with a list of the missing words to cut and paste back into the passage.

Topping and Tailing your Talk

One of the key ways in which you can differentiate for the whole range of students in your class is by using different kinds of talk. You can vary the way you speak when talking with individuals or with small groups. You can also incorporate different kinds of speech into your whole class sessions, by using a variety of words and different grammatical constructions (some simple, some complex).

A useful time to differentiate the way you speak is when giving instructions. As a teacher you will naturally use repetition when setting activities, to aid your students' understanding. Each time you repeat an instruction, rephrase it slightly to introduce more complex vocabulary, sentence structures or ideas. So, you might say 'I want everyone to pick out **five words** in this piece of writing that you think are really good. So, I'm looking for **five key examples of effective vocabulary** in the text that we've been studying.'

With your very able students use more complex vocabulary and speech patterns. With your least able students (or with those who have EAL) simplify your speech, whilst still pushing them slightly beyond where they are at the moment. In addition, challenge your top end students to use more complex language within their speaking, thinking and writing. This encourages them to build their higher order thinking skills.

Consider the following words: notice how they all have very similar meanings, but that to understand and use them correctly requires different levels of thinking skill and understanding:

✓ make notes, highlight, annotate
✓ tell, describe, detail, specify
✓ show, demonstrate, exemplify
✓ tricky, hard, difficult, complex
✓ idea, thought, notion, concept

With older students, you can drop in more complex terms related to a specific subject area, to stretch the students and to build their conceptual understanding. For example, in a novel or a play, the following terms mean almost the same thing:

- ✓ stress, friction, conflict, dramatic tension
- ✓ hidden, suggestion, implication, sub text, nuance

Talk with your students about how language can convey different kinds of meaning in subtle ways. Encourage your most able students to use exactly the right word in exactly the right context. This kind of focus on high quality talk, accurate expression and subtleties of meaning is great for encouraging higher order thinking.

The teacher can also differentiate talk in the classroom through the way that he or she uses questions with the class. Closed questions will help you check for understanding – have the students actually listened to and understood what you have been saying? Open-ended questions, with the opportunities they offer for extended evaluative, creative and lateral thinking, are great for stretching the top end of the class.

The Second T:

Time

The Second T: Time

It is fascinating to play around with time and timings in the classroom, and to explore the different effects this has on your children's learning. You might adapt the amount of time you give different children to complete an activity, with the most able being challenged to finish the task more quickly. You could adapt the moment in time at which you give a particular student a certain activity. For instance, giving some students a task that will appear in the next day's lesson, so that they can get a feel for the material ahead of time. This can work well both for the most able, and also for those who struggle, depending on the nature of the activity.

Hand in hand with the concept of time and timing goes the notion of deadlines. And as you will know from your own working life, there is nothing quite like a deadline to focus the mind and to force you to get on with something. Most people work best under some kind of time pressure, because the need to 'get it done' over-rides any concerns about the quality of what they are producing. By having a short, specific deadline to work towards, you force your students to stop procrastinating or aiming for perfection. If there is very little time available, they simply have to get on with it.

Writers sometimes talk about having an 'internal editor' who sits on your shoulder as you write. This is the voice that says: 'you can't write that' or 'people will think that's rubbish'. By forcing yourself and your students to work under the pressure of time, you silence that inner, negative voice. Encourage your students to get a first attempt down on the page, because they can always go back and improve it once they have a first draft. Indeed, the very act of going back and improving a piece of work is the perfect way to develop editing, reflective and evaluative skills.

Playing with Time

The chance to play with time is a very creative aspect of your role as a teacher. Enjoy a bit of experimentation with this part of your practice: don't worry if sometimes things go wrong, you will learn from that as well. I can still vividly remember being given one minute to do a life drawing in an A Level Art class. The picture was one of the best I produced during the entire two year course, because of the simplicity and focus forced upon me by that time limit.

Here are some ideas about different ways that you can play around with time and timings:

✓ Adapt the amount of time you give different groups of students to complete the same activity. Those groups who were given the shortest time could compare what they achieved within the time.

✓ Set some activities with very short time spans – 30 seconds, one minute, or two minutes at the most. This creates a powerful sense of pace and is a great way to stretch the thinking of the most able and to push the poorly motivated. Set really clear targets within the short time span – ask the students to achieve a certain number of words or ideas, or a specific end product.

✓ Now try doing the same activity, but give your students twice as much time to complete it. Talk together about what happened to their learning, motivation and behaviour. Did they focus more or less? Did they produce more or less? And what about the quality of the ideas that they devised?

- ✓ Ask your students how much time *they* think they need for an activity. Sometimes, give them as much time as they request; other times, ask them to complete the activity in half that amount of time. You could also try giving them double the amount of time, to see what happens.
- ✓ When your students are working on an activity, give them constant reminders about how much time they have left. Use countdowns as the time runs out. Remember, time can be flexible. If you have only given them two minutes, but you quickly realise that they need twice that amount, then simply make the two minutes last for four minutes. No one will complain, I promise.
- ✓ When you have planned ahead to use worksheets or other printed materials, sometimes give them out *before* the lesson in which you are going to use them. Your more able students could complete a worksheet at home and then do a follow up task in class. They could prepare a short starter activity to teach the new skill or concept, or devise a similar worksheet of their own. Your less able children could use the time to get used to the new material, or to look up some of the words that you will be using in a dictionary. Encourage parents to support students in preparing for future lessons, as well as in reinforcing what has already been learned.
- ✓ Give your students a series of activities to complete within a lesson, ones that gradually increase in difficulty. Set the challenge of seeing how far they can get in the lesson time. You could set a target for the amount they must complete, you could get your students to decide on a target for themselves, or you could set this up as a competition to see who completes the most.

✓ Think about how you use the time of the staff members who support the children in your classroom. Do you tend to sit them with one group for a whole lesson? Try asking them to move from group to group, giving about fifteen minutes focused support to each one.

Making Time Concrete

Use both visual and aural methods to make different lengths of time clearer to your students. This will give a sense of energy, pace and focus to the learning. It will help your students learn how to make the best use of time (very helpful for when they are doing exams in the future). It can also help you encourage your students to gradually increase the amount of time they can concentrate on one activity. You can give different amounts of time to different students, or groups of students, by using individualised methods of timing. Put the children in charge of letting you know when 'their' time is up.

Here are some different strategies for making time concrete:

✓ Use a large sand timer when setting whole class activities. When I'm working with large groups I use a fantastic giant yellow plastic PlayM8 timer so that everyone can see how much time is left (goggle PlayM8 to find out more). The fact that it is yellow, and huge, really grabs the attention.

✓ Use smaller sand timers or stop watches to keep individuals on task with their personalised time targets. Those children who struggle to stay on task, or who need constant reassurance, really benefit from the use of a visual timer. Promise to return to check up on the child once the sand runs through the timer.

- ✓ Download a timer or stopwatch onto your interactive whiteboard to use with the class. Allow one of your children to hit 'go' and another to tell the class when it is time to 'stop'.
- ✓ For some kinds of activities, try using short clips of music that give a sense of pace and urgency. For instance, when the students are collecting resources and equipment, or tidying up at the end of a lesson. The 'Mission Impossible' music works very well for urgent tasks.
- ✓ Beat some drumsticks on your desk, or play a slow downwards scale on a keyboard, to give a countdown to your class.

Long Term Activities

Activities that take place over an extended period of time can be very useful for extending and enriching the learning of your students. Set tasks that allow students to extend the amount of time they devote to them, depending on their own personal sense of motivation. Open-ended projects, that can be developed at home as the students wish, are great for allowing the very able to shine. Interestingly, these vaguely defined projects can hook your least well-motivated students as well, because it gives them a chance to work on something that they are really 'into'.

Sometimes allow your students to choose a topic of their own, as well as giving them topics linked to learning in class. Make it clear that there are literally no boundaries to how much time and effort your students can devote to projects outside of school. Encourage them to think outside the box when it comes to how they are going to present their findings or their work. It could be done as a written project, but equally it could be done as a website, a blog, a collage, a sculpture. Keep the parameters very vague to encourage creative thinking.

When you're using long-term projects, suggest to your students that they can return to working on them at any time when they have a spare moment within class. Use this idea as part of the 'top and tail' technique, as something for the students to do if they finish an activity early, or at any spare moments during the day.

As well as playing around with time within your own lessons, consider where it is most valuable for your students to spend *their* time. Perhaps they would benefit from an hour in the library, researching more complex ideas? Or maybe some of your students would learn more if they went to a different, older year group for some subjects or topics? Don't be afraid to take time and stretch it, mould it, bend it, adapt it, to better suit your needs and those of your students.

The Third T:

Targets

The Third T: Targets

Just as timings help your students to focus on reaching a goal, so a well-chosen target will encourage them to aim for a specific objective. Ideally, you want a target that is just slightly difficult for the child to reach. Those students who are really able or well motivated can strive to achieve a high target. Those students who struggle to learn, or those who lack motivation, will also benefit from the careful and considered use of targets. The more personalised the targets, the better they work for differentiated learning. Encourage your students to participate in setting their own targets, and in reviewing the progress they have made towards reaching their goals.

Targets for the Teacher

We all respond well to targets, and that includes the teacher, as well as the students. Use personal targets to encourage yourself to differentiate more effectively for your students.

✓ When you are working out the learning objective for a lesson, consider whether it is (or should be) the same for everyone. If you are completely honest with yourself, have some of your students already achieved the objective you had planned to set? If they have, consider whether they need to revisit it or not, or whether you should be creating a different kind of learning goal for them.

✓ Consider setting several layers of learning objective in your lessons. Have one main objective that you want to ensure everyone achieves, then one or more others that you will try to achieve with the most able students. A good way to define this within your lesson plan is: all must … some may … a few might.

✓ Set yourself the goal of speaking to every single child in your class in every single lesson that you teach. You may be amazed at how difficult this actually is. Make a special effort to talk to those students who normally pass under your radar. Typically you will talk least to those students who are quiet or who never make a fuss. Interestingly, although we often teach to the middle of a class, we tend to talk most to those students at the top or the bottom of the ability range.

✓ If you are struggling to find time to differentiate every lesson, set yourself the target of three lessons a week where you will focus really strongly on creating differentiated learning activities. If you are a primary school teacher, choose a variety of subjects to target for full differentiation each week. If you are a secondary school teacher, focus on a variety of age groups or on different classes within each year group.

✓ Alternatively, nominate one or two students each week, as your 'differentiated learners'. When you plan an activity for the whole class, figure out one way to differentiate the learning so that it will particularly suit these particular learners. Use your mark book to keep a list of the 'differentiated learners' you have already targeted, so that over the course of a term every child gets a chunk of really high quality, personalised learning.

Targets for the Students

The timing techniques discussed previously are useful for creating short-term focus in lessons. Using targets with your students will help them focus both on short and long-term goals. As the teacher you must have a clear vision of what you want to achieve, and you must create a strong motivation within your students to reach those goals. You can create targets for a single activity, for the lesson as a whole, for the week, for the term or indeed, for the year. You can also set targets that encourage higher levels of motivation.

- ✓ At the start of a lesson, explain to your students how they can excel within that lesson. What can they do, say or show you that will make you believe they have really achieved their best?
- ✓ For those students who lack motivation, or who struggle with focus or behaviour, explain how they can prove themselves within the lesson. Again, what can they do, say or show you that will make you believe they are really trying their best?
- ✓ Use really specific targets to push students to work within set boundaries. For example, ask them to write a story with exactly 20 words (not 19 or 21, but exactly 20). Demonstrate your high expectations, by insisting that they meet their goals precisely.
- ✓ Share successful examples of learning with the class, to demonstrate a target towards which the students can work. Go through the example together, identifying the key features that made it a success. For their next activity, ask the students to set themselves one of these key features as a target. One useful way to find these sample pieces, that show specific skills, is to dig out some of your own exercise books or essays from when you were younger. Alternatively, I also like to write my own examples to use with students, so that they match the children's learning needs exactly.

- ✓ Celebrate difference within your class, making it clear that we all have strengths and weaknesses, and that everyone is of equal value to you. Praise those children whose strengths lie in non-academic areas: those who are kind, or good friends, or who always cheer everyone up.
- ✓ Create a 'Star of the Week' award in a variety of different categories, not just in the academic fields. Your stars could include: the hardest worker, the most creative student, the student who has been the best friend to others, the student who has taken the most risks in their learning, and so on. You could create an 'X Factor' style learning display on which you include photos of your stars of the week. You could also involve your children in voting on who should win some of the awards.
- ✓ Use targets to control noise within your lessons. Set a target for the appropriate level of noise during each activity. Ask a student to be 'noise monitor', and to decide whether the class met your target. It can work well to choose a student who is normally very noisy to make this decision. This will encourage him or her to think about how noise impacts on the learning of the rest of the class.
- ✓ When you use praise, make it very specific. What exactly did the student do well? What previously agreed target did they achieve? Be fairly tricky to please, depending on your knowledge of the individual child. Ensure that praise keeps its value as a currency by having high expectations, and by making praise difficult to earn.
- ✓ Set a topic-based project, and ask the students to create their own targets for what they will do in each lesson when working on the project. Towards the end of the lesson, ask them to reflect on whether they met the target they set themselves, and if not, to think about why

not. What could they do in future to make sure they achieve their targets?

✓ Set a variety of targets for assessment, depending on what you know about an individual child's strengths and weaknesses. Then, when you come to mark, focus on these differing targets to see what has been achieved. For instance, some students might be set a target to do with the layout of the activity, other students might be asked to focus on using punctuation correctly, others on taking risks with their ideas and their learning.

Personalised Target Setting

Find the time to get your students to create personalised targets, preferably at the start of term. Where possible, involve parents and carers in the target setting process as well. This strategy is so valuable that it is worth putting aside any concerns about how much time it might take out of lessons. Indeed, some schools set aside a full day for teachers to meet one-on-one with their students, to review progress and set targets for the future. If it is not possible for you to give over the time to do this, ask your students to work out their personalised targets at home with their parents' help.

To create personalised targets, encourage your students to think about and analyse their strengths and weaknesses. What do they do well right now? Where is there room for improvement? Get the students to be as specific as possible about the ways in which they will meet their goals, by setting themselves specific aims. For instance, if a student's goal is to 'make my writing look neater', their specific aims might be 'remember to always underline the title and date' and 'make the tops of my T's a bit taller'. Refer to the targets set frequently in class, and when you are assessing your students' learning. Look back at the targets together at the end of each term, to see how much progress each student has made.

The Fourth T:

Teamwork

The Fourth T: Teamwork

The ideal classroom situation is for the teacher and the students to work together to achieve their best, creating an ethos of cooperation within the 'whole class team'. Of course this is very hard to achieve, but it is certainly a great aim for which to strive. When you achieve an ethos of teamwork, the children support and help each other, you support and help each of them, and they help you out too when you need. You get to know each student as an individual, and gradually differentiation becomes embedded within your classroom practice. The learning environment and classroom atmosphere supports the learning of every child.

As well as your whole class team, you can also use smaller teams (i.e. groups) to help you differentiate more effectively. Working within a small group format is brilliant for differentiating learning, because the group members can support and boost each other's learning. In a group we can talk through our thoughts with others, share our difficulties, pool our resources, bounce ideas off each other and build on the thinking of the group. People generally feel a lot more relaxed when learning in a group, than they do when working individually. There are lots of ideas for using different kinds of groupings towards the end of this section.

Creating a Team Feeling

You can use a variety of techniques to create this vital team feeling within your classroom. The day-to-day language you use with your students is particularly important. When you talk with your students use 'we', 'us' and 'our' rather than 'I', 'you' and 'your'. Make it clear that everything you do is aimed at improving the students' chances of success. The approaches you use are for everyone's benefit.

Encourage your students to take individual responsibility for the learning of the whole class team, whenever and wherever possible. Encourage the students to give you feedback on their own learning, and on how effectively you are pitching the lessons. Make sure your students feel confident enough to let you know if an activity was too easy or too hard. Encourage them to give you feedback about which teaching techniques helped them learn most effectively.

Refuse point blank to allow students to be disparaging to each other. Jump on every single example of negative or uncooperative attitudes. This is tough going at first, but if you persist, it will make a difference. Make it clear that you view peer-to-peer negativity as being just as bad as if a student was rude to you. Maintain the same standards for how the students treat each other, as for how they treat you.

I met a primary school teacher once who had been warned that her new class were renowned as being extremely uncooperative. Before the school year began, she had a 'Team Year 5' t-shirt made at a t-shirt printing shop. She framed it and put it up on her classroom wall. In their first lesson together, she emphasised that they were all part of 'Team Year 5'. Her assumption was that everyone would work together to create success for all members of the class team. What a brilliant example of teacher creativity!

Create a learning and behaviour contract together with your class, or put the students in charge of doing this themselves. Ask all your students to literally 'sign up' to the contract, by signing their names on the paper. Give them each a copy to take home, and laminate a copy to go on your classroom wall. When your students break one of the terms of the class contract, show them their signature as proof that they have all signed up to the deal.

Getting to Know You

In order to differentiate successfully for your class team, you must get to know your students. And that means not just gaining an understanding of their academic abilities, but also genuinely getting to know them as individuals. For the primary school teacher, with only 30 or so children in his or her class, this should be reasonably simple given a bit of time. For the secondary school teacher who works with lots of different classes, it is harder to truly know each individual student. Extra curricular activities can be a great help, because you get to know students on a more personal level when you meet them outside of lessons.

It is tempting to believe that the best way to get to know more about your students, and their varying levels of ability, is to set them a test. Certainly, a formalised assessment or levelling system is useful in gauging what a child already knows or has remembered. However, a test will not tell you much about a child's levels of motivation. Often, it will not actually tell you much about a child's deeper understanding of a subject. Typically, the results of a test will mainly tell you who is good at taking tests.

It could be that the child who only answered half the questions in an assessment is actually your most gifted student. Perhaps that poor mark is telling you that he is completely switched off by school and by learning. Perhaps that poor mark is telling you that he freezes in exam style situations. Perhaps that poor mark is telling you that he misinterpreted the questions, or indeed that you wrote the questions in an ambiguous way that could easily be misunderstood.

In every single moment of every single lesson you have a chance informally to assess and to get to know your students. This is what the very best teachers do (often in a completely instinctive and perhaps subconscious way). As you ask a child a question, watch for hesitation and uncertainty in his answer, or for an answer that shows a particularly intelligent take on a subject. Notice who puts their hands up to answer (showing understanding, confidence or at the very least motivation), and who very rarely steps forwards. Gain a sense of each child as an individual, as far as you possibly can.

To a large extent, all the data in the world is no substitute for your gut instinct and your 'sense' of where a child is at currently. (You may prefer to call it your 'professional judgement' when talking to managers or inspectors). I can usually tell by looking at a student's face and body language whether he is engaged and interested in what I am teaching. This is not something you can tell through a formal assessment, or through sheets filled with data. Teaching is an art form as well as a science.

To boost your knowledge of your students:

✓ View every single interaction as a chance to get to know the student as an individual, and where they are currently with their learning. This includes when you are talking to them one to one, when you are marking their work, when you are doing a whole class Q&A session, and so on and on.

✓ Find out about your students' interests, their likes and dislikes, the hobbies they have at home, their favourite television programmes, what games they enjoy. Take an interest in the answers they give you, and sometimes adapt the learning to take account of what you find out.

✓ Set an activity early on, which gives you a 'feel' for what these young people are like. For instance, if they were marooned on a desert island, what five objects would they take with them and why? Ask younger children to bring in a favourite toy for a 'show and tell' session, then look at what they brought in, and figure out what that tells you about them.

✓ Use a learning preferences questionnaire to find out more about your students. Take account of what you discover by incorporating a wide range of teaching and learning approaches. The more of a mixed bag of activities you use, the more likely you are to 'click' with each individual student.

✓ When using more formalised assessments, remember to assess your students' oral abilities, their levels of creativity, their willingness to work well in a group, and other skills, as well as their academic achievements.

✓ Use formal assessments towards the end of a topic or a term, to see what the students have actually retained and understood. Sometimes, tell them *not* to revise for an assessment, so that you can figure out what has stuck properly, and what they don't yet fully understand.

✓ Hold a series of student/teacher conferences, so that you can talk to your students one on one. If you struggle to find time to do this, you could set a long-term project in order to free up some time within lessons.

✓ Use samples of a student's work to figure out their strengths and weaknesses. As soon as you know which class or classes you will be teaching, ask the students' previous teachers for samples of their work. You could ask the students themselves to show you two examples of their learning from the previous year: one that shows a particular strength, another that shows a specific weakness that they would like to overcome.

✓ Use observations to help you figure out where your students are now, and where they need to go next in their learning. Use both whole class observations, and also observations of individual students. Sometimes, when you set the whole class off on an activity, give yourself permission *not* to go round to help individuals. Instead step to one side for a while and watch how different individuals are working.

✓ Do a detailed observation of one particular child, to identify the 'next steps' in learning that are required. This is an approach now used very widely in early years settings. During your observation, focus on aspects such as the child's concentration levels, motivation and language use, as well as on the subject specific skills they are demonstrating.

Group Work and Differentiation

Group work offers a fantastic format for differentiating learning. Consider for a moment what happens when you work or learn within a group: sharing ideas, building on one another's thinking, taking on different roles, helping those who are struggling. Whereas an individual activity is just that – if the individual can do it, great, but if he or she cannot, help will probably end up coming from the teacher. And the teacher has 30 or more individuals to help.

When you use a group format for differentiated learning, you need to manage it carefully, to maximise the benefits. Firstly, it sounds obvious but do make sure that it is actually a group activity rather than just an activity being done while sitting in groups. Choose group activities that require all members to make an individual contribution, in order to be successful.

Think carefully, ahead of time, about which students should go in which groups. Sometimes you will want to group by ability, particularly when you are setting different tasks for different groups. At other times, you may want to mix abilities within groups, perhaps specifying different roles for different group members, or allowing the children to mix and match the roles as they wish. At other times, you may wish to use a random method of grouping.

Here are some different grouping strategies that will help you differentiate learning:

✓ **The 'Text Team':** The students are grouped according to their reading level, with different texts being given to each team.

✓ **The 'Think Tank':** The students are assigned different roles within the team, either by the teacher, by a vote within the group, or by a process of self-nomination. The roles that the students take on could include: ideas person, resource gatherer, chair person, timer, and so on. If you are working with young children, try giving the different roles an animal 'character' to help the students understand the requirements of the role. For instance 'The Owl' is wise, and so makes a good chair person. 'The Squirrel' is great at gathering things together, and so is the perfect resources person.

✓ **The 'Focus Group':** The students are given a specific focus for the learning that is going to take place in their group. For instance, you could use Edward de Bono's 'Thinking Hats' approach, with one group wearing the white hat and looking for facts, while another group wears the green hat and takes a more creative approach.

✓ **The 'Expert Groups':** The teacher divides up a topic into various areas, and gives each group one area on which to focus or to research. The individual groups summarise and teach what they have learned to the class.

✓ **The 'Jigsaw Groups':** The activity is split up into parts, and the children within the group each get one part on which to focus. They share their ideas with the children in the other groups, who are focusing on that same part. The children then create the 'jigsaw' – the overview of the topic – created by slotting the pieces together.

✓ **The 'Teacher Talkers':** One group receives additional teacher talk time. Sometimes this is the lowest ability group, but other times it is a top or middling group that gets the extra input.

✓ **The 'Self Chosen' Groups:** The teacher identifies four aspects of a topic to be covered, or alternatively gives four problems or questions for the class to explore. The teacher allocates one corner of the classroom for each aspect of the topic. The students then move into the appropriate corner of the room, depending on which aspect, problem or question they wish to cover.

Sometimes it works well to use random methods to create groups. You might number the children around the room, putting all students with the same number together in a group. But on a more creative note, you could hand out playing cards or give out pictures (animals, famous people) to denote groups.

The Fifth T:

Thinking Skills

The Fifth T: Thinking Skills

In order to differentiate effectively, you need to use your thinking skills to their maximum. You must plan the learning so that all your students can access it at the most appropriate level. This means using lots of creativity and lateral thinking, because you're going to have to come at the 'problem' of differentiation from many different angles. You will want to encourage your students to use their thinking skills to the maximum as well, during your wonderfully well thought out lessons.

Sometimes lessons are about learning new facts, remembering facts learned previously, practising old skills or picking up new ones. In these lessons, the children will be using mainly lower order thinking skills. Some children will be able to access the activities easily, or will already understand the content of the lesson, while others may struggle to 'get it' at all. When the children are using mainly lower order thinking skills within a lesson, you have to do the higher order thinking yourself to differentiate the tasks for your different learners.

Where you plan lessons that encourage the use of higher order thinking skills, the students can access and complete the activities at a variety of different levels of complexity. In other words, your students will naturally differentiate many higher order activities by virtue of their own approach to those activities. Higher order thinking skills include lateral and creative thinking, theorising, deduction, evaluation, reflection, and so on. These higher order skills are about using and applying knowledge and skills in new contexts or situations. Often, it is possible to mix in plenty of opportunities for higher order thinking within what might otherwise be a fairly mundane lesson.

A great way to incorporate higher order thinking skills is to use lots of cross curricular links and connections within your lessons. Challenge your own thinking by using approaches that would not normally be seen together within a particular subject. For example, you could link art with maths by using a sculpture activity with your students. You could link English with science by getting the children to write a postcard from space to tell someone facts about the Universe.

Practical Activities for Higher Order Thinking

Higher order thinking is about encouraging your students to apply the knowledge or skills they already have in a variety of contexts and situations. It is about *actively* thinking and learning, rather than *passively* learning from the teacher. When the students understand *what* they are learning, *why* they are learning it, and they have some measure of choice in *how* they learn it, they are far more likely to engage their higher order thinking skills.

To help your students develop their higher order thinking, and to differentiate more effectively, try the following approaches:

✓ When you start a new topic, ask your students to list the questions they would like answered during your programme of study. They could list their questions on sticky notes, which you display on the wall. They could then add further sticky notes with answers on them, as you learn more about the new topic and their questions are answered.

✓ Take an abstract concept (metaphor, forces, place value, photosynthesis, climate change) and make it as concrete as possible, so that it is accessible for all your students.

41

For instance, when studying how plants grow, get your class to dig an area in the school grounds and plant some seeds. By exploring the concept in a real life situation, the students can apply the ideas that they are learning.

✓ At the end of a day or a lesson, ask the students to decide on the three most important things that they have learned. Once they have decided what their three things are, they should rank them in order of importance, and say *why* they chose to rank them in this way.

✓ Encourage your students to cross-pollinate their learning between different subjects and formats. The ability to reframe one thing (e.g. a painting) as something else (e.g. a piece of music) requires your students to use their creative and lateral thinking.

Choice and Thinking Skills

At appropriate times, give your students an element of choice in their own learning. Encourage them to consider how they prefer to learn, and also how they personally learn best. You can offer your students choices about what, how, when and where they wish to learn. By offering choices, you ask the students to play their part in differentiating learning. It is valuable to offer choices around learning because:

✓ It helps your children to build the skill of 'metacognition' – the ability to think about their own thinking.

✓ It encourages them to use their higher order thinking skills, as they analyse and evaluate their preferred approaches to learning.

✓ It can be helpful for increasing motivation, as we all like to have a measure of control over what happens to us.

Of course, complete freedom of choice is not necessarily a good thing: I am sure we all know at least one student who would 'choose' to sit and do nothing all day. Choice needs to be managed by the teacher in response to what he or she knows about the students. Generally speaking, schools have a habit of keeping the control in the hands of the adults, rather than handing it over to the children. However, now that knowledge and ideas are so freely available online, we need to help our children learn how to manage choice, and how to make good decisions.

At first, try offering a fairly limited range of choices, keeping a measure of overall control. Gradually increase the options as your students get used to the idea of making good choices. Set clear targets around the choices, so that the students have a goal for which to aim. Keep your expectations high for all, not just for the most able. Use a variety of activities to make up your different choices, so that you appeal to every student in the class.

To incorporate more choice into your classroom, you could:

✓ Offer a number of different formats in which a task can be completed – as a report, as a poster, as an essay, as a letter, as a blog entry, and so on.
✓ Give a choice of resources with which to work: books, magazines, pamphlets, websites, newspapers, podcasts, films, and so on.
✓ Use a visual system to show the different levels of complexity of each task. Ask your students to think about which level of difficulty best meets their learning needs. Red equals a hard task, amber equals a medium level of difficulty, and green is an easy task. Challenge all students to choose at least one 'red' task to complete

during the lesson; the most able students could be challenged to choose two.

✓ Offer choices about how students will learn about a topic area. For example, they could choose the order in which they learn the various parts of the topic. They could also choose the area of the topic that they would like to study in the most detail.

✓ Use a 'work stations' approach, setting up several different activities within your classroom. The students could choose from these as they wish, spending as much time as they want at each particular work station. Alternatively you could give the students a specific target to achieve, for instance, to visit at least three work stations during the lesson. Interestingly, this mirrors how learning takes place within the foundation stage (or early years) curriculum. In the preschool years, children are given a choice from a range of activities (or 'continuous provision'), set up by the teacher or practitioner in response to what he or she knows about the children.

How to Encourage Risk Taking

The ability to take risks is a key aspect in certain types of higher order thinking – particularly within imaginative, creative and lateral thinking, but also when extending logical and critical ideas. Indeed, we need to take risks to learn anything new, because we can never be good at something without getting it wrong lots of times first. You need to encourage your students to see mistakes as a way to learn, rather than as something to be avoided.

Some students get hung up on making sure that every finished piece of work looks neat and pretty, sometimes to the detriment of its content. Interestingly, this is often a problem faced by able students who are striving for perfection. Other students may find it really hard to get going on an activity, for fear of whether they will do it well enough. Typically, those students with poor motivation, or those with weak skills will struggle to get started. When your students are constantly concerned about what others will think about their work, this stifles the opportunities for extending thinking and learning.

Help your children learn to take risks in their learning and their thinking (and take lots of risks yourself as well to model the process). To do this:

✓ Use activities that are about the process, and not about the end product. For instance, set the class a quick piece of writing to generate ideas and then do something completely unexpected with it. The students might edit it until it has half the original number of words, they could turn it into a paper aeroplane to share ideas around the class, they might scrunch it up into a snowball and have an 'ideas snowball fight', or they could just throw it away without showing anyone what they have written.

✓ Don't see ideas as the 'property' of one person – encourage your students to pass them around the class, sharing them freely amongst each other. You can do this easily with sticky notes.

✓ Encourage your students to share, to add to and to build on the ideas of others. Split the class into groups and give each group a large sheet of paper (A1 size) with a different question or challenge at the top of each one. Give the class a short time target of about three minutes per question. During that time they must list their thoughts or ideas at the top of the paper. At the end of the time they should fold over the paper so that their ideas are hidden, then pass the paper on to the next group. Repeat the process until each sheet of paper returns to its original starting point. Now open out the sheets to see what everyone has written.

✓ Show yourself doing something badly, in front of your class. Let your students see you taking risks, failing, but still trying again. Choose an activity that you cannot do very well yourself, for instance, juggling. Ask your students whether any of them can do it better than you. Help them understand that, in order to get better at any skill, we first have to do it badly.

✓ Celebrate risk, and failure, by praising the willingness to make mistakes in front of your class. Make it clear that you prefer to see a child trying, and getting something wrong, than not trying at all.

✓ Encourage an independent mindset in your students by using the 'Three before Me' approach. With this technique you insist that your students try at least three approaches to answer a question or deal with a problem before they ask you for help. The approaches they choose might include: to think again, to ask a friend, to consult a book, to look online. Have a poster on your classroom wall to remind the children to try 'Three Before Me'.

Thinking Skills for the Teacher

A key part of your skill as a teacher is to think about how different tasks and activities work for your learners, and the kind of conceptual knowledge, skills and understanding they need to complete those tasks. You must then set a task that is *just a little bit too difficult* for their current level of skill or understanding, and support them in achieving that step forwards.

One of the most exciting and interesting aspects of the teacher's job is the creativity you have to use to plan for learning. Your skill allows you to take a complex, abstract idea and bring it to life for your students, at a level and in a way that all of them can access. You are responsible for motivating them to learn, and for encouraging them to see learning as a creative, exciting and ongoing process.

When you make learning concrete and based in reality, it is easier for your less able students to access. Where the learning is abstract and theoretical, this stretches the thinking of your most able students. It works well to begin by teaching a concept through a concrete, hands-on activity, and then gradually moving it into a more abstracted and theoretical form.

For example, I once watched a brilliant science lesson, in which the teacher introduced Newton's Third Law. First, he asked a child to stand on a skateboard, and challenged the rest of the class to move the child without touching him. The other children eventually figured out that what they needed to do was to ask their classmate to swing his arms, thus creating a force. By giving the child a weight, the teacher showed how the child would move even further. The class moved on to firing some water-powered rockets in the playground, to see what they could observe. Finally, they learned about the scientific theory behind what had been going on, and wrote down the details in their books.

One of the most vital higher order thinking skills that the teacher can use is the ability to think in a linked up way. This might take the form of linking various subject areas together, to teach a new skill or concept. It might also be about the creative thinking that the teacher does during the planning stage, and how he or she links a resource to some learning, or ideas in different subjects together.

For Instance …

Imagine that the learning objective in a Geography lesson is: *To learn the names of the continents and to ensure that the children can label them accurately on a world map.*

A lower order thinking skills approach to this task might involve the teacher explaining what each continent is called, writing the names of the continents up on the board, then asking the students to write the names onto a map. Those who finish early could be asked to colour in their maps. Some children will find this task easy to complete, will remember the names easily or may know them already. Other children will struggle to do much beyond labelling their maps by copying from the board, and are unlikely to retain the information.

Here are some possibilities for higher order thinking approaches to this particular learning objective. Some of these ideas are realistic for use in the classroom. Others show you what happens when the teacher really sets his or her creative thinking to work:

✓ Split the class up into groups, and assign a different continent to each group. The groups should then (a) research the animals, habitats and cultures of their continent, (b) come up with a way to memorise the name and location of the continent (c) prepare a short presentation about their continent to teach to the rest of the class and (d) create a three dimensional map of their continent, to include objects, photos, collage, painting, video, and so on. All this information could then be shared in a 'work stations' lesson, where the children 'visit' the other continents.

✓ Get the children to work together to create a giant map of the world in the playground using outdoor chalks. The children could then play a version of 'Port/Starboard' in which they must run to the correct continent when the teacher (or a student) calls out the name.

✓ Create a slideshow of photos from the different continents on your interactive whiteboard. As each image shows, the children must call out the name of the continent where that photo was taken, or click the correct button on their student response pads.

✓ Find partner schools in each continent through an online penpal website. Get the children to write emails to children in those continents, asking them for information about the places where they live.

✓ And finally, an imaginative approach that will obviously be beyond the average school budget (but we can dream). Split the class up into groups and book a flight for each group to visit one of the continents. Each group is tasked with taking photos, making a film, and living for a week, in their continent. When they arrive back at school, they share what they have learned with the rest of the class.

Thinking Skills in the Plenary

The plenary, or final section of the lesson, is a great time to develop your students' thinking skills. You can use this part of the lesson to check the understanding of the weakest students, and to stretch the most able. The evaluative and reflective discussions that take part towards the end of a lesson are ideal for boosting higher order thinking. Here are some ideas for differentiated learning in the plenary:

✓ Write 3 top tips for approaching the activity you have just done, or for learning the skill you have just learned, to share with the other students in the class. Alternatively, write 3 top tips for how a younger student could learn this skill, and test them out on a class lower down the school.

✓ Get the students to write questions they would like answered on sticky notes at the start of the lesson. At the end of the lesson go through these questions and check whether the students have their answers. Alternatively, pass the question sticky notes around the class, and ask the students to write an answer to someone else's question on the back.

✓ The students write definitions for three key terms that they have learned in the lesson. Give your most able students the hardest words to define.

✓ Show some anonymous samples of work on your interactive whiteboard. Get the students to grade it, saying whether it is good, average or weak and why they believe this.

✓ Ask an able student, or a group of students, to summarise the lesson, rather than doing it yourself.

✓ Get the students to leave the piece of work they have done in the lesson face up on their desks. The students can then set off on a 'great work' hunt around the room. When they see an example of 'great work' they should record it by taking a photo, by making a note or by putting a sticker on it. They could then report back about what they found to the rest of their group.

✓ Ask the students to predict what you are going to be learning in the next lesson, justifying the ideas that they give. Why do they think you are going to move onto this area next? Hopefully they won't say 'because it's on the next page in the text book'.

The Sixth T:

Things

The Sixth T: Things

Things, or to use the more technical sounding term 'resources', are a great way to differentiate for your students. The umbrella term 'resources' can of course include a host of different kinds of things. It could mean a source of additional support and help, such as a teaching assistant or a visual dictionary. Equally, it could mean something used to inspire and motivate the students, such as a fascinating object or a really interesting text.

The best resources for differentiation (and generally, for high quality teaching and learning) are those which:

✓ trigger the students to use their higher order thinking skills;

✓ encourage the teacher to use his or her higher order thinking skills;

✓ create a sense of interest and curiosity within the students;

✓ relate to the experiences and interests of the teacher/students;

✓ bring a sense of the real world into the classroom;

✓ offer the children a multi sensory experience;

✓ originate with the students sometimes, as well as with the teacher;

✓ are big, colourful, unusual, fun or weird;

✓ are something you would not normally expect to see in the classroom.

People as a Resource

People are a fantastic resource for differentiation: visitors and experts brought in from outside, the students that you have within your class, children from other classes, and of course you and the staff who work with you. Perhaps the very best use of the teacher as a resource is the one to one time he or she can dedicate to an individual child or a small group. You have probably noticed how much your students love it when you give them individual attention.

To use people as a resource for differentiation:

✓ Use your students as 'experts' on a subject, topic or theme. By asking a child to act as an expert you can really motivate those students who lack engagement. The student's expertise does not have to be academic or even school based. The child might be an expert on a favourite pastime from outside school (playing computer games, fly fishing, chess, karate, camping, etc.).

✓ Encourage students to bring their own texts, research materials and resources into the classroom to use within lessons. There is something very special for a child about having 'their' stuff in the school environment.

✓ Ask your students to reflect on their own experiences, and on things that have happened to them. By grounding the learning in their personal experiences, your students are far more likely to retain it.

✓ Make sure you ask your teaching assistant to work with the most able, as well as with the least able and those with difficult behaviour. Use your expertise as a teacher to work with individuals who are struggling – you are the most highly qualified person in the room, so place a high value on your own time.

✓ Ask able, confident students to act as teachers for the others, for instance by teaching part of the lesson, or by pairing up with a weak student once they have finished their own work.

✓ Use resources to find out more about your students. Ask each of your students to bring in one object or item that says something about them as an individual. Use the information you glean from looking at their objects to figure out how best to differentiate for them.

Objects as a Resource

I am a huge fan of objects in the classroom – especially objects that your students didn't expect to see when they came into school that day. Objects inspire both the teacher and the students to think creatively. Objects can support learning for the least able, or boost those students who struggle to get motivated. They can extend the thinking of the most able students, by encouraging them to make links, to think creatively, to observe in detail or to look in a fresh way. Objects can also engage and enthuse your whole class, as a starting point for learning something new. Encourage a variety of responses to the objects you bring into your classroom, so that every learner gets something out of interacting with them.

Take a simple resource – a cardboard box, for instance – and ask your students where they want to go with it. How do they want to use it? What might they turn it into? How could they reinvent or re-imagine it? The creative and lateral thinking involved in these decisions is brilliant for boosting the learning and confidence of your students. Now take that same cardboard box, and figure out how you might incorporate it into a lesson. What could you put inside it? What could you ask your students to build from it? Thinking creatively about a simple resource is a brilliant way to build your imagination powers.

Here are some more examples of different objects, and how you might use them in a differentiated way in your classroom:

Clothes: The students are given a selection of scarves, bags and hats and are asked to choose words to describe them (textures, colours, how they are worn, what materials they are made from). The students are given a choice of activities, graded by difficulty, and asked to complete at least three activities during the lesson. A simple task could be to write a list of words and definitions to describe the clothes. The children could choose whether they need to use a dictionary to complete this task. A more complicated task could be to write the script for a fashion show, in which these new designs are being presented.

Natural objects: The teacher hands out some pine cones in a maths lesson and asks the students to look at them closely, to see what patterns and numbers they can observe. Some able groups of students are asked to go online, to find out more about Fibonacci numbers in nature, and to report their findings to the class at the end of the lesson. Other groups are asked to go out into the school garden and bring back samples of flowers and seed heads. They are asked to count the number sequences and draw pictures to show the spirals within these natural objects.

Objects to inspire curiosity: The students come into class to discover that someone has left behind a padlocked treasure chest. On the treasure chest is a large handwritten sign saying 'Do Not Open'. There is no sign of a key. This activity could go in a variety of different directions. Some children could write a letter to the pirate who owns the chest, trying to persuade him to open it. Other children could write a description of what they think is inside. Others could draw a treasure map, showing where the chest was buried.

Texts as a Resource

When you're exploring ways to differentiate for your students, look at the variety of texts that are available to you and think creatively about how they might be used. Consider how the different types of texts might suit your different learners and their differing ways of learning. Make sure the reading age of the texts you use matches the needs of your students.

What kinds of text might motivate your children best? Have a look at the following list, and think about some individual students in your class. Which texts would appeal most to which children?

- ✓ Magazines
- ✓ Newspapers
- ✓ Comics
- ✓ Non-fiction
- ✓ Pamphlets/Booklets
- ✓ Manuals
- ✓ Novels
- ✓ Short stories
- ✓ Online texts – encyclopaedias, blogs, websites, tweets, etc.
- ✓ Snippets and scraps of text, including sticky notes
- ✓ Lists
- ✓ Letters
- ✓ Diaries
- ✓ Text messages
- ✓ Postcards

When you are considering how to teach a theme or topic, think widely about the variety of texts you might be able to use. Ensure a good mixture of texts, including some with pictures, graphics and diagrams to appeal to those who prefer a visual way of learning. Offer your most able students the chance to research and study deeply by giving them access to more complex texts.

When working with text in class, you can differentiate by making some simple adaptations to the text itself:

✓ Ask able students to work with a long, unedited piece of text (or the whole story/novel/play/research journal), while other students focus on a shorter extract. This allows the most able students to look at extracts in their wider context, for instance developing their thinking about linked themes within a novel.

✓ Encourage avid readers to read widely – give them a list of a range of texts by the author you are studying in class. Let them and their parents know about other similar books that they might like to read at home.

✓ Use detailed writing frames for those students who struggle, whilst asking your most able students to help prepare writing frames for the rest of the class.

✓ Adapt the vocabulary on any worksheets that you use. Use complex words, phrasing and grammar for the most able; use text boxes, graphics and simpler language for those who struggle with literacy.

✓ Challenge the students to learn and use complicated technical terms within different subjects – for instance, 'pathetic fallacy' and 'dramatic irony' in English lessons.

✓ Offer key word banks, lists of words and laminated word cards, both to support understanding at the bottom end, and also to stretch thinking at the top end.

Self-created texts

Give your students lots of chances to create texts of their own. These self-created texts can be used to support differentiated learning within lessons. For instance, you could get your students to make their own word books or dictionaries as they come across new vocabulary. When you are whole class teaching, give the students mini whiteboards on which to make notes or try examples or show their thinking. Ask the whole class to show you an answer on their mini whiteboards, so that you can check for understanding.

Create a class blog, so that your students get used to having a real audience for their writing. Students could take on a variety of differentiated roles in updating the blog, according to their learning needs. Some could write blog entries, others could take photos and upload them, others could respond to comments left on their blog. Mix and match the roles so that everyone gets a chance to develop different skills.

As well as encouraging your students to create texts, consider when it would be useful for you to create texts of your own. By doing this, you can tailor the texts so that they match exactly the learning you want the students to accomplish. For instance, when doing a session on writing for different audiences recently, I wanted some small snippets of texts written for different audiences, but around the same topic. So, I went ahead and wrote my own. I like to create my own texts, because then I can get them to match exactly the learning objectives I have planned for the class.

The Seventh T:

Technology

The Seventh T: Technology

In recent years, new technologies have opened up a whole new world of possibilities for differentiated learning. Technology offers us a real chance to match the learning more closely to the child, because it allows for a high degree of personalisation and interactivity. However, we must use technology with great care. Certainly, it is not as simple as sticking a child in front of a computer and saying 'get on with it'.

In many ways, we are still feeling our way in terms of getting the very best differentiated learning out of the internet, digital cameras, interactive whiteboards, and so on. You need to apply your skill as a teacher when thinking about how to use technology in a way that works well for your students. Above all, we should not lose sight of the fact that it is the flesh and blood teacher who has to decide *how* to use the technology. It is the teacher who can inspire his or her students to learn and to achieve their very best.

In terms of meeting the learning needs of all children, new technologies allow even those children with very significant special needs to access education. These 'assistive technologies' allow us truly to differentiate for those children who would otherwise struggle in a mainstream classroom environment. For instance, children with severe communication disabilities can now communicate using a specially adapted computer.

Some of the many ways in which technology can help us to differentiate include:

✓ **Laptops and tablets:** By using laptops/tablets, the teacher can let the students work at their own pace, using a variety of software programmes or apps.

Students (particularly those who struggle with literacy) are often very well motivated by the chance to work on a computer.

✓ **Educational websites:** Many internet sites use animations, which are typically very appealing to your less able students. Similarly, many online games allow children to learn in a hands-on, visual and interactive way.

✓ **Online teaching programmes:** These programmes allow the children to learn and practice skills at their own pace, thus offering a very personalised method for learning. The teacher is given instant feedback on how well the children understand the activities they have been doing. You can incorporate personalised targets, to boost the individual student's motivation to move onwards through the programme.

✓ **World education games:** Your children can now go online to compete with school children from right across the world, in the 'World Education Games'. Challenge your students to see how they fare against others from around the globe.

✓ **An interactive whiteboard:** An interactive whiteboard allows you to differentiate for those children who learn in a hands-on way, and it is also helpful for those children who struggle to pay attention. Get your kinaesthetic learners up to the front to manipulate objects or ideas on the board. Boost the confidence of your shy children in front of their peers, by choosing them as volunteers to use the board.

✓ **Video/audio clips and podcasts:** You can boost differentiation through the use of online video clips, videos you make yourself, audio clips, and podcasts. You might offer children reinforcement of the learning, through letting them view a video clip or listen to a podcast on a subject. You could film yourself introducing a starter activity, and then play it back to the class, as a great way to help you engage and motivate your students. You might film or record yourself giving feedback on a piece of work, rather than writing your comments. In fact, this is a useful tip when you need to give detailed feedback, because it makes the process of marking much faster.

✓ **Recording devices:** You can offer your children the chance to record their learning using a recordable microphone or other recording device. For younger students, you might add 'talk buttons' to a display, to aid understanding. These are small buttons that allow you to record a short clip of sound, which can be stuck onto a display or in an area of your classroom.

✓ **Student response systems:** With these systems, the students respond to questions posed by the teacher, using a remote controlled clicker. (Think 'Ask the Audience' in the TV programme 'Who Wants to Be a Millionaire?'). The questions might take the form of a vote on a topic, or a quiz to check for understanding. These systems are useful for differentiation, because they help you work out whether your teaching has reached every student in the class. You can use them to gauge the students' level of interest in a subject or topic area. In addition, they appeal particularly to students who like an interactive approach to learning. And finally, they encourage your quieter students to get involved, without having to speak out loud in front of the class.

✓ **Moodle/Virtual Learning Environments:** Using a moodle or VLE, both teachers and students can upload examples of work, share ideas and information, take online courses, and so on.

When you are using technology, make sure that you hand over the reins to the students as often as you can. Typically, they will be more adept at using most types of technology than you are.

Graphics and Differentiation

Many of the new technologies developed in the last twenty or so years support a very visual way of learning, which chimes well with many modern learners. For those students who struggle to work with text, digital images can be a good way to put across their ideas.

✓ Encourage your students to use photos as a way to present their learning. For instance, taking photos of the steps in a science experiment.
✓ Use comic strips as a way into literacy, particularly for the less able. Your students could both read and write comic strips to help them learn.
✓ Get the students to post photos of their work on your class blog, or on your school website.
✓ et homework activities that involve taking photos, or creating other images using different kinds of technology. Older students might use a programme such as Photoshop to manipulate the images they take.
✓ Take photos of good examples of learning – extracts of writing, paintings, sculptures, experiments – and share them with the children.
✓ Show your students a close up photograph of an object, a place or an animal. Ask your students to figure out what it is.

✓ Ask your able students to critically analyse photos and images, to develop their higher order thinking skills. What does the image 'tell' the viewer? Are there hidden messages within the photo that they can 'read' in a metaphorical way?

✓ Use photographs to inspire creative thinking, for instance asking the children to imagine stepping into the photo and turning right – what do they see?

✓ QR codes are a fairly new introduction in the world of technology. These codes are basically barcodes with information. When they are scanned with a smart phone or a table, they reveal added details such as websites, text, pictures, contact details, and so on. You could post QR codes around the school, and send your students on a hunt for information. You could also use a QR code to give extra support, so that a child who needs help scans the code to access additional resources.

Of course, as well as technology offering a great boost to differentiated learning in your classroom, it also gives teachers many new ways of finding great resources and sharing great ideas. We can choose from teaching forums, educational e-books, social networks, and so on and on. All these offer us fantastic new ways to learn how to reach and teach every single child.

CPSIA information can be obtained
at www.ICGtesting.com
Printed in the USA
LVOW13s0000250717
542452LV00019B/802/P